Tax Haven Ireland

'An extremely important, and possibly the best, book to have been written about one of the world's biggest and most dangerous tax havens. It skewers the self-serving myths of crooked Irish elites to show how going down the tax haven route not only inflicts harm on other countries – it hurts its own population too.'

Nicholas Shaxson, author *Treasure Islands: Tax Havens and the Men who Stole the World*

'Excellent insights and analysis showing how corporations and the rich are addicted to tax avoidance to the detriment of normal people. Informative and enjoyable to read.'

Prem Sikka, University of Sheffield

'An important book – it exposes industrial scale tax avoidance being organised by the Irish elites and enjoyed by the world's major corporations. It blends detailed research with impressive insight. It deserves a wide readership.'

Richard Boyd Barrett TD, People Before Profit

'An important book that deserves a wide readership. The claims that Ireland is a tax haven have been growing over recent years. This book adds important evidence to the claim and makes a passionate call for a more equal society.'

Professor Eoin Reeves, University of Limerick

'A policy of consistent denial by the government, along with lazy media treatment of the issue, has meant that Ireland's status as a tax haven is an ongoing controversy. This book goes a long way in resolving this argument.'

Terrence McDonough, Emeritus Professor of Economics, NUI Galway

'A must read for anyone interested in understanding how global capitalism works in the twenty-first century.'

Dr Stewart Smyth, Birmingham Business School, University of Birmingham

Tax Haven Ireland

Brian O'Boyle and Kieran Allen

First published 2021 by Pluto Press
New Wing, Somerset House, Strand, London WC2R 1LA

www.plutobooks.com

British Library Cataloguing in Publication Data
A catalogue record for this book is available from the British Library

ISBN   978 0 7453 4532 1   Hardback
ISBN   978 0 7453 4531 4   Paperback
ISBN   978 0 7453 4535 2   PDF
ISBN   978 0 7453 4533 8   EPUB

This book is printed on paper suitable for recycling and made from fully managed
and sustained forest sources. Logging, pulping and manufacturing processes are
expected to conform to the environmental standards of the country of origin.

Typeset by Stanford DTP Services, Northampton, England

Simultaneously printed in the United Kingdom and United States of America

Contents

Figures and Tables

Figures and Tables

Abbreviations

CGT	Capital Gains Tax
CSO	Central Statistics Office
CRO	Companies Registration Office
CFC	Controlled Foreign Company
CPT	Corporation Profit Tax
DIRT	Deposit Interest Retention Tax
DTT	Double Taxation Treaty
ECJ	European Court of Justice
FDI	Foreign Direct Investment
GDP	Gross Domestic Product
GNP	Gross National Product
HNWI	High-Net-Worth Individuals
IFSC	International Financial Services Centre
LDCs	Least Developed Countries
SIPC	Securities Investor Protection Corporation
SPV	Special Purpose Vehicle
TNC	Transnational Corporation

Acknowledgements

This book would not have been possible without the support and advice of a number of people. Richard Boyd Barrett, Alex Callinicos, Rachel Farrell, Terrence McDonough, Eoin Reeves and Stewart Smyth each read drafts of the document and offered important suggestions to improve the text. Stewart also asked a number of his colleagues to look over the book from a radical accountancy perspective. Cillian Doyle offered us important advice on the nature of Russian money flowing through the International Financial Services Centre (IFSC). He also read the book and gave insightful comments.

Prem Sikka read the book in draft form and was kind enough to send a number of important details about the role of the big four accountancy firms in the tax avoidance network. Nick Shaxson's work was an inspiration for much of what we wrote in Chapter 2 and he gave us important encouragement when the book was nearing completion. We also benefitted from employees of law and accountancy firms who spoke to us on condition of anonymity. Collectively, these people improved our book and none are responsible for any errors that remain.

Beyond these direct supports, the book benefitted from the work of a number of specialists in the area, including Richard Brooks, Christian Chavagneux, John Christensen, Emma Clancy, Sheila Killian, Richard Murphy, Ronan Palan, Jim Stewart and Gabriel Zucman. A number of these researchers have connections to the Tax Justice Network, which has been an invaluable resource in writing this book. We have also benefitted from the work of Oxfam, Christian Aid and a number of important anonymous entries to Wikipedia.

No book is possible without the support of those we love. In this context, Brian would like to thank his partner, Emma Hendrick. Her patience and support were not only invaluable in the completion of this book, they were essential in a project that took many more hours than was first expected. Brian would also like to thank his daughter, Keela, who brought joy to the house and helped keep him sane when down the rabbit hole of tax evasion. Finally, Brian would like to pay tribute to his mother, Deirdre, who tragically took her own life in 2018. Deirdre was a bright light in a world that is all too often dark. Her example inspired Brian to fight for a better world and her own struggles were bound up with the injustices that are laid out in this work. It is to her memory that Brian dedicates his part of the book. Kieran Allen would like thank Annette Mooney for her patience and forbearance while this research was carried out. His section of the book is dedicated to her.

As this book was being finalised, the authors received news that Terry McDonough had passed away. Terry was a longstanding comrade of the authors and an important presence on the Irish left. He will be greatly missed

Introduction

In 2015, researchers investigating global tax evasion made a shocking discovery. Ireland, with less than 0.1 per cent of the world's population had become the biggest tax haven on the planet. The route to this discovery, made by Thomas R. Tørsløv and his colleagues, lay in discrepancies in how corporate profits were being declared across different jurisdictions.[1] Ordinarily, businesses declare profits between 30 to 40 per cent of their wage bill, but for Ireland the declared ratio was closer to 800 per cent. A year later, official data from the Central Statistics Office (CSO) further corroborated these findings, showing that each employee in large manufacturing firms was responsible for €687,000 in gross added value, or nearly 30 times more than would be expected.[2] This could only be explained in one of two ways – either these workers were hired for their superhuman capacities, or their employers were funnelling profits made by foreign workers through the Irish taxation system. When they tackle this question at all, the Irish elites strongly argue that the first explanation is the correct one. According to their narrative, Ireland is now a high-technology, high-value economy, often targeted for unfair criticism by those who have been less successful in attracting foreign direct investment (FDI).

It is our contention that this narrative is strategically deployed by government ministers, tax planners and economists to create cover for tax avoidance on an industrial scale. Each year, foreign companies send about €100 billion of profits through the Irish tax code for no other reason than to avoid their taxes. This is more than three times the amount needed to eradicate global hunger and the evidence that reveals it is hiding in plain sight in official statistics. Despite this, however, there is not yet a full-length book detailing the historical development, the internal mechanics and the social consequences of Tax Haven Ireland. This book was written to close that gap.

The first chapter introduces readers to some of the less savoury aspects of the Irish tax haven, as we explain why the world's biggest pornography company relocated to Dublin and detail how Irish high-net-worth individuals (HNWIs) and domestic companies avoid their taxes. Once this is done, in Chapter 2 we move on to explain the inner workings of the international tax evasion network, linking it to key turning points in the development of twentieth-century capitalism – particularly the decline of the British Empire after the Second World War and the development of neoliberalism during the 1980s. Chapter 3 lays out the key stages in the development of the Irish offshore system, beginning with the foundation of the state and ending with the collapse of the Celtic Tiger in the Great Recession. The inner connections between domestic corruption and global corporations are central to this narrative, as the Irish ruling class gradually convinced the world's biggest companies to share their abuse of national sovereignty. Tax evasion usually works on the basis of an input–output model, as profits get funnelled in before being funnelled back out again once they have been sheltered from taxation. Chapter 4 explains how this process is organised in Ireland, outlining the key profit shifting mechanisms developed by the ruling classes and detailing some of the evidence found in Ireland's national statistics. Chapter 5 complements this analysis with a look at the key sectors involved in Tax Haven Ireland – namely the corporate law firms who fix-up the deals, the corporate services firms who help them along and the corporate accountants who make sure everything seems legal and legitimate. Chapter 6 explains the historical roots, and sectoral specialities, associated with the International Financial Services Centre (IFSC). Established as a back office to the City of London in 1987, the IFSC has become the biggest shadow banking centre in Europe and the fourth biggest on the planet. It has also become home to 40 per cent of Europe's Financial Vehicle Corporations, as well as establishing an important presence in the insurance and reinsurance markets, the aircraft leasing sector, investment banking and internal group financing. The IFSC houses the most important tax haven participants and creates a bridge between financial companies and the financial dealings of multinational companies. Chapter 7 analyses these multinational companies, highlighting the role of tax avoidance in attracting US firms, in particular, into Ireland. The chapter also details the controversy surrounding Ireland's tax deal with Apple Inc. and highlights the synergies between companies with high levels of intellectual property and Ireland's tax avoidance techniques – particularly in big tech and the pharmaceutical industry.

Lacking a strategy for domestic industrialisation, the Irish elites have traditionally put a disproportionate amount of their wealth into domestic property speculation. Tax Haven Ireland developed tools to encourage this during the Celtic Tiger years and used the period after 2008 to engineer a wall of foreign money to reflate the property sector after it had collapsed. Chapter 8 tells this story, linking the suffering of hundreds of thousands in Ireland's ongoing housing crisis to the wider recovery strategies of the Irish establishment. Over the last number of years, Ireland's role as a tax haven has been highlighted by a US Senate Inquiry, the European Commission, the European Parliament and numerous academics, charities and tax justice organisations. Despite this, however, the Irish elites have insisted that the country is an early adopter of anti-tax avoidance legislation and is unfairly labelled as deviant by its economic competitors. In Chapter 9 we set out to demolish these arguments by highlighting the contradictions in the official narrative, revealing that, far from adopting the best international laws to stop tax avoidance and evasion, the Irish elites do everything in their power to help these practices to continue. The final chapter, Chapter 10, focuses on the social consequences of the Irish offshore system, explaining how many people in the underdeveloped world die annually through strategies aided and abetted by the Irish establishment. Most Irish people are made worse off too, as a tiny minority undermine democracy, hollow out public services and hold back wages and conditions. Tax avoidance destroys lives and the fabric of society, as we seek to explain in this chapter.

As this book goes to print yet another financial scandal has broken in Ireland, as 16 executives at Ireland's largest stockbroker firm, Davy, were found to have been on two sides of a bond deal, illegally – organising it, while secretly buying the bonds themselves. Unsurprisingly, they failed to inform their own compliance team or the original owner, himself a member of the so-called Maple 10 – a group of property developers who bought Anglo Irish Bank shares *with the bank's own money* during the dying days of the Celtic Tiger. So far, there is little particularly new in this sordid affair, except that it has created so much anger among the Irish public that all of the executives have been forced to resign while the company has had to put itself up for sale, in a bid to survive. This reminds us of two things we want to highlight in this book. The first is that corporate Ireland remains a cesspool of cronyism and corruption, despite all the talk of reform. The second is that people power is capable of rooting this out and creating something far more progressive. If this book helps to convince readers that we need a radical transformation of politics on the island of Ireland, our efforts will have been more than worthwhile.

1

Porn, Tax Dodging and Exploitation

In 2012, one of Ireland's leading law firms, Arthur Cox, helped to bring the world's largest pornography company, Manwin, to Dublin. It was an extraordinary move for a firm that is one of the most respectable in Ireland.

Arthur Cox has been linked to the political elite since its very foundation. The company was started in 1920 in the maelstrom of the Irish Revolution when tens of thousands took up arms against the British Empire. Its founder, 'old man Arthur', had little interest in such subversive activity, but had an eye on securing a privileged position within the new state. Schooled at the exclusive Belvedere College by the Jesuits, he mixed in the social circles of conservative nationalists, and when they took power, Cox knew that his day had come.

In the words of his admiring biographer, 'perhaps no individual outside the cabinet benefitted more from this shift than Arthur Cox'.[1] Legal contracts, paid from the Free State's coffers, soon came his way, but so too did commissions from foreign firms eager to have an inside track on the newly independent Irish regime. One significant detail illustrates how embedded Arthur Cox was among the 'Belvedere boys' who came in to run the state. In 1940, he married Brigid O'Higgins, widow of the assassinated Free State Justice Minister, Kevin O'Higgins. O'Higgins had been the strong man inside that early regime and had secured his position by ordering reprisal executions on anti-Treaty republicans during the Irish Civil War. For the rest of his life, Cox referred to his new wife as 'Mrs O'Higgins', as in, for example, 'It's time Mrs O'Higgins and I went to bed'.[2]

His legal firm duly prospered in an Ireland that was proud of its adherence to Catholicism. At the time, the Irish were celebrated – or rather celebrated themselves – as the most Catholic people in the world – a beacon that shone through global darkness – ever ready to pray

1

for the conversion of godless Russia or pagan England. The new state put unmarried mothers into Mother and Baby Homes, banned foreign 'indecent' films lest they become 'occasions of sin' and even clamped down on jazz as a threat to Irish civilisation and morality. The key figure behind this shadow theocracy was John Charles McQuaid, Catholic Primate of Ireland and Archbishop of Dublin. And it was to him, at the ripe old age of 70, that Arthur Cox went to become a Catholic priest, just after Brigid O'Higgins had died. Becoming a Jesuit normally required spending 14 years in training, but in a tribute to his piety, loyalty and respectability, McQuaid allowed old Arthur to do the training in just two years. He then set off as a missionary to Northern Rhodesia to convert African babies.

How times change! Ireland, a country once renowned for its rigid Catholic morality, was now welcoming the biggest porn firm in the world and a company founded by a late entrant to the priesthood was its legal agent. Arthur Cox teamed up with another law firm, A&L Goodbody, to allow Manwin to establish subsidiaries in Dublin. They were housed in a building used by Grant Thornton on the river Liffey, but no signage was ever displayed. The legal work was complex and costly because Manwin had just merged with another US porn operator, RK Netmedia, and the merger had to be approved by the Irish Competition Authority. The Minister for Jobs, Enterprise and Innovation has the power to block any deal deemed to be against the public interest, so to make sure it got over the line, Arthur Cox and A&L Goodbody stood ready to deal with any complications. Then there was Manwin's practice of setting up complex corporate structures. It wanted a holding company – a legal entity often used to strategically place intellectual property in a tax haven – to hold its shares and ultimately reduce its taxes. But it also wanted a billing company and a content company which had the rights to use its pornographic movies. In all, a schedule of 60 pages of titles that Irish Manwin subsidiaries could use was lodged in the Irish Companies Registration Office (CRO).

Porn is big business and MindGeek, the name which Manwin adopted a year after its registration in Dublin, is the largest corporation within the industry. It seeks to normalise pornography as a way of making it more accessible and profitable. This involves a number of dubious techniques, including paying for clips of its videos to be inserted as product placements into the American film *Don Jon* (2013). Or organising a 'family friendly, non-pornographic design contest' for potential advertisers and running a campaign to plant trees. The last enterprise was billed as 'giving America some serious wood', because MindGeek would plant a tree for every 100 users of its 'Big Dick category'. It has even offered a $25,000 scholarship to students who wrote the best essay on 'How do you strive to make others happy?'[3] The aim of all this, to quote the Vice President of Pornhub, Corey Price, is 'to make porn acceptable to talk about'.[4]

One does not have to be an evangelical fundamentalist or a sexual prude to see something distinctly unpleasant about this enterprise. The porn industry presents itself as a liberator of sexual pleasure and desire, but it arguably has about as much relationship to genuine sexual desire as McDonald's has to nutritious food.[5] Pornography treats sex as a commodity, packaged with fantasies of domination and violence. Many of the scenes in the top-rented pornographic films contain physical and verbal abuse, with one study of the best-selling porn videos finding that 88 per cent of scenes contained physical violence, usually by men against women and often where women appeared to enjoy it.[6]

MindGeek's commercial success arose from encouraging porn users to load their favourite films onto its portals for free, spreading them throughout the World Wide Web like wildfire. The pay-off for its owners comes from the sales of advertising and the enticement of customers on to paying services. Through this strategy, the company has grown into a global behemoth, and its control over studios has had some seriously negative effects. For one thing, there has been a decline in the wages paid to many of the women involved. The sexual activity has also been 'spiced up' with increasingly risky behaviour, including more extreme rape scenes and 'gonzo' porn. Katrina Forrester describes the pattern,

> Riskier acts are incentivized. According to one analysis of an industry talent database, women entering the business now will do more, and more quickly, than they once did: in the nineteen-eighties, they would wait an average of two years before a first anal scene; now it's six months.[7]

Behind an industry based on the exploitation of women are men in suits, the respectable figures of capitalist enterprise, whose only motivation is the profitability of the bottom line. MindGeek was originally owned by a German tech geek named Fabian Thylmann, who used his software engineering skills to set up the algorithms to power his customer base. He expanded his business by linking up with a Wall Street hedge fund that gave him a high interest loan of $362 million. The trustee for this loan was CB Agency Services, which was based in Delaware, a US state famous for being a tax haven and, coincidently, a state that gave rise to the US President, Joe Biden. Behind it lay a controlling company, Colbeck Capital Management, led by two former Goldman Sachs' employees, Jason Colodne and Jason Beckman, who operated out of an exclusive office just off Central Park, New York. To spread the risk on their loan, they sold it off in tranches to other financial sharks anxious to get a slice of the action. One of the buyers was the Fortress Investment Group, run by former Princeton graduates, who were directors of UBS and former partners of Goldman Sachs.

Meanwhile, the original founder of MindGeek landed himself in trouble when he was unceremoniously arrested and extradited from Belgium to Germany to face charges of tax evasion and only escaped prison by agreeing to pay a €5 million fine. Worried that his legal difficulties and his association with the porn industry would leave him with 'a mark on his back', he sold his shares to a senior management team based in Montreal, Canada.[8] The new owners of the company are Feras Antoon and David Tasillo and their only concern is making money.

This brings us back to why MindGeek hired Arthur Cox to help set up its operations in Dublin. The clue lies in the complex corporate structure that has been set up by MindGeek. The address for its global headquarters is 32 Boulevard Royal, 2449 Luxembourg, an inauspicious building with no signage to indicate the nature of its business. A journalist from *La Presse* describes her visit,

> On the intercom, a receptionist tells us that no leader of MindGeek is on site. Not today nor tomorrow. 'Nobody works here, nobody works from here,' she says. On the fourth floor, where the group's head office

is officially located, there is flat calm in the middle of the afternoon. The silence is total.[9]

The real headquarters for MindGeek is actually 5700 km away, along the Décarie Expressway in Montreal, where 900 people are employed. It is a Canadian company with an offshore financial structure and the reason for this curious anomaly is that MindGeek's main interest, aside from porn, lies in dodging tax. It chose Luxembourg for its fictional headquarters because it is a tax haven with a notional tax rate on profits of 29 per cent, but where most foreign companies never pay anything near that. Instead, the multinationals meet with state officials to effectively set their tax rate as close to zero as possible through a host of incentives they can avail of. Dividends or interest payments received from loans, for example, are not subject to corporate income tax, while income derived from intellectual property is exempt from any form of wealth tax. No wonder that hundreds of North American companies have located themselves in Luxembourg or that in 2014 alone $416 billion in investment flowed there.[10]

MindGeek arrived in Ireland for the same reason it went to Luxembourg – it wanted another tax dodging paradise, connected to a wider network such as the Netherlands, the Cayman Islands or Bermuda. Using a series of tax treaties that link these countries together, a multinational like MindGeek can structure its operations so that it pays hardly any tax in any of them. They merely have to contact legal agents such as Arthur Cox and some expert 'tax planners' for a little help. A description of MindGeek's corporate structure shows how this all works. MG Content Limited was set up as a subsidiary of MindGeek's Ireland Holding Company which, in turn, is a subsidiary of its Luxembourg headquarters. In 2014, it recorded a profit of $23 million for the distribution of its porn around the web, but it claimed these profits were eaten up by $20 million in 'administrative expenses' much of which were paid to other subsidiaries within its empire.[11] As a result, it only paid $253,426 in tax, or an effective rate of 1.2 per cent on its original profit.

Another company, MG Billing, takes in subscriptions from paying customers. In 2015, it earned a staggering $427 million in revenue and declared a profit of $234 million, yet it paid a mere $145,301 in tax – an effective rate of 0.06 per cent in tax.[12] Yes, you read that right – it is a hundred times less than 6 per cent. No wonder the porn merchant contacted a legal company historically famed for its Catholic respectability. It had found a paradise for dodging taxes in a land once renowned for its Saints and Scholars.

TAX EVASION AS 'AVOIDANCE'

In 1989, Leona Helmsley – a New York billionaire – hit the headlines when she announced, while on trial for tax evasion: 'We don't pay taxes. Only the little people pay taxes.'[13] The 'we', Helmsley was referring to was herself and her property-speculating husband, while the sentiment she expressed was an early version of the American Tea Party – a right-wing sect that sees tax (on the rich) as theft. Very few of the Irish rich would put it so crudely, but many of them undoubtedly think it. In polite circles, the well-to-do refer to the need for 'tax avoidance' – a perfectly legal mechanism for reducing taxation – or if they want to be more technical about it – 'tax efficiency'. Both terms are then contrasted with 'tax evasion', which is defined as the practice of deliberately flouting the law.

Respectable people hire expensive accountants to minimise their taxes, presenting this as a game to outwit 'the taxman' by finding 'loopholes' in the legislation. Success comes either because of good luck or aggressive planning, with the latter preferred because it brings more certainty. Tax planners know tax law back to front and define their trade as 'ensuring the minimum tax is paid at the most opportune time'.[14] But that is not their only offering. Tax planners also organise the appearance of full compliance with the Revenue Commissioners so that wealthy people can simultaneously avoid tax and meet their full legal requirements. They also meet with Revenue when their clients are subject to audits and intercede on their behalf. And if that is not enough, they will even offer 'Revenue Audit Insurance to cover the professional cost of such encounters'.[15] No wonder the Irish rich want an accountant in the family rather than the priest they wanted in decades past.

A culture of tax avoidance is deeply embedded among the Irish upper classes. They regularly overstate their business costs while keeping every receipt that can be claimed from the taxman. These practices start when businesses are small, but as the wealth increases, so does the sophistication in avoidance. High-net-worth individuals have an array of avoidance measures to absolve them of their responsibility to wider society. To legitimise this behaviour, they insist that their wealth emerges through their own hard work and sometimes blame the poor for their poverty and fecklessness. This helps to breed a sense of entitlement among the rich who jealously guard their assets against the taxman and any redistribution to the working classes. In the past, Catholic theology was also used as the main ideological justification for minimal welfare provision, but in today's neoliberal Ireland, the case is justified with claims about personal choice and responsibility. Everyone supposedly gets what they deserve in a free-market economy, with tax becoming little more than theft from the successful.

The mainstream press is also in on the act. Instead of well-informed analysis on the ways the super-rich avoid their taxes, consumers of mainstream media are encouraged to ogle at their jet-setting lifestyles, while being constantly reminded of their philanthropic activities. *Irish Times* readers learned, for example, that a charitable foundation set up by the billionaire J.P. McManus and run by his wife and daughter, donated €1.7 million for community projects in 2016.[16] Denis O'Brien's Foundation tells how it funds human-rights defenders and does charitable work in Haiti. The Irish billionaire has also been made an Honorary Life President of the Football Association of Ireland, mainly because its senior management benefitted from O'Brien's financial largesse for many years. All this philanthropy then gets uncritical adulation from the mainstream press.

There is, however, a fundamental difference between individual philanthropy and redistribution of wealth through taxation. The philanthropist gets to choose where his or her money goes, but the taxpayer has no direct agency in these matters. Philanthropists can also claim credit for donating their money, whereas taxpayers must reside in a world of anonymity. Through his or her donation, the philanthropist strengthens a dependency relationship that can be endlessly exploited. If a recipient needs more money for example, they must learn the art of politeness and flattery. By contrast, the citizen who benefits from public spending can still denounce the state who provides them with resources. These contrasts are particularly relevant because many of Ireland's biggest philanthropists are also Ireland's biggest 'tax dodgers'. Dodging taxes is our preferred terminology for people who stay well within the law to avoid taxes. By using this terminology, we avoid the assumption that 'tax avoiders' hire smart people who find loopholes which dim-witted state officials have unknowingly left behind them. Instead we suggest that the Irish state actively connives in tax dodging by its wealthy citizens – effectively making 'evasion' legal.

Take one of Ireland's wealthiest men – J.P. McManus – as an example. Worth an estimated €2 billion, McManus is esteemed around his native Limerick for his classic rags-to-riches story and for being an exceptional philanthropist. He has hundreds of top-class racehorses, owns a stud farm, operates a foreign exchange trading centre in Geneva and has shares in Ladbrokes and Barchester, a company that runs old people's homes. He also hosts the J.P. McManus celebrity golf tournament in Adare Manor and was once a part owner of Manchester United. Yet according to the Irish Revenue Commissioners, McManus has not paid income or corporate taxes in Ireland for 20 years.[17] The reason for this seeming anomaly is that McManus is a tax exile who claims that his official residence is not in Ireland, but in Switzerland. The fact he built a Palladian-style mansion in Martinstown, Kilmallock that is 20 times the size of a three-bedroom house is deemed irrelevant. Under Irish tax law, someone who lives in Ireland for fewer than 183 days a year or 280 days over two years, is deemed not to be tax resident. Exactly how such timeframes are monitored remains unclear, however, because McManus owns a €55 million Gulfstream G650 jet and so he does not always buy airline tickets.

After the Celtic Tiger crash of the economy of 2008, there was a rise in public anger about tax exiles because the majority of people were suffering austerity. The government's response was to introduce a domicile levy of €200,000 on individuals whose income amounted to €1 million a year and whose assets were valued at over €5 million. Significantly, however, it did not follow a similar move in Britain whereby one had to automatically pay £90,000 for the privilege of being declared a non-resident.[18] If it had done so, it would have raised an extra €305 million for the hard-pressed Irish state coffers – which, coincidentally, was nearly half of what it hoped to raise in water charges. J.P. McManus, however, was one of a handful of individuals who paid that levy in 2012.

By coincidence, in the same year, he won $17 million in a three-day backgammon game with a fellow, US billionaire. Backgammon was a game once played in the court of French kings, but even these aristocrats never dreamed of the stakes involved in a billionaire contest. Either from pique or propriety, the loser withheld $5.2 million of the winnings to pay taxes to the US Treasury. So, the outraged winner took a case to a US Federal Court to get hold of his money. Then, in a supreme act of irony, McManus claimed he was an Irish tax resident, using the fact that he paid the domicile levy as his main evidence. Judge Nancy Firestone was having none of it, however, declaring that the levy was 'not a comprehensive tax on a person's worldwide income' and was not, as Mr. McManus asserted, 'substantially similar' to Ireland's income tax.[19] The domicile levy was peanuts to the Irish billionaire and the more relevant fact was that he did not pay income or corporate taxes to the Irish exchequer. It took a foreign judge to cut to the heart of the matter.

McManus' attempt to avoid his gambling tax spoke to a deep instinct of the Irish rich, namely that no state or Revenue Commissioner, whether in Ireland or the US, should touch their wealth. This same attitude indicates why so many Irish billionaires declare themselves tax exiles while continually flying in and out of Ireland. Of the 450 high-net-worth individuals identified by the Irish Revenue Commissioners, for example, 54 have declared themselves resident abroad and these tend to belong to the upper tier, the *crème de la crème*.[20] Thus: Denis O'Brien is officially declared as a tax resident of Malta; Dermot Desmond resides for tax purposes in Gibraltar; John Magnier has chosen Switzerland; and Michael Smurfit picked Monaco. Meanwhile, the domicile levy which was supposed to extract a contribution from the super wealthy has fallen into disrepair because, despite increased wealth, the numbers paying the levy and the amount they pay has declined.

Have a look at Table 1.1, provided in answer to a Dáil question.[21]

Further evidence of tax dodging by the super-rich emerged in September 2018, when the Comptroller and Auditor General revealed that of 334 high-net-worth individuals, 83 paid less tax in 2015 than the average PAYE (pay-as-you-earn) worker on €36,500. A further 143 paid less than €125,000 despite having assets worth more than €50 million each.[22] This is a dramatic indictment on the behaviour of wealthy individuals, but how do Irish corporations approach their taxes?

Table 1.1　Domicile Levy by Year and Amount Paid 2010–16

Year	Number of individuals who paid non-domicile levy	Amount raised (€ millions)
2010	32	3.43
2011	33	3.69
2012	24	2.44
2013	20	1.90
2014	13	2.02
2015	13	2.30
2016	10	1.40

According to the Companies Registration Office, there are 215,000 registered companies in Ireland, but only 153,700 of these made a Corporation Tax Return in 2017.[23] Of those making a return, 68,000 claimed that they made no profit in the year and a further 22,500 paid no tax because they availed of various reliefs.[24] That means just 29 per cent of the registered companies paid any tax at all. But even this figure is an overestimation for Irish companies, because the list includes subsidiaries of giant US multinationals as well as tiny one-person businesses. Multinationals pay the lion's share of the taxes in Ireland with just ten companies paying 40 per cent of the total taxes.[25] This occurs after these multinationals use Ireland's lax tax rules in what the EU Commission describes as 'aggressive tax planning'.[26] We shall deal with their activities in later chapters, but the figure suggests that substantially less than 29 per cent of Irish companies must be paying any tax at all. To get a handle on this it is useful to note that there are two main types of Irish registered company. The first are companies with less than ten employees. These make up 92 per cent of the 215,000 registered companies and pay no tax or very little.[27] For three quarters of the minority that paid tax in 2018 for example, it amounted to less than €10,000 annually or less than the amount a single person on a salary of €40,000 pays in income tax.[28]

The other important type is an emerging Irish multinational. Such companies are regarded as success stories because they have outgrown their home base. Once again, however, they appear to have a dislike of paying tax because just 4 per cent of all corporation taxes comes from such companies. To see how they operate, we will take a company which could hardly have a more Irish sounding name, Glanbia – an amalgam of two words, *glan* meaning clean and *bia,* meaning food. Clean food is what the company seeks to provide with brands such as Avonmore, Premier Milk and Killmeaden Cheese, household names across Ireland. But there is nothing clean or pure about Glanbia when it comes to paying their taxes. Thanks to the whistle blower, Antoine Detour, the source of Lux Leaks, we have some idea of how the company avoids its tax liabilities. Here is what happened. Glanbia set up two companies incorporated in Luxembourg and transferred €1 billion into them.[29] Being cash rich, these companies then lent money on to other subsidiaries within the Glanbia group. This allowed the classic tax planners' manoeuvre to come into operation – playing two tax codes off against each other. Luxembourg does not charge tax on interest received, but Ireland allows corporations to reduce their tax bills by claiming allowances for interest paid. If the interest rate the Luxembourg subsidiary charges an Irish subsidiary in the Glanbia group amounts to 20 per cent for example, this can be used to write down Irish tax obligations. But the interest earned by the Luxembourg subsidiary is tax free. A tax planner of moderate intelligence need only set up one company in Luxembourg and another in Ireland and adjust the interest rates to write off tax. They can then bring the interest rate up to a level that is near to, or equivalent to, gross profits of an Irish subsidiary to reduce the tax bill to as close to zero as possible. Luxembourgian authorities facilitate this manoeuvre by extending the definition of loans to include hybrids that are almost like owning shares.

The address used by Glanbia for its Luxembourg subsidiary was also used by members of the Sisk family to set up Trefoil Luxembourg. The Sisks own one of the largest construction companies in Ireland, but once again show a distinct lack of patriotism when it comes to paying taxes. Like Glanbia, Trefoil Luxembourg lent another Sisk subsidiary, Ventris Ltd €14 million. Ventris had to pay back the loan at a fairly high interest

2
Global Plunder

A list of the greatest villains of the twentieth century would include some familiar names. Adolf Hitler and Joseph Stalin would undoubtedly make the list, but the group of British aristocrats who helped to pioneer the global tax evasion system would be unlikely to feature. Men like the City banker, Alfred Suenson-Taylor, 1st Baron Grantchester, or his brother, Charles, who together helped to fund the first neoliberal think-tank known as the Mont Pèlerin Society. Or, Sir Anthony Fisher, the British businessman who bankrolled hundreds of right-wing think-tanks in a bid to shape the economy of the late twentieth century. Through their efforts, men like them painstakingly created an influential network of businesspeople, politicians, economists and philosophers dedicated to rolling back the post-war consensus – including its trade-union rights and welfare provisions. They also encouraged a number of offshore British territories to provide the conditions for capital to move more freely into less regulated areas of the global economy. Their first major success came in the late 1950s, when Suenson-Taylor, Fisher and others convinced the Bank of England to establish a euro-dollar market in the City of London. This was done to protect the fortunes of the declining British Empire by attracting much needed American finance into the City. But it would also prove to be the first crack in the system of regulated exchange rates known as the Bretton Woods system. Since then, the City has become the epicentre of a vast network of tax-dodging activities designed to keep British capitalism in the front rank of the global system. The two inner rings of this network include the Crown Dependencies of Jersey, Guernsey and the Isle of Man, together with British Overseas Territories, including the Cayman Islands, Bermuda and the British Virgin Islands. The outer ring includes former British colonies such as Hong Kong, Singapore and, of course, the Irish Republic.[1] With its colonial past and geographical location, the Irish Financial Services Centre (IFSC) was seen as the perfect administrative back office for London investment bankers, making it a significant link in the most important tax-dodging network on the planet.[2] This system now ensures that vast quantities of the world's wealth gets funnelled into Britain via the City.

But it is also responsible for the deaths of millions of people in the Global South who are denied basic welfare services, food and water as a result. Research by the Drop the Debt Jubilee 2000 Campaign estimated that around 7 million people die needlessly each year as money gets moved out of their reach, often into tax havens.[3] Oxfam put the figure at closer to 8 million people, in what the economist of debt Raj Patel famously denounced as genocide using financial weapons of mass destruction.[4] All told, the combination of global debt and tax evasion pioneered by respectable men from the British establishment has been responsible for more deaths than the First and Second World Wars combined. Hitler and Stalin are rightly denounced for their barbarous destruction, but men like Fisher and Suenson-Taylor got to die safely in their beds with vast wealth in their bank accounts and their reputations untarnished. By allowing global corporations to suck wealth out of the world's poorest countries, the Irish rich also have blood on their hands.[5] Tax dodging is very far from a victimless crime because the hundreds of billions stolen annually has devastating consequences for lives and societies. To understand the nature of this system, we now turn to the development, and current role, of tax havens in the global economy.

THE DEVELOPMENT OF TAX HAVEN CAPITALISM

Capitalism has always been an international system with a more advanced core interacting with a weaker periphery.[6] Historically, the most powerful countries often colonised their weaker rivals, but during the twentieth century, financiers in the core of the system began to spot a less aggressive way to make money. Instead of relying on naked force, they began to bribe legislatures in poorer parts of the system with the promise of much needed investment in return for pro-business laws and lower taxation. This then acted as a downward lever everywhere else, as the owners of capital threatened to move their wealth into these places if their own legislatures refused to follow suit. Tax evasion has existed in one form or another since taxes were collected, but the development of tax haven capitalism took place in three key phases – the period after the First World War, the period after the Second World War and the period after 1970. Let's look at each in turn.

The nineteenth century was a time of empire building, with all the major economic powers jostling for wealth and global position. Britain started the century in the lead, but the rise of Germany, from 1880 onwards, eventually led to more than a decade of global conflict, as the First World War was quickly followed by a series of European revolutions. The success of the Bolshevik Revolution in Russia in 1917 was followed by short-lived revolts in both Italy and Hungary. There were also major upheavals in Germany and Austria, with the threat of social revolution hanging over the former until 1923. It was in these conditions that the rich in Central and Eastern Europe began to look for new ways to put their assets beyond the reach of democratic forces.[7] In Britain and France the imposition of post-war taxes gave the richest families similar incentives for hiding their money. An opportunity arose for a sovereign state willing to shelter the wealth of the European elites – and Switzerland duly obliged.

Switzerland had remained neutral throughout the war, allowing it to escape the social upheaval witnessed in other countries. It was also characterised by two features that have since become synonymous with tax haven capitalism – domination by financial interests and poorer regions willing to support themselves through cut-throat, pro-business competition. Swiss bankers established a national cartel as early as 1912 and pressurised their national legislature into helping them compete for foreign money.[8] The result was a set of stringent secrecy laws that, in turn, facilitated a tenfold increase in foreign assets under their management over the next 20 years.[9] Buoyed by this initial success, Swiss legislatures then went a step further by making any breaches of banking secrecy a criminal offence. This allowed Swiss bankers to deal with anyone with the means to pay them – including a loan of 850 million Swiss francs for the Nazis' push into Russia during Operation Barbarossa. They also hid valuable European artwork for Adolf Hitler and Joseph Goebbels throughout the 1940s in a bid to keep part of the profit for themselves.

In addition to extreme levels of banking secrecy, Switzerland was one of the innovators of interstate tax competition. Like the United States, Switzerland is a system of autonomous regions – known as cantons – held together in a federation. After the First World War, these various cantons began to compete with each other on issues of taxation in a way that mirrored the United States at the turn of the twentieth century.

During the 1890s, Wall Street bankers spotted an opportunity to use the sovereignty of less developed US states as a lever to drive down their costs and regulations. Led by a New York corporate lawyer named James Dill, they drafted extremely pro-business legislation for the poorer states of New Jersey and Delaware. Legislatures in New York and Chicago were then suddenly faced with two equally unpalatable options – obey the bankers who currently resided within their own jurisdictions or lose the business to poorer rivals. In the wake of the First World War, Zurich bankers adopted an identical strategy, writing pro-business laws for one of the poorer cantons in the Swiss federation – Zug. Like its US counterparts, Zug was encouraged to take a slice of the incorporation market in return for driving down the costs of doing business everywhere else. Legislatures in Zurich and Geneva were then faced with the same Hobson's choice of adjusting their own tax offering or risking the consequences of capital flight into rival locations. Nicholas Shaxson captures the nature of this process,

> Offshore is not just a place, an idea, a way of doing business. It is also a process: a race to the bottom where the regulations, laws and trappings of democracy are steadily degraded, as one arrangement ricochets from one fortified redoubt of finance to the next jurisdiction, and the offshore system pushes steadily, further, deeper onshore.... In giving freedom to finance, people in democratic nation states lost their freedom to choose and implement the laws that they wanted.[10]

Whatever the social consequences, this process proved particularly lucrative for the havens themselves. Delaware currently hosts 60 per cent of all US Fortune 500 companies for example, while Zug has managed to incorporate one global company for every four of its citizens.[11] Since the 1930s, Liechtenstein, Luxembourg, the Netherlands and Belgium have also sold aspects of their sovereignty to global corporations – making these countries some of the current centres of global tax dodging.[12] Another centre was developed out of the remnants of the British Empire after the Second World War.

Although Britain was on the winning side in the Second World War, it quickly became apparent that the US and the Soviet Union were the new global superpowers after the war. Britain remained a key military ally of the US, but it was also an economic rival in the post-war capitalist system. The tensions and contradictions between a rising US and a diminishing UK helped to spawn the next phase of tax haven development. The US strategy after the war was to tie its major allies into a Bretton Woods financial system underpinned by the US dollar. This would help the dollar to replace sterling as the global reserve currency, thereby cementing US leadership of global capitalism. Today, 87 per cent of world trade has the dollar on at least one end of the deal, giving the US monetary authorities incredible financial power.[13] In the 1950s, 40 per cent of trade was still contracted in sterling – but the UK authorities could see the writing on the wall. Britain could no longer expect to be the centre of financial contracts when most trade happened outside its legal jurisdictions. To make matters worse, the Empire was crumbling under the strain of diminished economic resources and increased resistance in the colonies.

The City of London, so long the heartbeat of the global economic system, was in danger of becoming a second-rate financial centre. To guard against this eventuality, the British elite developed a two-pronged strategy. One part of this strategy involved using its overseas territories and the Crown Dependencies as a network of tax haven jurisdictions linked to the City. The other part, developed after 1957, was to consciously create a major UK offshore centre through the development of the so-called euro-dollar market.[14] Instead of the City of London functioning as the centre of a formal Empire, it would become the centre of a vast network of offshore jurisdictions.[15] Taken together, these decisions have made Britain into the primary driver of tax haven capitalism since the Second World War. Of the eleven remaining UK Overseas Territories for example, seven are tax havens, including Bermuda, the Cayman Islands and the British Virgin Islands. In addition, the Crown Dependencies of Jersey, Guernsey and the Isle of Man, as well as the IFSC, have become successful outposts of the City of London.[16]

This offshore web provides British finance with three key strategic advantages. First, and most importantly, tax havens hoover up vast wealth and foreign investment from around the world, before channelling it into British capitalism. Second, they function as less regulated storage centres for global financial assets, and third, they function as 'a money-laundering filter that lets the City get involved in dirty business while providing enough distance to maintain plausible deniability'.[17] Collectively, these advantages helped the UK to maintain its role in the heart of the global economy, even as the Empire declined. This achievement wouldn't have been possible, however, without the turbo fuel of the euro-dollar market. In 1957, the Bank of England made a landmark decision in the development of tax haven capitalism. In order to comply with the Bretton Woods fixed exchange rate system, sterling had to be tightly regulated. This was proving problematic, however, as many investors wanted out of sterling and into the dollar for their trades. To cope with this challenge, the UK authorities decided to allow a market for dollars to develop within the City of London. As trade was taking place in a foreign currency, the Bank of England argued that they had no need for regulation, and because it was located in the UK, it was also beyond the reach of the US Federal Reserve.

The result was a massive offshore market that has since become the largest source of corporate finance anywhere in the world. This euro-dollar trade protected UK banking interests by allowing them to continue lending and borrowing – this time in dollars. It also provided a major boost to the City of London via the vast amounts of new liquidity coming in. The US authorities' attitude to the new development was consequently more ambiguous. They opposed the financial advantages accruing to London, but they also understood the importance of euro-dollars in further entrenching the dollar as the global currency and in allowing US banks to compete with their rivals. The upshot was a more-or-less unregulated market in the centre of what was supposed to be a tightly regulated financial system. This allowed big business to escape many regulations that they had previously faced and established a bridgehead for future deregulation in the 1970s. Assessing these issues, Palan et al. argue,

> The development of the Euromarket in the City of London proved to be the principal force behind an integrated offshore economy that combined London and remnants of the British Empire. The British Empire is supposed to have more or less disappeared by the 1960s. This is incorrect. The formal British Empire may have collapsed, but the British led off-shore world is alive and kicking. It is impossible to comprehend the success of the City of London…without the Euromarket and the satellite British tax havens. Formalities aside, we should treat the City of London, Jersey, Cayman Islands, BVI, Bermuda and the rest of the territories as one integrated global financial centre that serves as the world's largest tax haven and a conduit for money laundering.[18]

These developments have helped to make UK firms some of the biggest tax dodgers on the planet. Of the 100 largest companies currently listed on the Financial Times Stock Exchange (FTSE) for example, 98 have tax haven operations. Of these, the worst offenders are found in energy and banking, with Barclays, HSBC, Lloyds and Royal Bank of Scotland (RBS) using 1649 shell companies between them and Shell and BP using more than 1000 between them.[19] What they couldn't do, however, was save the economic system from its recurrent slide into economic and financial crisis. After 30 years of relatively stable development, the global economy crashed again in 1973 as profit rates fell and the price of oil went into overdrive. The oil crisis of 1973 signalled the end of America's overwhelming dominance of the global economy, as deficits began to rise and both Japan and Germany began to catch back up. Coming hot on the heels of the civil rights and black power movements, this loss of power at home and abroad forced the US elites into action. A number of major business leaders began to call for less regulation on their interests and the result was the political and economic project known today as neoliberalism. David Harvey has argued persuasively that neoliberalism is best understood as a ruling class offensive strategy designed to (1) reorient policy making in the core of capitalism further towards corporate interests, (2) allow firms to operate more freely across national boundaries, and (3) secure the power of first world capital through debt and structural adjustment in the developing world.[20] Secrecy jurisdictions were also central to this new strategy, proliferating massively on the back of far more liberal cross-border capital flows. Today, there are between 60 and 100 offshore jurisdictions vying for business in what Palan et al. have rightly defined as the 'golden age' for global tax havens.[21]

NEOLIBERAL TAX EVASION

Margaret Thatcher and Ronald Reagan are rightly synonymous with the development of neoliberal capitalism, but relatively little attention has been paid to the – no less important – role of tax havens in this process. In the aftermath of the Second World War, very few economists championed a return to liberal economics, as the carnage of the Great Depression was fresh in the minds of influential policy makers. The dominant trend was towards Keynesian economic management, and in these circumstances, the group of hard-line neoliberals around Friedrich Hayek and Milton Friedman could quite easily have become isolated, were it not for the backing of tax-dodging outposts. In 1947, Hayek received money from the Swiss Central Bank to form the world's first neoliberal lobby group – the Mont Pèlerin Society.[22] This organisation brought together right-wing philosophers and economists to produce theoretical arguments for a return to the free market. But they also forged practical links to the City of London through Sir Alfred Suenson-Taylor, who, along with his brother Charles, linked Mont Pèlerin to an array of anti-regulation City financiers. Collectively, these networks were to prove extremely influential in the neoliberal counter-revolution during the 1970s. But perhaps an even greater achievement was their role in the creation of the euro-dollar market in the late 1950s. We saw earlier that after the Second World War, the US had hoped to dominate global trade by anchoring rival currencies around the dollar. This gave the US monetary authorities significant power while it lasted, but it also put restrictions on private financiers who lost their ability to speculate on currency flows and market volatility. Eurodollars helped the bankers get around this problem at the same time as the Vietnam War was creating vast deficits for the US Treasury. With massive quantities of dollars flooding into the City throughout the late 1960s, and the war dragging on interminably, US President, Richard Nixon, was eventually forced to take the dollar out of the Bretton Woods system in 1973.[23] This turned out to be the beginning of the end for the more regulated capitalism of the post-war era, as it set the scene for the end of currency exchange and capital controls by Reagan and Thatcher less than a decade later.

From a relatively marginal set of ideas, neoliberalism quickly became the new orthodoxy, as governments suddenly began to fear capital flight into less regulated parts of the global economy. Tax havens were absolutely central to this process, moreover, providing the impetus to establish the euro-dollar market in the first place and providing the bolt holes for capital to move once the breach had occurred. By the 1990s, Democratic US President Bill Clinton and Labour Party leader Tony Blair had both embraced the logic of neoliberalism in a process that signalled the decimation of post-war economic management. Blair's in-house sociologist, Anthony Giddens, tried to dress this up as a 'Third Way' between neoliberalism and social democracy, but the truth was that the neoliberals had carried through a political coup d'état that Friedman and Hayek could scarcely have dreamed of.[24] Instead of responding to the needs of their electorate, governments increasingly tied themselves to the wishlists of (potentially mobile) capital, reducing taxes and scaling back regulations in a reactionary race to the bottom. This has allowed corporations crucial leverage over political decision making in ways that have undermined the democratic process ever since. Some statistics on the taxes and incomes of the rich will help illustrate the point:

- Taxes on US corporations fell from 50 per cent after the Second World War to 22 per cent today.[25]
- Nominal corporation tax rates fell by ten percentage points (35 to 25 per cent) from 1995 to 2007 in the European Union.[26]
- Income taxes paid by the rich fell significantly, with Reagan cutting the top rate from 70 per cent to 28 per cent and Thatcher from 83 per cent to 40 per cent.[27]
- The richest Americans went from receiving 30–35 per cent of national income to 45–50 per cent in the last 35 years.

- The UK exhibited a similar pattern, with the richest 1 per cent increasing their share of 'after tax income' from just 3 per cent in 1973 to 24 per cent in 2013.[28]
- On the other side, figures produced by the US Federal Bureau of Labour Statistics, show that the average American worker earned a lower real wage in 2006 than their counterpart in 1970.[29]

The cross-border effects have, if anything, been even starker. A recent report by Oxfam calculated that for the first time in recorded history, the top 1 per cent of the world's population are richer than the bottom 99 per cent combined. Even more extreme, the world's eight richest men have a combined wealth in excess of the bottom 3.6 billion people – partly by virtue of decades of structural adjustment in the Global South.[30] If one effect of the oil crisis was the end of the Bretton Woods system, another was a series of financial imbalances that eventually led to debt servitude for many of the poorest people on the planet. This began when the oil-producing countries in the Middle East found themselves with massive surpluses of petro-dollars as the price of oil went up fourfold in the course of 1973. Much of this cash duly made its way to investment banks in London and New York and so the job of ironing out the global imbalances soon fell to Wall Street and the City of London.

With their own economies in a slump, western financiers began to create shadow bank transfers in the euro-dollar markets to lend this money to poorer countries in Asia, Africa and Latin America.[31] These loans provided higher interest rates than those that could be achieved in the West, but they also came with important risks as debt exploded across the Global South. Between 1970 and 1977, the debt of the least developed countries (LDCs) went from €300 million to €13,427 million.[32] This made sense for the power brokers in the western establishment, but it put the world's poorest people on the hook for debts that were extremely large and not of their making. To make matters worse, these debts were generally denominated in US dollars and contracted on the basis of variable interest rates. When the second oil crisis struck in 1979, the cost of these loans quickly became unsustainable, as interest rates increased and countries began to suffer domestic recession. By 1982, Mexico had declared bankruptcy, followed by Brazil and a host of other LDCs. Fearing the consequences for their own banking systems, Reagan and Thatcher turned this problem into an opportunity by using the International Monetary Fund (IMF) to restructure the debt in return for longer-term structural changes in the debtor economies.[33] Each time the process was the same, as private debts accumulated through tax haven lending were transformed into public debts administered by IMF officials. The results of this have also been consistently devastating, with academic work by Davison Budhoo and the Jubilee 2000 Campaign independently putting the deaths from structural adjustment policies at between 6–7 million annually.[34] Meanwhile, the financiers who caused this devastation have been handsomely rewarded for their efforts. David Harvey estimates that from 1980 until 2005 the world's poorest people were forced to transfer $4.6 trillion to their wealthy creditors in a process he defines as 'accumulation by dispossession'.[35] Reflecting on the role of tax havens in this process, Altamura writes,

> After the collapse of the Bretton Woods' system in 1973…Western commercial banks assumed an increasing role in transferring huge amounts of dollars accumulated by oil-exporting countries to Less Developed Countries (LDCs) *through the so-called 'recycling' mechanism of the Euromarket*…In the short-term, the privatisation of credit proved to be a profitable bet and it allowed the renaissance of the banking sector after the 'embedded liberalist' regime of Bretton Woods. Besides, these international flows of money provided the basis for the financial globalisation to come. On the longer-term, many LDCs became subject to the imperatives of private institutions and prisoners of a 'debt trap' throughout the 1980s. *We can only imagine how the destiny of LDCs and of the modern financial system would have been with the regulation of the Euromarket*…[our emphasis].[36]

The trajectory of capitalism since the 1970s means that we will never know the answer to Altamura's speculation. What we do know, however, is that tax havens have been at the very centre of our increasingly globalised, neoliberal economy. In the Global North, offshore jurisdictions have functioned as battering rams to wages and conditions, undermining democracy and dragging politics to the right. In the Global South, their influence has been even more pernicious in helping to create the conditions for endless austerity and the deaths of millions of people.

THE DIRECT EFFECTS OF TAX HAVEN CAPITALISM

One of the most arresting features of Albert Einstein's General Theory of Relativity is the discovery of black holes. These are massively dense phenomena exerting huge gravitational pulls on anything in their orbit. One of the arguments in this book is that tax havens function in an analogous way to more visible parts of the global economy. On the one hand, they hide huge 'alternative economies' which we know very little about and certainly cannot measure accurately. But in addition, tax havens exert a wider pull on the visible economy in many detrimental ways. Here we look at three direct effects in terms of lost revenues, organised criminality and global financial instability.

Lost Revenue

Tax havens cost the worlds' taxpayers trillions of dollars annually, but measuring the exact cost is no easy matter. The actors involved typically use these jurisdictions to evade their responsibility to the rest of society, meaning that open and transparent information is difficult to come by. Added to this, there are a host of different measures available, all trying to capture overlapping but slightly different phenomena. One thing that is reasonably well defined is the amount of assets held offshore by high-net-worth individuals. Understanding the wealth of the super-rich offers lucrative business opportunities to a host of private companies that have consequently tracked this aspect of the offshore system. In 1998, a Merrill Lynch/Cap Gemini report estimated that the wealth of the super-rich amounted to $27 trillion, of which one third ($8.5 trillion) was held offshore. Richard Murphy updated these figures for 2008, finding that the offshore component of this wealth had grown to $9.7 trillion.[37] Using a slightly different measure, Boston Consultancy Group came up with an overall figure of $38 trillion, with an estimate of $9 trillion held offshore.[38] A fourth estimate from Mc Kinsey and Company lends weight to this number, with a figure of $9.45 trillion held by the rich in offshore bank accounts.[39] Finally, Gabriel Zucman has used discrepancies in international financial statistics to come up with a figure of $7.6 trillion.[40] Working on the basis of an annual return of 7.5 per cent to the owners of these assets, Palan et al. estimate that the money saved by HNWIs through secrecy jurisdictions is roughly $255 billion annually.[41] This is more than twice the amount given in development aid, but to see the true extent of the human cost, consider the facts about access to safe drinking water.

The United Nations Education, Scientific and Cultural Organisation (UNESCO) recently concluded that 1.75 billion people currently lack access to safe and dependable drinking water.[42] As many as 60 per cent of rural families in LDCs suffer this form of water poverty with up to 25 per cent of urban families similarly affected.[43] UNESCO have estimated that an investment of just $10 billion per year over a ten-year cycle could eradicate water poverty for the whole of humanity. Just 4 per cent of the tax evaded by the super-rich in any one year could transform the lives of 300 million people currently suffering from water-borne diseases, but instead, the entire system has been stacked in the interest of a tiny elite. To understand just how concentrated this group really is, the Tax Justice Network estimates that one third of all private financial wealth and nearly half of all offshore wealth is owned by just 91,000 individuals or just 0.009 per cent of the global population.[44] Perhaps more than any other, this statistic exposes the lack of democracy at the heart of our system, and more worrying still is the fact that individual tax dodging is only the tip of the iceberg. By far the biggest tax evaders are the world's Transnational Corporations (TNCs) who use secrecy arrangements and transfer pricing to avoid truly staggering amounts of taxation. The opaque nature of the practices they deploy makes it difficult to gain accurate estimations, beyond the fact that the figures are substantial.

In 2009, Christian Aid made a stab at calculating the total capital flow from bilateral trade mispricing into the EU and the US from non-EU countries, estimating the number at $1.1 trillion for the period 2005–7.[45] Whether this figure is accurate or not is difficult to tell, but the fact that trillions are going missing annually seems very plausible. Using a concept known as the tax gap, Richard Murphy has estimated that 16 per cent of the total tax-take in the UK is being evaded annually, or 6 per cent of Gross Domestic Product (GDP).[46] The tax gap draws on objective data to calculate the difference between what companies announce in profits and what they actually pay in tax. Using a similar measure, the Internal Revenue Service calculates a 16 per cent annual tax gap in the US amounting to 2 per cent of GDP.[47] Official figures for the French economy put the loss at roughly 3 per cent of GDP annually.[48] Using the size of the global shadow economy as his guide, Murphy has also estimated that around 5 per cent of global GDP is being lost to tax authorities across the world, giving a total figure of $3.98 trillion annually.[49] These losses are truly astonishing, suggesting that an amount equivalent to German GDP, the world's fourth largest economy, is being lost every year through tax evasion and avoidance. The big winners are the rich and powerful who avail of tax havens and secrecy jurisdictions. The big losers are the rest of humanity, particularly those least able to afford it. Murphy has this to say about the problem,

> Large parts of the world's population are being denied opportunity… because of the activities of a relatively small number of accountants, lawyers, bankers and wealth managers in tax haven states. The real cost of that activity is seen in the unnecessary deaths of children in infancy, in the denial of proper education to children, and especially girls; and in the inability of countries without the necessary infrastructure to develop their economies as they should. The cost to the long-term wealth of these nations is incalculable…. Those among the 99 percent of the population who think they have lost out as a result of tax haven activity are absolutely right – they have.[50]

Criminal Activity

In 2015, 11.5 million documents from the Panamanian corporate law firm, Mossack Fonseca, were leaked to journalists. What quickly became known as the Panama Papers revealed an elaborate web of wealth and corruption involving politicians, heads of state, drug dealers and terror networks. When the European crime agency, Europol, cross referenced its database against the Panama leaks, it found 3469 probable matches – with 1722 organisations likely to be involved in money laundering for criminal enterprises, 516 matches connected to Eastern European crime gangs, 388 linked to VAT fraud operations, 260 cigarette-smuggling operations, 116 names linked to Islamic terror networks and 99 linked to organised drug crime.[51] In Britain, most of the headlines focused on the stockbroking father of the then Tory Prime Minister, David Cameron. Ian Cameron had been the head of an offshore fund known as Blairmore Holdings, which 'had avoided ever paying tax in Britain by hiring a small army of Bahamas residents – including a part time bishop – to sign its paper work'.[52] It also transpired that David Cameron had once owned 5000 units in Blairmore Holdings, which were only sold in 2010.[53] More ominous still was the fact that in 2013, Cameron had written to the European Council in a bid to have trust funds like his father's excluded from criminal investigations into tax avoidance – although no charges were ever brought against him in a court of law.[54]

What the Panama Papers made crystal clear, however, is that the current network of corporate havens provide opacity to global elites on *both sides of the law*. Indeed, tax havens have been central to organised crime for nearly a century. During the 1930s, for example, Mayer Lansky helped to create the biggest crime syndicate in US history with the help of offshore accounts in Switzerland and the Bahamas.[55] Without this link it would have been virtually impossible for the Mafia to launder their money, making tax havens an essential part of the American organised-crime story. More recently, Maingot found that 75 per cent of all sophisticated drug trafficking operations use offshore secrecy locations to launder their proceeds.[56] He also found that drug money was the primary catalyst for the spectacular growth of Caribbean secrecy jurisdictions from the early 1970s onwards.[57] In 2012, one of the UK's biggest banks, HSBC, was fined nearly $2 billion by the US authorities for widespread offshore money laundering involving Mexico's Sinaloa Cartel and Colombia's Norte Del Valle Cartel.[58] Drug gangs have brought chaos to the poor across the cities of Mexico, with the Sinaloa Cartel involved in a vicious turf war that has so far claimed the lives of 77,000 people.[59] Despite this fact, HSBC allowed $881 million to flow through their branches and knowingly excluded $670 billion from their monitoring systems over a long period of time. HSBC was essential to Sinaloa's operations, but the bank never lost its licence and none of the senior executives faced any criminal charges. Instead, they agreed to pay minimal fines before moving on with their profit making.[60] The signal this sent to the corporate world was crystal clear – fraud and corruption will be punished with fines, but no one that matters will ever go to jail. This is not just an informal understanding, moreover. According to Nicholas Shaxson, 'US banks may…legally accept proceeds from a range of crimes, such as handling stolen property – as long as the crimes are committed overseas'.[61]

Terror networks are similarly implicated in the murky world of tax evasion. Right-wing commentators used to rail against the menace of Islamic State, but dig even slightly into the detail, and it becomes clear that terrorist organisations rely on the same offshore system that supports the resources of the western elite. Figures from Global Financial Integrity estimate that the flow of illicit weapons, guns and natural resources runs to \$650 billion annually.[62] Until relatively recently, Islamic State was one of the major players in this trade, with \$2 million in revenue from oil sales every day. These sales were made to governments and firms across the world with help from offshore companies to conceal their true origin. Clean money and guns flowed back in again via these same offshore financial intermediaries.[63] Similar patterns have been discovered by Transparency International (TI) in relation to the City of London. According to TI director Robert Barrington, London is awash with cash stolen from Russia and laundered in the City. To take just one example, more than 50 per cent of company-owned, luxury London homes are registered in tax havens, with the British Virgin Islands and Jersey particularly prominent. Like the drug dealers, terror networks have been aided and abetted by the world's financiers, exposing the hypocrisy of the so-called 'war on drugs' and the 'war on terror'. In reality, western elites have used the latter to generate fear and racism at home, while cynically profiting from the same offshore methods that allow organised crime and terror to proliferate. Nicholas Shaxson captures the essence of this hypocrisy,

> The drug smugglers, terrorists and other criminals use exactly the same off-shore mechanisms and subterfuges – shell banks, trusts, dummy corporations – that corporations use. We will never beat the terrorists

or the heroin traffickers unless we confront the whole system – and that means tackling…the whole paraphernalia of off shore. It is hardly surprising in this light that…. the US success rate in catching criminal money was 0.1% meaning a 99.9% failure rate. *Laundered proceeds of drug trafficking, racketeering, corruption and terrorism tag along with other forms of dirty money to which the United States and Europe lend a welcoming hand* [our emphasis].[64]

From this vantage point the real war is being waged by the rich on the rest of us.

Financial Instability

Before Covid-19, the Great Recession from 2007 to 2013 was the deepest and most sustained economic dislocation since the 1930s. Most commentators have accepted the role of complex financial innovation in the global crisis, but there has been comparatively little focus on the role of low tax, low regulation jurisdictions. Tax havens have greatly increased the opacity and secrecy of global finance in a number of ways. By engaging in tax and regulatory competition (arbitrage), tax havens have created a race to the bottom that has helped to let big finance completely off the leash. Every time a global financial corporation is faced with potential regulation, a tax haven is on hand to make sure that they have a cheaper option overseas. One method of reducing costs is to move financial operations into the so-called shadow banking sector. This involves moving out of the global regulatory system, overseen by central bankers and effectively into the shadows (hence the name), using operations known as Special Purpose Vehicles (SPVs). Companies that do this forfeit central bank support, but they can also engage in riskier behaviour, with less money needing to be held in reserve.

The so-called shadow banking system that subsequently developed, often in low tax jurisdictions, proved to be a major factor in the Great Recession.[65] When the Financial Inquiry Commission attempted to assess the size of shadow banking in the USA, it found that it was actually larger than the traditional banking sector.[66] This means that a less regulated, more opaque and riskier banking system has grown up alongside the regulated banking that most people are aware of. SPVs typically have lower equity-to-loan ratios than traditional banks, making them more vulnerable to sudden shifts in market conditions. Thanks to the incentives offered by tax haven authorities, they also typically carry much higher levels of unsecured debt. Shadow banks typically claim onshore tax reliefs for their enormous borrowing offshore, giving them perverse incentives to increase their leverage. For these reasons, hedge funds in particular have created all manner of toxic assets in a bid to increase their profitability. The result was, and is, an accident waiting to happen. By definition, the risks involved in shadow banking are difficult to perceive. They only become fully apparent in the midst of an economic crisis, at which point the lack of central bank support becomes a major problem.[67] Shadow banks, generally domiciled in tax haven locations, were major players in the recent crisis. Here, we reproduce three examples to illustrate this point.

In December 2008, the biggest Ponzi scheme in history was rumbled on Wall Street. Since the 1970s, investors had assumed that Bernie Madoff made successful returns through skilful investment decisions. In reality, he was merely depositing their money in offshore bank accounts before paying the past year's returns with next year's investment money.[68] Stephen Harbeck, chief executive of the American Securities Investor Protection Corporation (SIPC) and official receiver to Madoff's brokerage business, labelled the Madoff scam a 'highly complex hybrid fraud', perpetuated by creating SPVs for each individual investment. Madoff used New York Mellon Bank to squirrel funds into offshore accounts in the Caribbean and Europe, but money flowed the other way too. For example, French investors used Undertakings for Collective Investments in Transferable Services (UCITS) funds quoted in Dublin and Luxembourg to invest $500 million in the Madoff Ponzi scheme. Two Irish funds also invested in Madoff's firm, raising questions about the role of the IFSC in this elaborate web of offshore finance.[69] When this scheme was finally rumbled, it had cost investors nearly $65 billion.

During the early 2000s, Royal Bank of Scotland went from being one of the biggest banks in Scotland to becoming the fifth largest bank in the world.[70] On the face of it, much of this was down to the genius acquisitions of its chief executive, Fred Goodwin, who helped the bank to post profits of £10.8 billion for 2007, or a whopping £1 million for every hour.[71] As in the case of the Madoff scheme, however, all was not as it appeared. One part of the RBS business model involved complex international tax avoidance schemes known as structured trading. These were massive deals, often around £6 billion at a time, which moved money into secretive offshore entities with ambiguous or dual corporate status. The idea was to trick the authorities so that RBS *and* a foreign partner could each claim tax relief on the same deal. Most of the time the resulting profits flowed from the taxes that were being avoided, with the underlying deals actually losing money. As usual, banks in the Cayman Islands and other Caribbean Islands were involved, costing the British and US treasuries at least £500 million in forgone taxes.[72] When the Great Recession came, RBS was one of the biggest casualties, posting a loss of £28 billion in 2009 – the biggest in UK corporate history. Fearing the wider ramifications of the bank's collapse, the British taxpayer was forced to pump £45 billion into the bank for a 70 per cent share. Since 2008, the bank has lost a further £58 billion, causing untold damage to working people across the UK. Fred Goodwin has meanwhile retired with an annual pension of £700,000.

Our final example comes from closer to Ireland itself. During the financial crisis of 2008, a little-known investment bank known as Depfa plc collapsed, before receiving €124 billion from the German authorities.[73] This proved to be Germany's single largest bailout, but the bank in question was originally registered in Ireland. Like many of the funds operating out of the IFSC, Depfa Bank accumulated massive assets (loans) on the back of very little equity capital. Their business model was incredibly risky, moreover, because they promised to purchase variable rate bonds even when no one else was prepared to. This meant that Depfa became an insurance company for other players in the market without properly hedging the risks for itself.[74] Ordinarily, these kinds of trade would be a red flag to the financial authorities, but the Irish regulator, Patrick Neary, infamously stated that he had neither the expertise nor the interest in regulating this form of subprime lending.[75] With interest rates falling – following the collapse of Lehman Brothers – Depfa haemorrhaged money and quickly folded. In this instance, the Irish taxpayer was sheltered from the immediate fallout thanks to the

3
Making Treasure Ireland

The mainstream account of Ireland's economic development is deliberately misleading. The narrative begins with a contrast between the first decade of laissez-faire policy making and a 25-year period in which economic nationalism became the order of the day. Then, in a watershed moment for the Irish economy, Seán Lemass and T.K. Whitaker jointly set Ireland on the path to a more successful economy, with a series of liberal initiatives from 1958 onwards. After an interlude of failure during the 1970s and 1980s, the period from 1994 to 2008 is celebrated as a 'Celtic Tiger' that allowed Ireland to overtake its European rivals after decades of relative under-achievement. The crises associated with the Great Recession and Covid-19 are then acknowledged, but the overarching narrative remains that Ireland has been better able to weather these challenges thanks to its ability to attract foreign direct investment (FDI) and foster a knowledge-based economy. The country's low corporation tax invariably plays a starring role in this account, with most Irish people strangely able to explain how the 12.5 per cent rate helps to make the country 'economically successful'.[1] There is also a sense that Ireland got lucky with its geographical location, its English language and its modern education system, but also made its own luck as an early adopter of neo-liberal policy making. Like all good stories, this one touches on aspects of Ireland's development, but it is more self-serving ideology than accurate economic history.

It is true that the first decade of independence was based on the continuation of liberal economics, but this was done to serve the bankers and landowners who populated Cumann na nGaedheal, rather than the interests of the wider population. It is also true that Fianna Fáil (FF) wanted to create a new class of Irish business owners during the 1930s, but this aspiration was never dropped when Lemass and Whitaker took over – it was merely pursued under different conditions. The best way to understand the different economic strategies pursued over the last 100 years is to see them as a series of initiatives designed to secure the wealth and privilege of the domestic elite. The first decade saw the dominance of liberalism and austerity budgets as the government sought to uphold the dominance of existing property relations on the one hand, with subduing a rebellious population on the other. From 1932 to 1958 there were attempts to pursue more domestically focused industrialisation, but the relative failure of this policy meant that from 1958 onwards, the entire establishment rowed in behind a unified strategy of tying the fortunes of Irish capitalism to those of the global elite. This model has had a number of iterations since that time, but in broad terms the state has used its sovereignty to attract foreign capital with all manner of (often tax-based) incentives, at the same time as it has protected and nourished a domestic elite in banking, agriculture and construction. The dynamics established between foreign capital, domestic capital and the state have also led to a deeply embedded culture of cronyism and corruption which went right to the top in at least two administrations since the 1970s. During the 1980s, for example, one of the most corrupt Fianna Fáil administrations established the Irish Financial Services Centre (IFSC) to support investment banks in the City of London and to take advantage of the European Single Market. This was the birth of an Irish offshore centre that has since grown to become one of the world's foremost tax havens. The rest of this book will look at the inner mechanics of this process, but before we get there, we need to recount Ireland's historical path to this destination.

PREHISTORY OF TAX HAVEN IRELAND

The Irish state was born amid the throes of revolution and counter-revolution that gripped Europe in the early twentieth century. After the First World War, an impoverished population rose against the British Empire for national freedom in order to better their own lives. Land seizures, factory occupations and mass strikes were all part of a pattern of agitation that ran from 1918 until 1923. However, following a Treaty with Britain and a vicious civil war, the genie of social rebellion was put firmly back in the bottle. Despite their role in the struggle for national liberation, the new leaders of the Irish Free State were deeply conservative. One of their number, Kevin O'Higgins, put it succinctly when he said he despised 'the attitude of protest, the attitude of negation, the attitude of sheer wantonness and waywardness and destructiveness which…has been to a large extent a traditional attitude of…the Irish people'.[2] The aim of the new Cumann na nGaedheal government was to uproot any revolutionary instinct among the Irish population and create a state that would facilitate the development of local Irish capitalism.

Besides their own inherent elitism and conservatism, the roots for this strategy lay in the 'development of underdevelopment' that initially characterised the independent nation. Through a series of Land Enclosure Acts stretching back to 1604, the British ruling classes had gradually created the conditions for the world's first industrialised economy, and in the process, they had reshaped Ireland to meet the needs of the metropolis.[3] Millions of British peasants had been pushed off the land to facilitate industrialisation and, over time, a symbiotic relationship emerged between British factory owners and Anglo-Irish landlords. Karl Marx correctly noted that Irish land was 'the bulwark of the English landed aristocracy' but he also pointed out that English factory owners had common interest with them 'in turning Ireland into mere pasture land which provides the English market with meat and wool at the cheapest possible prices'.[4] British manufacturers needed grains and livestock to feed their workers and the Anglo-Irish landlords were more than happy to oblige. The 'development of underdevelopment' that resulted can be seen in the fact that when the new Irish government came into power in 1922 only 4.3 per cent of the entire Irish labour force was working in manufacturing.[5] Ireland was effectively a meat and grain house for British capitalism, with thousands of ships commissioned to export agricultural produce to Bristol, Liverpool, Glasgow and London. Even during the darkest days of the famine, almost 4000 vessels carried food across the Irish Sea to these more profitable outlets.[6] British industrialists and the Anglo-Irish landowners therefore became staunch allies, alongside the financiers who linked this trade through the City of London.

At the time of independence, 97 per cent of Irish exports went to the British mainland and the Minister for Agriculture, Patrick Hogan, was determined to keep it that way.[7] With more than half the population working the land, Hogan argued that 'national development in Ireland for our generation at least, is practically synonymous with agricultural development'.[8] This led to a set of laissez-faire economic policies emphasising 'free trade, low taxes and government spending, modest direct intervention in industry and agriculture and parity with sterling'.[9] This so-called 'treasury view' model was justified on the basis of Ireland's economic comparative advantages, but there is no doubt that it also helped to bankroll Cumann na nGaedheal's principal economic backers – the major farmers and financiers.[10] In keeping with their wider strategy, the new government also adopted the British system of corporation taxes, applying both a traditional income tax on profits in addition to a new corporate profits tax (CPT) introduced in Britain to pay for the war. Meanwhile, Cumann na nGaedheal also handed the state's monetary policy to private bankers in 1927 who unsurprisingly decided that their future economic success lay with a strong currency and high rates of interest payments.[11] This meant tying the Irish punt to British sterling at parity, but it also meant that Irish manufactured goods would become immediately uncompetitive. Indeed, according to Conor McCabe, the 'value of the Irish pound was set at such a disproportionately high rate that it became a significant hurdle in the development of indigenous Irish industry'.[12] This was an acceptable casualty of the wider strategy, but agricultural prices fell dramatically throughout the 1920s, meaning there was little progress in that sector either. Despite the well-known slogan of 'one more cow, one more sow, one more acre under the plough', there was no increase in 'the number of cows, other cattle or pigs, while the area under crops fell by nearly one fifth between 1922–32'.[13] In a process that was to become depressingly familiar throughout the twentieth century, Cumann na nGaedheal supported the interests of an economic minority without being able to move Irish capitalism onto a successful trajectory that could potentially benefit the majority. Working people gained nothing economically from the first decade of independence and many smaller property owners began to feel deeply alienated. The Wall Street Crash (1929) signalled a major downturn in the Irish economy and when Fianna Fáil were elected in 1932, the time had come for a shift in direction.

During the late 1920s, Fianna Fáil cultivated the support of smaller farmers and businessmen by promising a new protectionist strategy that would break from the British. Party leader Éamon de Valera, denounced the new Ireland as little more than an 'Outgarden of Britain' and when his party came to power they imposed a series of tariffs and quotas to build an indigenous industrial base.[14] During the depression years of the 1930s, Ireland largely withdrew from laissez-faire capitalism and by 1936, Fianna Fáil had increased tariffs on more than 1000 goods by an average of 45 per cent.[15] Meanwhile, de Valera's decision to stop paying land annuities further contributed to an Economic War (1932–8), with tit-for-tat tariffs erected on British coal and Irish beef. Although this hit big farmers particularly hard, they were unable to challenge the move towards economic nationalism.[16] Fianna Fáil ministers successfully argued that the country's reliance on agricultural exports kept Ireland economically enslaved despite its formal political independence. Economic nationalism therefore dominated from the 1930s until the 1950s, thanks to support from industrialists, many workers and smaller farmers.[17] In line with their industrialisation strategy, FF passed the Control of Manufacturers Act (1932), which made it mandatory that all new production facilities would be at least 51 per cent Irish-owned and declared that at least two thirds of all share capital would be owned by Irish citizens.[18] Shielded from the rigours of international competition this new policy had some initial successes. Industrial production grew by nearly 50 per cent between 1931 and 1938, industrial employment rose by 57,000, and the sectoral composition broadened out to include clothing, footwear and engineering.[19]

The enforced self-sufficiency of the Second World War initially added further weight to this strategy, but the success of economic nationalism was intimately bound up with its limitations. Although Irish industry developed, it was almost entirely geared towards a small domestic market with limited opportunities for expansion.[20] Historically, successful protectionism entails a two-stage strategy, with tariff walls initially erected before being reduced as domestic industries become sufficiently established. In the Irish case this strategy was never possible, however, because of the limited size of the Irish market and the ongoing dominance of financial interests. With a domestic market of less than 4 million people, indigenous manufacturers lacked the customer base to expand to the levels required for international competitiveness. Irish companies were never big enough to become market leaders and they suffered greatly from a lack of modern technologies.[21]

Added to this, the link to sterling meant that Irish banks were reluctant to release the credit that might have allowed domestic firms to become more competitive. In opposition, Fianna Fáil had vigorously attacked the banks, with Sean McEntee claiming that they were 'bleeding the Irish farmer, crushing Irish industry, [and] investing Irish money abroad'.[22] But even though there had been banking commissions in 1926 and 1934, monetary policy remained steadfastly controlled by financial interests – even after Fianna Fáil took power. Reflecting on the power of the bankers in this period, Conor McCabe had this to say,

> It was a testament to the power of the banks in the Free State that, after sixteen years, two commissions, and one international financial crisis, their ability to dictate the pace and direction of Irish economic growth to suit their own business agenda to the detriment of almost all other aspects of Irish economic and social life remained undaunted.[23]

It is equally telling that Fianna Fáil could build a cross-class alliance on the basis of a nationalist model that still left the currency tied to sterling. De Valera and Lemass were serious about ending the horrors of colonialism, but they never managed to wrest full control of the economy away from their own domestic bankers. An independent central bank had to wait until 1943 to be established, and as the 1950s rolled on, Ireland fell further and further behind economically. Between 1951 and 1958, Gross Domestic Product (GDP) rose by less than 1 per cent per annum and the limitations of the protectionist model were definitively revealed by the fact that GDP per capita slipped from 75 per cent to 60 per cent of the European average.[24] Another change in direction was required, this time focused on the potential of FDI.

THE TURN OUTWARDS

During the first 30 years of independence there were genuine differences between Cumann na nGaedheal and Fianna Fáil, but three decades of relative economic decline eventually brought their policies into alignment with each other. By the late 1950s, Fianna Fáil accepted the insurmountable challenges that lay in protectionism, while the successors to Cumann na nGaedheal, Fine Gael (FG), came to see industrialisation as the essential driver of post-war Irish capitalism. Both sides also realised that state sovereignty could be better leveraged to create the conditions for foreign investment to help lift the domestic economy. Central to this new direction were Seán Lemass and T.K. Whitaker. Lemass became Taoiseach in 1959 with a determination to modernise the economy through a new generation of domestic profit-seeking businessmen.[25] Whitaker, who worked in the Department of Finance, developed an important document for this new strategy, known as the Programme for Economic Development. This prioritised the allocation of scarce resources to growth and accumulation, suggesting that if sufficient capital was not available from domestic sources every effort should be made to obtain it from abroad.[26] The shift outwards had actually begun in the early 1950s, with the establishment of the Export Board (1951) and the Industrial Development Authority (IDA) (1952). However, it was the introduction of an Exports Profits Relief Tax in 1956 that marked the first steps on the road towards Tax Haven Ireland. This scheme, which offered foreign manufacturing companies a tax exemption on profits for up to ten years, was defined by Kennedy et al., as 'probably the most important incentive of all in attracting foreign enterprise to Ireland.'[27] To coincide with Whitaker's change of policy direction, the Control of Manufacturers Act was also dismantled and a series of tax reliefs for the purchasing of plant and machinery were introduced. In 1959, the world's first Free Trade Zone was also established around Shannon Airport and the IDA began touting Ireland internationally with promises of 'no tax' and 'double your after-tax profits' to US investors.[28]

Investigating this period for a recent 'Review of Ireland's Corporation Tax Code', Seamus Coffey notes that a number of the tax incentives introduced at the time were quickly expanded – with a capital allowance of 20 per cent in 1956 moving to 100 per cent by 1978, for example.[29] There were also generous discounts for the physical depreciation of capital goods that ranged from 10 per cent to 25 per cent annually.[30] This was the first sign that the Irish elite were willing to use the state's taxation policy to attract foreign businesses and, for a time, the new strategy seemed to be paying off. Real output increased by 4.4 per cent per annum throughout the 1960s and by 1983, there were almost 1000 foreign enterprises in the state. Collectively, these accounted for 70 per cent of the new employment and 90 per cent of the increased exports in tradable goods.[31] Reflecting on the wider changes that were occurring, Cormac O'Grada, had this to say,

> At the outset few foresaw the rapid growth in the foreign sector, but direct foreign investment in Irish industry soon became the corner-stone of government policy.... The remarkable transformation of the economy between the late 1950s and the early 1970s may be largely attributed to the arrival of the multinationals.[32]

This transformation also created new dynamics between the different branches of domestic capital, foreign capital and the state. At first, there were hopes that FDI would create linkages with Irish industrial and manufacturing companies, but it quickly became apparent that the foreign sector was not particularly interested in such ties. This soon created what Barry has defined as a 'dualistic industrial structure' characterised by a more technologically advanced foreign sector leaving behind its domestic counterparts.[33] On the other hand, the influx of foreign capital was actually a fillip for those industries not in direct competition with FDI – such as banking, construction and professional services (law, accounting, tax planning etc.). The arrival of foreign capital absolved the banks of their need to provide domestic credit for investment, allowing them to more easily uphold the peg with sterling. There were also profit-making opportunities for accountancy and consultancy firms, but it was in the area of property and construction that the biggest shift was to occur. Land assets are unique in capitalism, being fixed in supply and immovable across borders. This gives their owners what P.J. Drudy has usefully described as a 'double monopoly', allowing domestic property developers to profit from foreign investors looking for premises to be built and better infrastructure to move their commodities.[34] By 1973, there were more than 350 IDA-sponsored companies in the state, occupying 15 million square foot of industrial floor space – all of which had been built in the previous decade.[35] An Office Premises Act passed in 1958 was also important in opening up profitable opportunities for domestic developers, who were then able to increase employment in the sector by 42 per cent during the 1960s. These somewhat contradictory impacts on the different sectors of the economy drove policy making in important directions. Time and resources were increasingly devoted to attracting and servicing the needs of global corporations, but the state was also busy creating patronage networks to protect the interests of the Irish elites.

Here again, land and construction held a number of advantages that quickly drew capital into the sector. Regulation influences every area of a capitalist economy, but rarely is this influence as direct and consequential as it is in the markets for land and property. Although state-sponsored infrastructural projects are undertaken with public money, most of the benefits actually flow to private property holders. A government-commissioned report, the Kenny Report, found that between 1961 and 1973 the average price of serviced land in Dublin increased by 530 per cent, for example, when the corresponding rise in the consumer price index was just 64 per cent. More pointedly, the report insisted that the vast majority of this increase was completely unearned, coming directly from the investment made by local authorities.[36] Favourable (re)zoning decisions are also crucial for profitability, making it essential for developers to remain on good terms with decision makers in the civil service and the governing political establishment.[37] Being on the inside gives developers crucial advantages in securing successful zoning decisions and puts them in the frame for contracts secured through the IDA and the state. Having already shown a willingness to provide tax advantages to foreign investors, these dynamics soon fostered the second key ingredient in the development of Tax Haven Ireland – cronyism and corruption.

Fianna Fáil had always considered itself the 'builders' party' and in 1965 they established a semi-clandestine fundraising group known as TACA, through the offices of Haughey Boland on Amiens Street in Dublin.[38] Those lucky enough to be asked to join were already party loyalists, but TACA moved their relationship to a whole new level, with 500 businesspeople invited to pay an annual subscription charge of £100 (roughly €2150 today).[39] This was expressly designed to forge links between the party hierarchy and the business community, with one side relieving the other of money in return for direct access to government ministers.[40] Some members of the group also gave up a day a month to actively fundraise for Fianna Fáil, while others were happy to lobby ministers at various functions. The property developer, Patrick Gallagher, summed up their thinking when he suggested that 'Fianna Fáil were good for builders and builders were good for Fianna Fáil and there was nothing wrong with that'.[41] There may have been nothing wrong with it from the point of view of private builders, but the willingness of Fianna Fáil to take money from developers was soon influencing key aspects of government policy.

During the protectionist era, FF prided themselves on launching a major house-building programme to lift working class families out of poverty. In the 1930s, there were more houses built in the public than the private sector, but by the 1950s, FF were scaling back on direct construction, and encouraging local authority tenants to purchase their houses. By commodifying the housing stock in these ways, FF were consciously creating a market for domestic capitalists in areas that had been more limited in the previous economic regime. This policy had an impact more-or-less immediately.[42] Table 3.1 captures the relevant data.

Table 3.1 Public and Private Housing Output and Public Housing Sold to Tenants, 1920s–2007

	1920s	1930s	1940s	1950s	1960s	1970s	1980s	1990s	2000–7
Public Housing	6920	38,450	20,768	52,500	29,124	61,953	42,893	20,184	46,926
Private Housing	10,910	31,657	37,164	49,188	64,835	176,230	182,203	275,186	468,318
Public Housing Sold to Tenants	zero	zero	zero	zero	64,490	59,566	46,204	17,204	10,649
Percentage (%) of Public Housing Built	39	55	36	52	31	26	19	7	9.1

Source: 'From Asset Based Housing to Welfare Housing? The Changing Function of Social Housing in Ireland'.[43]

By the late 1960s, FF also made sure that the state was the major tenant for private sector office developments, with more than 50 per cent of private office blocks occupied by government departments using taxpayers' money.[44] TACA was eventually wound down in the 1970s, but not before the die was cast in terms of cronyism and corruption.

EVASION NATION

The period from 1973 to 1993 is widely regarded by mainstream commentators as a failure, as two major oil crises trapped the economy in a spiral of stagnation, inflation and serious balance of payments difficulties.[45] Most of the world responded to the oil crises of 1973 and 1979 by replacing Keynesian demand management with neoliberal austerity, but for the first time in their history, Irish governments began to run budget deficits in the hope of replacing foreign demand with government initiatives. Fine Gael won the 1973 election on the promise of increased spending, and for the first three years of their term, they fulfilled their mandate – including a budget deficit of nearly 7 per cent in 1975.[46] This level of deficit spending was gradually reduced in the last two years of the FG–Labour government, but it was ramped up again by Fianna Fáil in the early 1980s.[47] Despite this, economic growth averaged just 1.5 per cent from 1979 to 1986 – with total employment falling by 100,000 people and more than 200,000 people leaving the country in search of employment.[48] For mainstream commentators, Charles Haughey's greatest crime was to initiate a series of 'giveaway budgets' when he came in to office in 1979. But from the point of view of Tax Haven Ireland, Haughey's role in two other initiatives were far more significant and long lasting. The first was his role in the 'Ansbacher' tax scam which worked by pretending domestic savings were overseas when they were really in Dublin. This allowed the domestic rich to avoid their taxes and signalled that Tax Haven Ireland was 'open for business'. The second was his drive to establish an International Financial Services Centre that could service the needs of global capital. IFSC firms often pretend that foreign profits should be booked in Ireland when they are really created in other countries. Let's look at each of these initiatives in turn.

For most of the twentieth century, Charles Haughey was regarded as a giant among his colleagues, but when he died in 2006, Haughey was despised by the general public as the biggest tax cheat of them all. Over the course of his career, Haughey took the equivalent of €45 million in bribes and corruption payments from businessmen, including the financier Dermot Desmond, the hotelier P.V. Doyle and the retailer Ben Dunne. This staggering amount, representing 171 times his legitimate salary, shows just how endemic corruption was at the time.[49] Indeed, one of those intimately aware of the business elites throughout the period alleges that Haughey was effectively an inside man for a coterie of wealthy businessmen anxious to have one of their own at the very top of the political establishment.[50] Haughey would need to be well looked after, however, with one of his own accountants, Des Traynor, tasked with facilitating dodgy payments from business leaders into Haughey's many bank accounts.[51] During the 1980s, this allowed Haughey to live in a palatial mansion in Kinsealy, North Co. Dublin, replete with hired staff costing €5000 per year. He also had a yacht, a thoroughbred stud farm and his own personal island – all on a salary of around £7000 annually.[52] His colleague in government, George Colley, became so concerned that Haughey was granting favours to his friends that he insisted on all state contracts coming to him in the Ministry for Industry and Commerce before they were signed off.[53] Two official inquiries proved Colley's concerns well founded, but what also became abundantly clear was that Haughey was not acting alone. Corruption was endemic in the Ireland of the 1960s and 1970s as a network of executives, developers and mainstream politicians were busy using the state to further their own interests. The scandal that unfolded around Guinness and Mahon Bank's Ansbacher accounts, is emblematic of the period.

Des Traynor left Haughey Boland in 1969 for a Guinness and Mahon Bank that was already setting up tax dodging links with a bank in the Cayman Islands. Over the next two decades, Traynor masterminded an elaborate tax scam that benefitted 179 of the movers and shakers in Irish society with the imprimatur of the state itself. Set up in 1971, Guinness Mahon Cayman Trust (GMCT) allowed Traynor to take money from his wealthy clients under the pretence that it was moving offshore and so out of the clutches of the tax man. In reality, the money was resting in Stephen's Green, minutes away from the Irish Central Bank (ICB) in Dublin. This meant that client money was always at hand should they need it, and as an added bonus, the rich could write off the interest that they were supposedly paying abroad as an extra deduction against their taxes. To ensure their identities were protected, Traynor developed a system of memorandum accounts to track who really owned the assets, alongside a set of anonymity codes for added secrecy. Haughey was known as S8 and S9 for example, but within five years, the Irish Central Bank became aware of what was going on. During a routine inspection in 1976, chartered accounts from the ICB discovered loans backed by offshore accounts and immediately realised the potential for a scam. Digging a little deeper, it became obvious that 'there could be no reason for these arrangements other than to reduce the tax liabilities of the customers in question'.[54] Yet, rather than making moves to shut it down, they accepted a personal guarantee from Traynor that he would cease his operation over time.

At the same time, the Central Bank doctored its own internal files to refer to the affair as tax avoidance instead of more serious – and illegal – tax evasion. The fact that Ken O'Reilly Hyland was a major funder for Fianna Fáil, a director of the Central Bank and a holder of a tax-dodging account, tells us everything we need to know about large sections of official Ireland at the time. The idea of allowing financial criminals to wind down their own operation was an obvious fiction, particularly as the amounts flowing through the accounts increased rapidly once Haughey became Taoiseach. In 1979, there was IR £5 million on deposit, but just three years later this had grown to IR £27 million.[55] Despite this, the Central Bank never stepped in to shut it down or passed on their information to the Revenue Commissioners. Indeed, the whole sordid affair only came to light in 1997, when corrupt payments from Ben Dunne to Charles Haughey and former FG Minister, Michael Lowry, led investigators to accounts for nearly 200 people. Among them were many of the inner circle who had bankrolled Fianna Fáil, but it also included Fine Gael TD, Hugh Coveney (the father of Fine Gael senior politician, Simon Coveney), members of the Board of Cement Roadstone, a director of Allied Irish Bank and the hotelier P.V. Doyle. Haughey and the clique of politicians and businessmen around him had spent 25 years pretending their money was deposited offshore in what was the strongest possible signal that, when it came to tax dodging, Ireland was more than 'open for business' – its top leaders were tax evaders.

Haughey's more lasting legacy for Tax Haven Ireland was not, however, corruption payments from the cream of the Irish establishment. It was in finding a way to make tax dodging on a grand scale available to global companies – without the apparent whiff of corruption. This occurred through the establishment of the IFSC in 1987 under the direction of Haughey, billionaire tax exile Dermot Desmond, and a number of City of London bankers. The original proposal for an IFSC was drafted by Desmond, then head of National City Stockbrokers, in conjunction with the chief executive of Allied Irish Banks, Michael Buckley, for inclusion in the Fianna Fáil manifesto for the 1987 election. Initially, Desmond and Haughey faced opposition from civil servants in the Department of Finance, who were concerned that the scheme would undermine the tax revenues the state got from the banks.[56] But Haughey and his senior team pushed it through, conscious of the opportunities it presented for moving Ireland in to the tax-dodging big leagues. Meanwhile, the wider catalyst for their determination came from two interrelated opportunities created by Margaret Thatcher's government – the deregulation of the City of London in 1986 and the establishment of the Single European Market in the same year. This latter initiative created a market of hundreds of millions of customers that immediately incentivised US companies to find a friendly base inside the EU. Ireland proved remarkably adept at capturing much of this new investment, moreover, thanks to an existing range of international subsidies, which now included a 10 per cent tax rate for foreign manufacturing companies. In addition, the creation of a Single Market for financial services created the opportunity to provide tax and regulatory services on a hitherto unimaginable scale. One of the key legislative developments was known as the Undertakings for Collective Investments in Transferable Services (UCITS).[57] This meant that all financial products meeting a given standard could be approved in one EU country and sold in another. Immediately this presented the possibility of creating an Irish Financial Services Centre to manage the wealth of the global rich. The fact that rival tax havens like the Channel Islands and Liechtenstein were excluded from these arrangements further convinced the Irish elite to move more centrally into tax evasion and avoidance.

Instead of developing a domestic industrial policy, as a critical Telesis report had recommended in 1982, the Irish elites positioned Dublin to become a financial outpost of the City of London. The Taxes Consolidation Act (TCA) of 1997 was particularly important in this context, as it allowed Special Purpose Vehicles to compute their taxes as if they were trading companies and enacted a number of extremely generous tax advantages.[58] This might seem like a technical issue, but it was of huge importance to global corporations. Non-trading, or passive profits, were usually taxed at the rate of 25 per cent, but their re-designation as trading profits allowed a reduced rate of just 12.5 per cent. The TCA also laid the foundation for the new vehicles and structures used by IFSC law and accountancy firms to allow US multinationals to use Ireland as a conduit to avoid non-US corporation taxes. Most important of all, the act created the Section 110 Special Purpose Vehicle that would eventually make Ireland the number one location for securitisation in the European Union. These policies had the desired effect more-or-less immediately, with corporate giants such as General Electric, Heinz, Hewlett Packard and IBM establishing significant corporate treasury management operations in Dublin within the first year.[59] They were soon joined by major banks and investment funds, moreover, as the IFSC became one of the principal engines of Irish growth during the so-called Celtic Tiger. Added to this financial activity, recovery in the US, coupled with the success of the Irish rich in attracting FDI, meant that for the second time since the founding of the state the Irish economy was set to enjoy significant expansion. At the heart of it now, however, was a strategy of sharing tax privileges which the Irish rich had already secured with their foreign counterparts who ran the multinationals.

THE RISE AND FALL OF THE CELTIC TIGER

If the 20 years preceding the Celtic Tiger were a significant disappointment, the period from 1993 to 2008 appeared to be no less than an economic miracle. Ireland entered the 1990s with a GDP at just 60 per cent of the EU average, but over the course of the next 15 years this increased to 145 per cent.[60] Much of this was initially driven by multinationals setting up their routes into the European Single Market, as inward investment from the United States increased from 2.2 per cent of GDP to 49.2 per cent in the course of a decade. At one point, a country with just 1 per cent of the EU population was securing 25 per cent of all Greenfield US investment, thanks to a combination of relatively low wages by European standards and a pliant political class willing to allow foreign money to use Ireland as a convenient drop off point within the EU. In 2003, the Irish state also streamlined its corporation tax regime with a headline rate of 12.5 per cent for all companies trading in the state and a 25 per cent for all non-trading profits.

Ireland had historically struggled to employ its population, but within a few short years the numbers in work went from 1.3 million to 2.1 million.[61] The participation of women in the labour force was particularly impressive, growing from 435,000 to 787,000 in little over a decade.[62] This increase in people at work was the greatest single contribution to rising living standards, as labour markets gradually tightened and employers were forced to increase real wages. Walsh estimates that real wages rose by 34 per cent in the early years of the Celtic Tiger as economic activity went into overdrive. The right-wing Heritage Foundation explained the conditions for this 'Tiger Miracle' in the following remarks:

> Ireland has long had, and intends to sustain, low tax rates to attract investment. Smaller government [also] became part of the road to success. While cutting back on spending, the government took steps to promote business investment. A notable example was the adoption of a proposal to create the International Financial Services Centre (IFSC) in the old Docklands area of Dublin. The successful development of the IFSC shows the strength of cooperation between business interests and all parts of the state system that is such a strong characteristic of Ireland.[63]

After 40 years of relative failure, the FDI model seemed finally to be vindicated, but there were a number of problems lurking in the background. The first of these had to do with the nature of the foreign investment itself. Although there was a genuine spike in real investment in the early 1990s, a lot of the money flowing into Ireland came to take advantage of transfer pricing rules, treasury management operations and other forms of tax incentive. Reflecting on this phenomenon near the end of the process, O'Riain argued that 'clearly a boom in foreign investment did drive the rapid expansion in growth and exports.... But many of the best known foreign firms were simply moving goods through their Irish operations to take advantage of low tax rates, creating an entrepôt economy that provided the illusion of growth and development'.[64] This became all the more problematic, moreover, as real growth was gradually squeezed out by the contradictory dynamics of the Tiger's trajectory. Following a path first trodden by the Asian Tigers, inward investment initially created a booming economy before gradually pushing up prices and using up resources. This eventually undermined the attractiveness of the country for real investment, as wages rose and supplies of labour were harder to come by. At the time, people assumed that the Celtic Tiger had lasted unbroken for 15 years, but in hindsight it is more accurate to see it as a tale of two halves, with an export-led boom from 1993 to 2000, followed by a banking and construction bubble from 2000 to 2008.

The watershed moment came when a dotcom bubble burst in the US stock exchange, driving down activity in Ireland and US investment abroad. In the three years of the period 2002–4, investment into Ireland fell from $27 billion to only $9 billion, at the same time as export growth declined 'from an annual average of 17.6% between 1995 and 2000 to an average of 4.9% annually between 2001 and 2006'.[65] Behind the headline growth figures there was thus a considerable weakening of the productive base of the economy and a continual reliance on sectors that had traditionally supported multinationals.[66] Ordinarily, the scale of this decline in real activity would have crashed the Irish economy in the early 2000s, but there were two features of the tax haven model that initially delayed this crisis while making it more serious. The first of these had to do with the growing influence of financial services. In the early years of the century, the insurance market grew by a whopping 310 per cent and financial services by 159 per cent, partly offsetting the collapse in the export of manufacturing goods and services.[67] US firms also ramped up their entrepôt activity, with their Ireland-based subsidiaries declaring more profits in the Republic of Ireland than in any of their foreign counterparts. In 2004, for example, US companies declared $27 billion in profits in Ireland compared with only $19 billion in Canada and $5 billion in Germany.[68] The Trinity College Dublin academic Jim Stewart also found that 'financial investment' continued to grow through the twenty-first century, reaching 20 times the size of non-direct investment and 17 times the size of Irish Gross National Product (GNP) by 2011.[69] A lot of these financial flows represented 'hot money' looking for a place to hide from tax collectors, and did little to stimulate real activity in the economy. What it did do, however, was artificially increase the levels of GDP and provide employment for an army of tax consultants in companies like PricewaterhouseCoopers (PwC), KPMG and Deloitte. This is an important marker of a tax haven economy as financial flows came to dwarf activity in the real economy.

The second important development was a major expansion of domestic credit, primarily for the building industry. As noted earlier, an important aspect of Tax Haven Ireland has been the disproportionate role that banking and construction have played in the economy. In the early years of the Celtic Tiger, Fianna Fáil granted all manner of tax advantages to the building sector while encouraging domestic banks to borrow from European capital markets to fuel the expansion of construction. In 1997, the Minister for Finance, Charlie McCreevy, cut the rate of Capital Gains Tax from 40 per cent to 20 per cent in a direct giveaway to the construction sector. A year later, he extended tax breaks from an existing urban renewal scheme to rural areas in a move criticised by the Department of Finance because 'the majority of the beneficiaries of property tax relief schemes are high net worth individuals or corporate investors'.[70] The Department also worried that tax cuts in a booming economy would 'contribute to the emergence of asset price inflation and potentially destabilise the wider economy'.[71] How right they were. In the decade from 1996 to 2006, house prices rose 250 per cent across the state, and by an eye watering 551 per cent in Dublin.[72] Punch and Drudy worked out that if they had kept pace with the consumer price index, house prices should have risen from €73,000 in 1994 to €109,000 in 2007. In the event they actually rose to €323,000 or four times the rise in building costs, five times the rise in average industrial earnings and seven times faster than the consumer price index.[73] Fuelling this was a combination of cheap credit from abroad and major tax breaks from the state. According to the Revenue Commissioners, the combined cost of the various government tax reliefs in 2004 was €8.4 billion, or nearly a quarter of the total tax take.[74] Indeed, a former FF councillor and major property developer, Bernard McNamara, admitted as much, when he stated baldly that his move into property 'largely came about from the capacity to use tax breaks'.[75] But it also relied on easy money from the European monetary system as foreign banks funnelled money into a property bubble. At the start of the Celtic Tiger, the share of national income devoted specifically to house building was in line with the EU at 5 per cent, but a decade later 'this share had trebled, while other construction projects accounted for a further 6%'.[76] For the bankers and the builders, this created a veritable bonanza of profit-making opportunities. A paper by the former governor of the Central Bank, Patrick Honohan, estimated that the balance sheets of the six main Irish banks grew from a collective value of €85 billion in 1999 to just under €600 billion in 2008.[77] This was around four times the size of the real economy, much of it devoted to land speculation and property development. To see exactly where this money was going, consider Table 3.2.

Table 3.2   Selected Sectoral Breakdown of Non-Financial Corporation Loans 1999 and 2008

Year	1997 € (millions)	2008 € (millions)	Percentage (%) Change
Manufacturing	4498	8095	80
Construction	1962	24,351	1141
Wholesale/Retail Trade and Repairs	3331	12,103	263
Hotels/Restaurants	2677	10,537	293
Real Estate	3594	71,833	1899

Source: R. McElligott and R. Stuart. 'Measuring the Sectoral Distribution of Lending to Irish Non-Financial Corporates: Central Bank Financial Stability Report 2007', Central Bank and Financial Services Authority of Ireland, pp. 115–26.

Banking and construction eventually accounted for 30 per cent of Irish GDP as domestic demand largely replaced foreign investment in goods and technology. This not only drove the economy over the cliff, it also led to a resurgence of cronyism and corruption as a string of Fianna Fáil ministers, parliamentarians and local councillors were found to have abused their positions in return for payments. In the 1980s, the motivation had been to hang on to power in a period of crisis, but as the economy recovered, senior FF politicians thought that they should share in the largess of their major backers.

These were men like the former Minister for Foreign Affairs, Ray Burke, who developed a longstanding relationship with two corrupt builders, Michael Bailey and Tom Brennan, and Dublin Mid-West TD, Liam Lawlor, who was found to have 'sold his knowledge, expertise and influence as a councillor and as a TD...in circumstances that were entirely inappropriate and corrupt'.[78] Perhaps the most explosive findings of the Mahon Tribunal into corruption payments were made against long-time FF leader, Bertie Ahern. The former Taoiseach had tried to shield himself from scrutiny by refusing to hold any bank accounts for the period under investigation. Despite this, the tribunal investigators found vast unaccounted for sums clearly controlled by Ahern, and it rubbished his account of winning money on the horses and getting dig outs from sympathetic businessmen. In all, it estimated that Ahern had failed to account for £165,000, with the authors of the Mahon Report concluding that 'corruption affected every level of Irish political life' and that 'those with the power to stop it were frequently implicated in it'.[79]

In these conditions there was little incentive in reining in the bubble in construction, as house prices rapidly moved beyond anything that workers could afford. The model was bound to hit the rocks eventually and although the crisis broke in banking and construction there is an important path dependency that is often overlooked in mainstream commentary. For more than half a century, Irish capitalism relied on a development strategy based on foreign investment in financial services and manufacturing, domestic investment in construction and banking, and widespread corruption. During the Celtic Tiger, this created misplaced exuberance in Irish establishment circles, as employment and investment rose steadily through FDI. This neoliberal development model seemed to bypass the need for a domestic industrial policy, as the heavy lifting was being done by companies coming in from abroad. One of the preconditions for success was the policy framework provided by successive administrations, but it also relied on relatively cheap labour costs and a global economy that remained open and healthy. Irish labour costs were initially among the lowest in Europe, but over time the sheer success of the model put upward pressure on wages and conditions. This made inward investment less attractive, particularly when the US economy ran into trouble. An existing domestic industrial policy would have afforded the government more options in a crisis, but, as it was, they turned to the only sectors that had been sufficiently developed since the 1950s – domestic banking and construction. These sectors had been largely protected from direct competition and had remained profitable thanks largely to the patronage of the Irish state. It was these sectors that eventually drove the Irish economy over the edge as global capitalism faced its biggest crisis for 80 years.

Having had one of the biggest booms in capitalist history, Ireland now suffered one of its biggest ever reversals. Within a year, both the banking and construction sectors had collapsed, throwing hundreds of thousands out of work and piling pressure onto the state. The full horrors of neoliberal development were now on show, but rather than shifting to a more democratic form of economic planning, the Irish state used the global economic recession to move even further into tax evasion. In 2009, the Fianna Fáil government took the unprecedented step of hosting two austerity budgets in a twelve-month period. This was done in order to reduce social welfare payments and public sector wages and conditions. But they also quietly convened a Commission on Taxation in 2009, made up of bankers and consultants who were intimately connected to the inner workings of Tax Haven Ireland. This group was expected to find new ways to bring capital into a busted economy, and their key initiatives have not disappointed. The first was the Capital Allowances for Intangible Assets programme which has positioned Ireland as the foremost tax haven for companies using intellectual property. The second was to adjust the Section 110 Special Purpose Vehicle to allow foreign capital to power a recovery in the domestic property sector.[80] Collectively, these have made Ireland into one of the biggest tax havens on the planet.

4
Dirty Secrets

In June 2018, a group of academics investigating the nature of global tax evasion made a startling discovery. Based on a quantitative analysis of 'observable amounts of profits booked by multinationals', they concluded that Ireland was the biggest tax haven on the planet for 2015.[1] Indeed, according to their estimates, Ireland was responsible for so much profit laundering, that the flows of illicit money into the state were higher than all of the Caribbean tax havens put together.[2] In order to reach this conclusion, Thomas R. Tørsløv and his colleagues isolated a discrepancy in the amount of profits being booked by domestic companies versus their foreign counterparts. In non-tax havens these figures are broadly comparable and usually come in at between 30–40 per cent of the overall wage bill.[3] In tax havens, the profits of the multinationals dwarf those of their domestic rivals in ways that are simply not possible without profit shifting from other jurisdictions. The ratio of pre-tax profits to wages in the Irish case was 800 per cent, meaning each worker in a multinational was responsible for a profit of just over €184,000 versus an expected rate of €23,000.[4] Yet, even this is an underestimate when we realise that, according to the Central Statistics Office, each employee in large manufacturing firms was responsible for €686,949 in gross added value in 2016.[5] This suggests that these workers were 30 times more productive than their global counterparts or that profits were being moved into Ireland illegitimately.

When one looks at who pays Irish corporation taxes a similar picture begins to emerge. According to the Revenue Commissioners, 81 per cent of the total corporation tax take in 2017 came from what is known as its Large Corporates Division.[6] More importantly, 48 per cent of the tax was paid by just ten multinationals, indicating one of two things – either a tiny group of companies are making as much profits as all of the rest, or, more likely, they are funnelling vast profits through the state for a nominal fee.[7] The latter option would never be admitted by Revenue, of course, but the fact that Ireland is at the very centre of the tax evasion system has been further confirmed by a group of researchers working in the Netherlands. In 2017, Javier Garcia-Bernardo and his colleagues used sophisticated data analysis to investigate more than 70 million distinct ownership relationships between 98 million corporations.[8] This allowed them to build up an incredibly detailed picture of international corporate transactions, revealing Ireland as one of the world's five major *conduit tax havens*. According to Garcia-Bernardo et al., conduit tax havens are critical to the entire evasion and avoidance system because they link the world's 24 biggest *sink tax havens* to the major financial districts in London and New York.

This analysis, published in one of the world's most reputable scientific journals, not only improves our understanding of international financial flows, it also alerts us to the fact that tax evasion takes place within a complex network of havens that are themselves differentiated by geography, task specialisation and the origin of the flows within their territory.[9] In this chapter, we outline the inner mechanics of this complex system at the same time as we situate Ireland's place within it. In this way, the full workings of Tax Haven Ireland can begin to be revealed, using official data from the Industrial Development Authority and the Revenue Commissioners.

A CONCENTRATED AND FRAGMENTED SYSTEM

Defenders of capitalism like to exclaim the virtues of free-market competition as though the global economy was still characterised by countless relatively small operators all vying for consumers. This vision underpinned Adam Smith's famous idea of an 'Invisible Hand' regulating markets at the end of the eighteenth century, but today's global capitalism is dominated by a small number of major corporations who control markets rather than competing in them. Figures compiled by the Swiss Institute of Technology from the Orbis database reveal that 1318 global corporations control 80 per cent of global revenues, with just 147 corporations controlling 40 per cent of the entire network.[10] These corporate giants regularly block competitors from using their networks, merge to increase their market share and purchase successful rivals if they become too much of a threat. But they also fragment themselves into hundreds of different legal entities each with their own corporate and organisational structure. HSBC, for example, is composed of at least 828 separate corporate entities across 71 different countries for example. The world's biggest brewing company, Anheuser-Busch InBev, consists of at least 680 corporate entities located in 60 different countries.[11] This fragmentation recreates aspects of competition between entities within the group, allowing the parent company to benefit from managed levels of internal competition at the same time as it controls all the players in the market.

Multiple legal entities help to lower costs and achieve the maximum efficiency. They also increase the opacity of business operations so that only a small number of executives know where a company's assets are being held and where their profits are actually being produced. Having subsidiaries across a number of jurisdictions also hedges against the political decisions of particular governments and sets up a dynamic known as 'treaty shopping', wherein transnational corporations play governments off against each other in order to get the best deal for their various subsidiaries. Having multiple different entities also means companies can engage in 'transfer pricing' and 'treasury management functions' that allow them to reduce their costs, including their taxes. Between 50–80 per cent of global trade takes place in value chains linked to transnational corporations, making it essential to have a high number of corporate entities in order to manipulate internal prices and reduce business costs.[12] Finally, by having various internal entities, a number of accountancy tricks can be used to drive the company's overall tax liability towards zero. One way to do this is to apply for tax deductions for interest payments in a subsidiary country for money that is actually borrowed from another subsidiary within the group. A second way is to avoid the withholding of taxes on royalties or intellectual property by funnelling these payments through friendly jurisdictions with generous exemptions.

Collectively these arrangements afford global corporations' incredible power to hold on to their profits, at the same time as they manipulate the internal policies of democratic states. For this reason, it might seem like these arrangements are set up against the wishes of democratic governments, but the truth is, that the integration and fragmentation of the global corporate system is mirrored and supported by similar arrangements among states in the tax-dodging network. One of the myths about tax havens is that they are tiny islands in exotic places. The reality is that with flows of up to $15 trillion passing through them annually, these jurisdictions require both the complex legal systems of the world's biggest countries and, more importantly, their political imprimatur.[13] The United States, China, Western Europe and Japan currently make up around 70 per cent of the global economy and it is financial districts in each of these areas that operate as the major hubs for global tax evasion. Rather than seeing tax havens as deviant micro-states setting up an unwanted 'race to the bottom', it is therefore more accurate to see a global tax evasion and avoidance system made up of the following three primary components:

1. Financial Districts. These control and integrate the world's financial markets, house the major investment banks and provide the legal and political framework for the biggest owners of global capital.
2. Conduit Havens. These link up the system via low or zero taxes on the movement of capital, bilateral tax treaties and a highly complex legal system tailored for use by global corporations.
3. Sink Havens. These allow untaxed profits to end up in their territory, via low levels of democratic oversight, high amounts of domestic secrecy and extremely low or zero corporation tax rates.

In addition to this threefold characterisation of the players in the network, there is also geographical and sectoral specialisation that readers should be aware of. US corporations generally shift more of their assets through tax havens than any of their rivals, for example, because much of their profits are derived from non-US earnings. The Irish Financial Services Centre and Luxembourg play a key role in recycling much of these earnings into tax-free profits – with Wall Street playing an auxiliary role.[14] Companies on the European Mainland generally use the Netherlands, Switzerland and/or Luxembourg for their offshore activities, with the latter also operating as a major sink destination for money flowing from US corporates into Europe.[15] Since its conversion to state-capitalism in 1978, China has controlled more of its domestic financial flows than other major power, but it is also increasingly reliant on financial markets in Hong Kong and Taiwan, where Chinese technology firms often control their most important assets.[16] Japanese corporations generally use a combination of Singapore and Tokyo, while the City of London is the primary integrator of capital flows between Asia, Europe and the Caribbean.[17]

When we look at sectoral specialisation, we find that four of the big five conduit havens operate sophisticated holding company regimes. Switzerland specialises in personal wealth management, whereas for the Netherlands it is corporate treasury management that makes up the bulk of its tax offering. Delaware, Switzerland and Panama offer extreme levels of personal secrecy, while Cyprus pitches a reputation for transparency because it automatically exchanges information with other Organisation for Economic Co-operation and Development (OECD) countries. In line with the other conduit jurisdictions, Ireland has a very favourable holding company regime, but it also specialises in head office incorporation, insurance and reinsurance and treasury management functions. The reasons for each of these will be explained in due course, but for now it is worth summarising the nature of the tax evasion system as one in which four or five global centres are linked to between 60 and 100 sink havens by five or six important conduits. Ireland is one of these major conduits, moreover, explaining why Tørsløv and Garcia-Bernardo uncovered the findings that they did.

IRELAND'S INPUT–OUTPUT MODEL

Tax evasion is a complex process and a secretive one. The finer details are often difficult to uncover, but at the heart of the Irish system are three stages that are fairly easy to understand.

- Stage one involves funnelling profits that were created outside Ireland into the Irish tax net. Historically, this necessitated signing a number of Double Taxation Treaties (DTTs) alongside a method of incorporation that allowed companies to declare Ireland as their legal place of business even when it isn't their site of operation.

- Stage two involves using the state's legal framework to reduce multinational tax bills to close to zero. This can often be seen in the national accounts, particularly post-2015 when the primary avoidance mechanism changed.
- Stage three involves shifting dividends, interest and royalty payments back out of the country without any withholding taxes imposed on their foreign owners.

Let's look at each of these stages in more detail.

Stage One – Profits In

In order to shelter profits from foreign taxes, the profits must be shifted into Ireland in the first place. This has been happening to some degree since the late 1980s, but it was made considerably easier when the United States made changes to their tax code known as 'check-the-box' rules in the mid-1990s.[18] Until President Trump passed the Tax Cuts and Jobs Act (TCJA) in 2017, the US was one of only a handful of countries to have a worldwide taxation regime. Under this system income earned by US corporations anywhere in the world was originally liable to tax of 35 per cent paid when profits were repatriated to America. Like other worldwide systems, however, any tax paid in a foreign country would be discounted in the US at the rate at which it was paid. This meant that if a portion of the taxes were paid in Ireland at 12.5 per cent for example, the balance (22.5 per cent) would still be due in the United States. In 1996, the Inland Revenue Service changed these rules so that US multinationals could treat earnings from foreign affiliates as if they were separate from their parent group. By filling out an IRS form 8832, US corporations were suddenly allowed to pay their foreign taxes overseas, without any obligation to pay the balance in the States.[19] This was meant to give US companies a comparative advantage in an increasingly competitive global system and the message it sent to American executives couldn't have been clearer. While US companies were still expected to pay 35 per cent on their domestic profits, they were now free to go 'treaty shopping' in the rest of the world. The impact of these new rules on the amount of profits declared abroad can be seen in Figure 4.1.

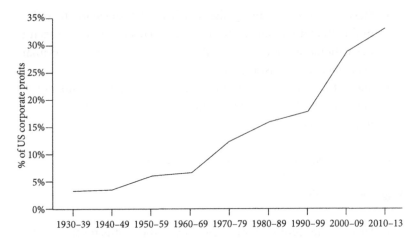

Figure 4.1 The Share of Profits Made Abroad in US Corporate Profits
Source: Bureau of Economic Analysis.

Treaty shopping was designed to ensure that the bulk of any benefits would flow to US shareholders. However, the new rules also tweaked the interest of Irish tax officials who were quick to spot an opportunity. Within a year of the Inland Revenue decision, the Fianna Fáil government undertook a mammoth overhaul of the domestic tax code with a view to making Ireland more attractive to US multinationals. The Taxes Consolidation Act (TCA) (1997) runs to an incredible 1518 pages, but from the point of view of Tax Haven Ireland, the most important initiatives were a set of intentionally ambiguous rules around establishing a company and setting up Section 110 Special Purpose Vehicles for international securitisation.[20]

Mirroring the American system, the TCA allowed companies to pay taxes on their global earnings, with a system of credits for any money paid overseas.[21] The test for determining where taxes should be paid was the company's *legal residency*, and this, in turn, depended on where their 'central command and control' (C&C) was located.[22] The C&C designation is legal jargon for where a company's key decisions are made and it was wide open to manipulation. Effectively companies now had three choices when it came to using the Irish corporation tax code. If they wanted to pay their taxes in Ireland, a company would incorporate *and* inform the Revenue Commissioners that its key decisions were taking place in the state. Alternatively, a company could also opt to incorporate in Ireland without necessarily paying taxes in the state. All the board had to do was declare that their key corporate decisions were being made elsewhere – a Caribbean island for example. This was a highly unusual step allowing companies to tell the US authorities that they were registered in Ireland while telling the Irish authorities they were operating overseas. In addition, the new TCA allowed companies to incorporate in a foreign country and still pay Irish taxes. Here, all they needed was a tax treaty between Ireland and the foreign country to declare their C&C function in the Irish state. Tax treaties define the legal standing of companies subject to them and include where taxes should be paid, which legal protections are in place and how disputes are to be managed.[23] On paper, they are signed to avoid instances of double taxation, but they are highly valued by multinational corporations because they can engineer instances of 'double non-taxation'. Tax treaties usually take precedence over domestic law and because they stipulate that companies in one contracting state cannot be treated worse than those in the second contracting state, they are difficult for traditional sink haven jurisdictions to negotiate.[24] After all, signing a tax treaty with a country like Bermuda would potentially mean companies in a non-tax haven being entitled to zero corporation taxes through a treaty that overrides domestic law. The fact that Ireland has been able to negotiate more than 70 bilateral tax treaties is therefore extremely important to the tax avoidance industry and plays a major role in selling the country to global investors.[25] When combined with the deliberately grey area around incorporation, moreover, these arrangements have allowed companies to funnel hundreds of billions into the Irish state. This achieves the first step in the Irish tax evasion input– output model. The next step is to run these profits through the Irish tax code, without letting ordinary taxpayers share in any of the advantages.

Stage Two – Profits Sheltered

The most visible aspect of Tax Haven Ireland is the unusually low headline rate corporations pay on trading profits. Ireland charges 12.5 per cent for trading profits, 25 per cent for passive income and 33 per cent for capital gains. However, these rates overestimate how much companies will actually pay, because the Revenue Commissioners apply a series of deductions to move from *Gross Trading Profits* to *Total Taxable Income*. The first of these figures captures the total amount of profits being declared in the state annually. The second figure captures how much of this declared profit is actually subject to taxation. Over the last few years, the gap between these numbers has been roughly €100 billion. Table 4.1 shows some of the recent figures that are publicly available.[26]

Table 4.1   Gap between Gross Trading Profits and Total Taxable Income in Recent Years (billions)

Year	Gross Trading Profits	Total Deductions from Trading Profits	Taxable Trading Profits	Passive Income	Total Taxable Income	Corporation Tax Receipts
2017	€159	€94	€65.1	€14.5	€ 79.6	€8.1
2018	€182	€101	€80.4	€15.6	€96	€10.2

Source: 'Summary of Corporation Tax Returns', Revenue Commissioners.

The idea that companies can declare €100 billion in profits that immediately drop out of the tax net might seem disconcerting. However, even these figures do not reveal the full scale of the benefits flowing to multinationals as they merge the foreign and domestic sectors. This helps to mask the activity of Tax Haven Ireland, so it is better to disaggregate the figures with statistics from the Industrial Development Authority (IDA). According to the IDA, 229,000 of the country's 2.29 million workers are in the multinational sector.[27] On average, these workers earn €66,000 per annum versus €46,000 in the domestic economy.[28] If we follow Tørsløv and his colleagues in assuming a global rate of profit in the region of 35 per cent of workers' wages we would expect a rate of profit per worker of €23,100 in the foreign sector and €16,204 in the domestic sector.[29] Based on these figures we should further expect foreign companies to be making roughly €5 billion profit in the domestic economy annually, with around €32 billion being made by their Irish counterparts. In actual fact, the level of profits being declared in the latest figures was €182 billion or *€145 billion ahead of what would be expected given the number of workers* *employed in the state.* What explains this discrepancy? The biggest part of the difference is the €101 billion being moved through the state tax free using a number of schemes to be outlined below. In addition, global corporations move a further €44 billion through the state which is taxed at around 10 per cent – a lower rate than they would be taxed abroad. This more than doubles the tax take on trading profits and is one of the reasons the Irish state acquiesces in this fiction. When this money is added to passive income from rents and royalties, etc., it makes up the €96 billion that the Irish Revenue Commissioners taxed in 2018.

Table 4.2 gives an approximate summary of how the Revenue Commissioners got to their Total Taxable Income for 2018.

Table 4.2   Total Taxable Income 2018 (billions)

Estimated Profits Created in the State (Taxed Close to Headline Rate of 12.5 per cent)	€37
Total Profits Shifted Into the State	€145
Portion of These Profits Shifted Tax Free	€101
Portion of These Profits Taxed Close to the Headline Rate	€44
Total Taxable Trading Profits	(€37 + €44) = €81
Profits from Passive Income	€15
Total Taxable Profits	€96

Instead of claiming tax on the approximately €37 billion trading profits being created by Irish workers, the Revenue Commissioners take a share of €96 billion. This allows the state to increase its tax take from the corporate sector from around €4 billion to around €10 billion annually.[30] For their part, global corporations get to move approximately €145 billion of profits through the Irish tax system while only paying taxes on one euro out of every three. This reduces their overall taxes on their declared profits to around 3–4 per cent per annum. We explore these figures in more detail below, but for now we need to unpack the two most important methods for actually reducing these taxes in the Irish context – transfer pricing and loan manipulation.

Transfer pricing (TP) involves manipulating internal prices so that most of the profits of a corporate group are booked in low tax countries.

This is possible because between 50–80 per cent of global trade now takes place between the various arms of a company without objective prices to guide them. Internal group members are meant to sell commodities to each other on an 'arm's length basis', mirroring what an external company would have to pay. However, it is extremely difficult for tax authorities to make sure that this occurs, particularly with trademarks, logos and other forms of virtual assets. A successful transfer price is one that undervalues internal commodities going to low tax countries and overvalues them in their higher tax counterparts. A survey of 850 multinationals in 2007 found that 77 per cent placed transfer pricing at the heart of their taxation strategy – and with nearly $50 trillion moving between the arms of corporations, this is an extremely lucrative process.[31] Take a look at Table 4.3 for some typical abuses.

Table 4.3 Typical Abuses of Transfer Pricing

Internal Trade	Commodity	Price Charged ($)
Czech Subsidiary to Parent Company	Water Plastic Seals	972.98 per unit
Chinese Subsidiary to Another Subsidiary	Gloves	4,121.81 per kilo
French Subsidiary to Another Subsidiary	Locks	3067.17 per kilo
US Company to Israeli Company	Missiles	52.03 each
Indian Subsidiary to Indian Subsidiary	Diamonds	13.45 per carat
US Subsidiary to Belgian Subsidiary	Car Seats	1.44 each

Source: Palan et al. *Tax Havens: How Globalisation Really Works.* 2000.

Despite the obvious dangers in this process, Ireland chose not to enact any form of TP regime until 2010, when it was put under pressure from the European Commission. Thereafter, a set of TP rules was established, but the rules were deliberately designed not to undermine multinational activity. One problem is the fact that Ireland has adopted the least favoured method acceptable under the OECD's transfer pricing rules – the transaction net margin method (TNMM).[32] This is meant to compare internally booked sales with those made from similar transactions on the open market, but it can be difficult to find effective comparisons when companies go to such long lengths to hide the real nature of their activities. A far bigger problem, however, is the fact that Ireland's TP rules are designed to only identify cases where Revenue suspect a firm has *undervalued* its Irish profits or overstated its expenditure.[33] This helps Revenue to protect resources in the domestic economy, but it is completely ineffective when dealing with global companies moving *higher than normal* profits into the state.[34] Ireland is awash with billions of euros funnelled here to take advantage of low taxation while the TP regime that has been put in place remains completely blind to this activity. It seems plausible that the state's 'one-way' system was designed to allow Ireland to comply with OECD anti-avoidance regulations at the same time as the rules have been crafted to allow TP to continue.

Loan manipulation is the second important method of reducing corporation taxes in the Irish context. Credit is essential for corporations who may want to invest when they don't currently have the capital, or to cover costs when they themselves haven't yet been paid. In an earlier phase of capitalism, investment banks took idle capital from companies who didn't currently need it before recycling it to others for productive investment. The state also underwrote this process, guaranteeing insurance for lenders' deposits and tax deductions for firms who borrowed to expand their production. The latter incentive took note of the fact that companies had to incur costs in order to make profits, so it allowed a company to pay interest to banks before they paid their profit taxes. Corporate tax law still reflects this older reality, but the truth is that today major conglomerates often use their own legal and organisational structures to *lend capital from one arm of the company to another arm in a different country*. This presents the possibility of getting a deduction for interest that is paid circuitously back to the company itself. Different states offer different types of allowances, but the Irish state is possibly the most generous of all – because it offers big tax allowances for any amount of interest that a company might pay. The higher the level of interest, the more profit that can be sheltered, and by artificially inflating the interest charges to almost the level of profits made, companies can approach a zero rate of tax. If they consider that too blatant, however, they can set the interest rates to just under their actual profits to arrive at a tax rate of between 1 per cent and 3 per cent. To make their gain, multinationals only have to find another tax haven where interest is not taxed. That way, they can have the best of both worlds – just like Glanbia did when it played off Luxembourg's tax code against Ireland's.

Given the difficulty in policing these practices, the most effective way to guard against this form of evasion is to limit the amount of debt that can be used to finance a company's operations. Most countries have a set of these 'thin capitalisation rules', but as of 2020, Ireland hasn't implemented any deemed effective enough by the EU Commission.[35] This is despite the fact that the state signed up to the EU's Anti-Tax Avoidance Directive (ATAD) and is expected to limit debt-based financing to no more than 30 per cent of earnings before interest, tax, depreciation and amortisation.[36] The directive was meant to be signed into law no later than 1 January 2019, but, true to form, the Irish state has sought a special derogation to put it off until 2024. This is a sign that multinational companies see the absence of capitalisation rules as vital to their taxation strategies – a point conceded by corporate law firm, Matheson, when they told investors that 'the most significant provision of the ATAD is likely to be the introduction of fixed ratio interest limitation rules'.[37] If the state is forced to close this loophole it will cause problems for multinational corporations, but Matheson remains confident that 'Ireland will exercise its discretion…to limit any adverse impact on implementation, particularly on the financial services industry'.[38] Since the late 1990s, transfer pricing and loan manipulation have been employed alongside Ireland's extensive network of DTTs to funnel vast profits through the tax code. The final job of the conduit network is to make sure this money gets back to its owners without attracting any withholding taxes.

Stage Three – Profits Out

One of the complications faced by any successful tax haven is the existence of what are known as withholding taxes. These are taxes on dividends, interest, royalties and capital gains that are traditionally levied at a higher rate than trading profits because these payments are gained through ownership rather than working – so-called 'passive income'. Ireland's success in convincing the world that vast profits were being made in the state, meant that there was now an onus on the Revenue

Commissioners to tax this income *before it moved back to source.* If an Irish person makes money on their savings for example, they are expected to pay a deposit interest retention tax (DIRT) at 35 per cent. If they make a windfall from selling shares, they are expected to pay Capital Gains Tax at 30 per cent. Withholding this tax is a function of the state but applying these charges to foreign incomes would quickly undermine the basis of Tax Haven Ireland. To get around this problem, the state established a very attractive holding company regime, based on deliberately weak controlled foreign company (CFC) rules and a set of withholding taxes that wealthy foreigners can easily avoid. Holding companies are the legal and organisational backbone of global conglomerates.[39] Their job is to separate ownership from management in a way that allows the owners sufficient oversight of their holding companies at the same time as it allows legal separation from day-to-day operations. Setting up holding companies and controlled foreign companies offers two key advantages from the taxation perspective. Firstly, multinationals can strategically place assets like intellectual property (IP) into holding companies based in countries with low levels of corporation taxes. This allows them to claim that profits from the sale of this IP should be moved out of higher tax countries into places like Ireland. Secondly, they can defer any withholding taxes that might arise on these profits by shifting the resulting royalties and dividends into controlled companies that are outside their own jurisdiction.[40] Rules around CFCs are meant to stop this practice from occurring, but Ireland resisted any such rules until 2019, before finally implementing a CFC regime that deliberately misses tax avoidance on passive income.[41] Writing about the benefits of the Irish regime for prospective clients, one of the state's leading corporate law firms, Dillion Eustace, had this to say,

> Ireland has become a destination of choice for holding companies due to its capital gains participation exemption, generous foreign tax credit system, membership of the EU, ever expanding double tax treaty (DTT) network, *lack of controlled foreign company rules, thin capitalisation rules and the general ability to pay dividends free of withholding tax* [our emphasis].[42]

Ireland officially applies withholding taxes to all categories of passive income, but the exemptions are so generous as to make these taxes almost meaningless. Take the dividend withholding tax as an example. On paper, the Revenue Commissioners expect people to pay a 20 per cent tax on the dividends they receive, but if an Irish registered company sends dividends to a second Irish registered company these charges don't apply. If an Irish registered company sends profits to an EU company or a company in a country bound by a DTT, the rate immediately falls to 12.5 per cent and, depending on where the money is sent, it can go even lower. On their prospectus to international investors, PricewaterhouseCoopers explain that dividend tax may be avoided entirely by 'non-resident companies that are resident in a country with which Ireland has a tax treaty or in another European country where the company is not controlled by Irish residents'.[43] This is because a number of these treaties allow withholding taxes to be paid in the receiving country – and for 23 of these, that rate is 0 per cent. Small wonder the Irish Development Authority baldly admits that multinational corporations are 'generally exempt from Ireland's 20% Dividend Withholding Tax...'.[44] The rules around interest-based withholding taxes are equally porous. We noted earlier how companies are increasingly using debt-based finance to lend to entities within their own group. This gives multinationals an ability to get tax breaks on interest that is paid to themselves, but it also results in a withholding tax on the income that they receive. If two different companies were trading at arm's length, the first would get a tax deduction for a genuine expense and the second would pay tax on a genuine income. But a company doesn't want to *pay tax on income it pays to itself*, as this defeats the purpose of lending in this way in the first place. The state ordinarily imposes a 20 per cent tax on interest income, but, according to the Industrial Development Authority, this can be avoided if the money is going to an EU or DTT country 'which generally taxes interest received from outside its territory'.[45] The assertion that interest will be stopped at the other end might seem legitimate, until one realises that 30 of the 72 countries that Ireland has DTTs with impose an interest withholding tax of 0 per cent.[46] Royalties received from Irish registered companies are also meant to be taxed at 20 per cent, but once again these taxes can be avoided by sending them through EU countries or those with tax treaties with the Irish state.

As before, there is an expectation that the country receiving the royalties will impose a withholding tax at the other end, but when 25 of Ireland's DTT counterparts apply a royalties rate of 0 per cent and a further 14 expect just 5 per cent – one begins to see the bigger picture.[47]

BECOMING A CONDUIT FOR INTELLECTUAL PROPERTY

The most important tax evasion strategies in the Irish case use the three stages outlined above, tailored specifically for IP assets owned by US multinationals. These so-called virtual assets – including items like brands, software and logos – are notoriously difficult to value and are therefore open to abuses from transfer pricing in intergroup trading. Indeed, this is particularly true when added to the benefits provided by Ireland's deliberately ambiguous rules around the incorporation of commercial entities. IP-based transfer pricing strategies have come into their own with the rise of the internet and the smart economy. However, state documents, released from the archives in December 2018, show that as far back as 1984 Fine Gael Ministers were seeking legal advice on how US corporations could avoid taxes by locating in Ireland. One document in particular, reveals former Taoiseach John Bruton writing to the then Finance Minister, Alan Dukes, stating that US multinationals were looking for European bases for their Foreign Sales Centres (FSCs) and that 'unless they were given favourable tax treatment in Ireland they would not locate here'.[48] Bruton has since gone on to be chairman of the Irish Financial Services Centre (IFSC) in a sign that his words were not only heeded – they were acted upon.[49] Over the next 25 years these schemes became so successful that by 2010 they were helping US multinationals to shield roughly €100 billion from their non-US profit taxes annually. Between 2004 and 2017 this created a war chest of more than €1 trillion making what has euphemistically become known as the 'Double Irish' – the biggest tax evasion tool in history.[50] Here, in outline, is how the Double Irish works.[51]

THE DOUBLE IRISH

Imagine a world that outlawed the use of transfer pricing and made sure that profit taxes were paid in countries in which sales are made. Assume further, that a US multinational sells a piece of software to a French company for €1000 and that the marginal cost was just €40, leaving €960 in profit. France currently levies its corporation profit tax (CPT) at 33 per cent, meaning that, in this hypothetical world, €320 would have to be paid. US executives don't want to pay these taxes, however, so they pay expensive lawyers and accountants to advise them on ways to keep this money for themselves. In our current system, one thing they could do is argue that the real value in this transaction was added from the intellectual property and that this is not housed in France, but in Ireland. It is very difficult to measure how much of this value is due to the IP, so lawyers for the US company will generally argue it's as much as 95 per cent. If this is accepted, then instead of paying €320 to the French revenue authorities, the company would pay €16 in France (33 per cent of the 5 per cent left over) and €114 in Ireland (12.5 per cent of the €912 transferred there as IP). But even €130 is far too much to expect from a US multinational. So instead of using Ireland to set up one company to house these IP assets – it could set up two different Irish companies (hence the name), one resident in the state for taxes and one with its C&C in a sink tax haven such as Bermuda. As we saw above, the US and Ireland each have different rules on how corporations are to be classified – and by exploiting these differences in the tax code, all of the ingredients for the Double Irish are in place.

- Stage one begins when the US company creates IP assets and sells the rights to an Irish incorporated company controlled from Bermuda – Ire(B).
- The US tax code assesses Ire(B) as genuinely Irish, allowing it to escape US CFC rules for recognised tax havens.
- Under Irish law, however, Ire(B) is controlled from Bermuda and is therefore *resident for tax in the Caribbean.*
- Stage two begins when Ire(B) licences the software to a second Irish company Ire(I).
- This company has unfettered access to EU markets, so it can sell the product to the French company without any tariffs.
- As before, 95 per cent of the profits flow back to Ire(I), but before they can be taxed at 12.5 per cent in Ireland, Ire(I) has to pay Ire(B) for the use of the latter's intellectual property.

- The cost of this IP always turns out to be more or less the level of the profits made, allowing the full €912 to flow back to Bermuda.
- This amount is taxed in Bermuda at a rate of 0 per cent, leaving €912 in the control of the US company.
- Historically, the Irish state imposed a withholding tax of 20 per cent on transfers into known tax havens, so to get around this problem, Ire(I) could send these funds via a Dutch company that is not faced with any such withholding charges.
- This made the scheme into a Double Irish with a Dutch Sandwich.[52]

The 'Double Irish' ultimately hinged on the ability of multinationals to incorporate in Ireland without becoming resident for taxation. This option resulted from a conscious choice by the Irish tax authorities and it is hard to believe that such a pro-business measure was not created to specifically exploit the difference in the respective tax codes outlined above. The US government was aware of these tax advantages for at least a decade before a Senate Committee, chaired by Senator Carl Levin, blew the practice open in 2013. This soon sparked an official enquiry by the European Commission, led by the Competition Commissioner, Margarethe Vestager, which was eventually to find Ireland guilty of allowing Apple to get away with more than €13 billion in unpaid taxes. When asked why one of the most powerful corporations in the world was paying virtually zero tax in the Irish state, the then Deputy Prime Minister, Eamon Gilmore, stated that these 'are not issues that arise from the Irish taxation system... They are issues that arise from the taxation systems in other jurisdictions and that is an issue that has to be addressed first of all in those jurisdictions'.[53] This response, from the leader of the country's Labour Party, was yet another indication of just how craven the wider establishment had become. The fact that the Irish elites were actually responsible for the 'Double Irish', was definitively settled less than two years later, moreover, when the Minister for Finance, Michael Noonan, made a song and dance about closing it. Under pressure from the European Commission, Noonan used his budget speech for 2015, to broadcast the fact that Ireland was 'pulling the shutters down' on the 'Double Irish' by making sure that companies that are incorporated in the state must also be resident for taxation.[54] What he didn't make a song and dance about, however, were the following facts:

- The scheme was left open for companies already using it until 1 January 2021.
- There are ways to continue to operate this scam using a number of Ireland's existing tax treaties.
- When the state had the chance to close all versions of the Double Irish, they chose not to do it.[55]
- The state had an even more effective tax dodge on the go and ready to replace it.[56]

To add insult to injury, Noonan also left two months from the date of his announcement – in October 2014 – before the new measures kicked in, leaving plenty of time for multinationals to arrange their affairs to avail of these structures for another five years.[57] But even those who didn't choose to take up this offer were left with ample opportunities after the official closure of the Double Irish. Although the government tightened up its own rules to make sure that companies incorporating in the state had to pay Irish taxes, they resisted calls to revise all their existing tax treaties to tighten the rules in a similar manner. This is important, moreover, as a number of these treaties supersede respective domestic laws and contain the same C&C test used in the original scam. This means that a company sending royalties to a noted tax haven such as Bermuda would merely have to switch them to a low tax country with an Irish tax treaty to continue to avail of these same tax advantages. Little wonder two partners at US taxation firm Bilzin Sumberg concluded that although the Double Irish was gone on paper,

> this does not mean that the objective cannot be reached in other ways. Ireland has an extensive treaty network. At least two of these treaties contain management and control residency standards and are in countries with similarly low rates. Specifically, it is possible to form an INR (Irish Non-resident company) under existing structures, with its management and control in Malta.[58]

In 2017, Christian Aid found evidence that both Microsoft (LinkedIn) and Allergan (Zeitiq) had realised the same thing and were using Ireland's tax treaty with Malta to replace the 'Double Irish' with the 'Single Malt'.[59] When this practice was raised with Michael Noonan by Sinn Fein MEP Matt Carty, he was dismissively told 'to pull on the Green Jersey' (the colour worn by international teams representing Ireland).[60] More importantly, when the Irish state had the chance to implement the one piece of OECD tax reform that would have ended all versions of the Double Irish, it refused to do so. Article 12 of the OECD Model Tax Treaty disrupts the residency-based aspect of the scheme by stopping companies from artificially moving profits from one country to another. To date, Ireland has made much fanfare about its participation in the OECD BEPS (Base Erosion and Profit Shifting) process, but 'when it signed the Multilateral Instrument, the Irish government opted out of Article 12 – a key part of the Instrument aimed at preventing...the Double Irish and its successors...'.[61] Christian Aid's report, meanwhile, found evidence that the amount of money flowing through the state has actually increased in the succeeding five years thanks to a second scam – this time based on a set of bogus Capital Allowances for Intangible Assets (CAIA).[62]

A GLOBAL SINK FOR INTELLECTUAL PROPERTY

Becoming the world's biggest tax haven took ingenuity on the part of a ruling class that has proven itself cunning and far-sighted. The 'Double Irish' was the most successful tax scam ever devised, but it did rely on an obvious fiction that was eventually seized upon by its opponents. Allowing companies to legally incorporate without paying taxes is a red flag for international tax authorities, and this, in turn, made it difficult to defend when these authorities began to scrutinise the arrangements in a bid to disrupt them. For now, the Irish state has found a way to protect a version of the Double Irish, but there is no guarantee that this will last. Maintaining a successful tax haven relies on constant innovation in preparation for a time when one scheme has to be wound down and another one enacted. Ireland faced just such a pivotal moment in the first quarter of 2015, but it had been preparing for this eventuality for a number of years.

In 2009, Fianna Fáil set up a Commission on Taxation in the midst of the biggest collapse in the Irish state's revenue in living memory.[63] This body included a range of people intimately connected to Tax Haven Ireland and, in a 560-page document that ranged over the entirety of Irish taxes, perhaps their most important recommendation was one that built on Section 291A of the TCA (1997).[64] In particular, they advised the state to extend a range of deductions for expenditure on *intangible assets* with the aim of securing a greater share of corporate profits at a time when they were badly needed.[65] Tax deductions for capital investment are well established in corporate law and hinge on the fact that profit is the outcome of investment, that itself, costs money. If, for example, a company spends €1 million on a piece of machinery that will anchor production for the next ten years, they are usually entitled to write off the cost of this machinery against their profits over the timeframe in question. A profit of €1 million a year would therefore be liable to tax at €900,000, with the other €100,000 allowed as a deduction for expenses.

One can argue about the merits of this tax break when workers who invest in their careers don't receive it, but historically it was a deduction that was difficult to abuse. Corporations used to buy their capital assets from external suppliers who sold it to them for a price that reflected its labour value. The machine was also used in a physical production process characterised by wear and tear, known technically as depreciation. Even if the equipment didn't break down physically, it would need to be replaced periodically in order for the firm to remain competitive. Now consider Capital Allowances for Intangible Assets in the modern corporate setting. The first major difference is that, typically, a company produces these assets in one arm of a company before selling them to a second arm at an internal price wide open to manipulation. This problem becomes even more severe when the assets in question are *intellectual property* such as brands or logos rather than physical assets like plant and machinery. It may be true that the Starbucks brand is crucial to selling coffee in their outlets, but it is hard to argue that the more these logos are used the more value they lose. It would be more accurate to suggest that Starbucks gains from the use of its branding and logos in a way that is the very opposite of depreciation. Even when intellectual property – such as software – is subject to a form of depreciation, it is extremely difficult to accurately measure this without a set of external prices. To get a sense of how open this measure is to abuse, read what KPMG wrote to prospective investors:

> A hypothetical company with an equity market capitalisation of €1,000 million, but tangible assets of €100 million can argue that the gap of €900 million represents its intangible asset base, which can be legally created and appropriately located.... Ireland's Capital Allowances for Intangible Assets Programme enables these intangible assets to be turned into tax deductible charges.... [W]ith appropriate structuring, the intergroup acquisition financing for the purchase of these intangible assets can also be used to further amplify the quantum of tax deductible charges.[66]

Allowing companies to claim that the gap between their market value and their tangible asset base consists of intangible assets is tantamount to writing a blank cheque for multinationals to be cashed on the basis of 'virtual assets' with made-up prices. The value that multinationals place on these assets must be vetted by one of Ireland's IFSC business and consultancy firms, but this is hardly a daunting challenge, given the role that these organisations play in the wider tax evasion system. The state's new virtual assets-based tax deductions ensure that companies with large amounts of intellectual property will be able to shift profits into Ireland tax free for decades to come.[67] And if this wasn't generous enough, they can get a second, interest-based tax deduction by funding the onshoring of the property to Ireland with loans from countries that don't apply any interest-based withholding taxes.[68] We outline the key phases in the CAIA strategy below.

CAPITAL ALLOWANCES FOR INTANGIBLE ASSETS (CAIA)[69]

- A US company develops software that costs €1 million to produce and sells this to a wholly controlled Bermudan company – Ber(1).
- Ber(1) revalues these intangible assets to €1 billion and books the gain in Bermuda tax free.

- An Irish subsidiary – Ire(1) – now purchases this asset for €1 billion in a process known as onshoring.
- Under the new CAIA rules, Ire(1) can write off the €1 billon paid for this asset against the taxes owed on its profits in Ireland.
- Another arm of the company, located in, for example Jersey – Jer(1), gives a loan to Ire(1) to purchase the intellectual property assets at an interest rate of 10 per cent.
- During the next ten years, Ire(1) charges out the use of these IP-based assets and accumulates profits.
- Over the same time period, Ire(1) claims tax relief on both the €1 billion purchase (under CAIA), and the intergroup loan interest.
- After ten years, the CAIA initiative has shielded €2 billion worth of Irish profits from any form of Irish taxation.
- This process can be repeated periodically to top up the virtual assets being used for the tax deductions.

Comparing this scam with the 'Double Irish', a number of notable points emerge. The first is that Ireland's role in the wider tax evasion system has shifted from specialising as a major conduit, to becoming a sink for hundreds of billions of assets brought onshore to cancel taxes on billions in profits now being booked through Dublin.[70] This gives the Irish state greater control of the process, and, as an added bonus, dispenses with the obvious fiction of an Irish-incorporated entity paying tax in Bermuda. Secondly, capital allowances for tangible assets is a well-established principle in corporate tax law, making an extension to intangible assets potentially more defensible in legal cases. Thirdly, CAIA is more lucrative for the state, as greater amounts of taxable income end up in the Irish system. The 'Double Irish' funnelled profits into Ireland on their way to Bermuda. The CAIA scheme works by funnelling profits through the Irish tax code with the increase in Irish corporation tax receipts clear for everyone to see. Finally, the very success of the scheme has also resulted in its one major drawback – the far more visible distortions it creates in Ireland's national accounts. Just how visible the new tax scam is can be seen in Table 4.4 from the Revenue Commissioners. The first column looks at the various ways that the Irish state gives tax deductions. The second shows how the actual profits that were taxed fell from €182 billion to €96 billion, just over half the original sum.[71]

Table 4.4   Calculation of Total Taxable Income Figure

	2018 (millions)	2018 (millions)
Gross Trade Profits (Less Deductible Amounts as Follows)		182,734
Trade Capital Allowances	79,019	
Trade Loss Forward (and Current Trade Losses)	10,287	
Group Interest Charges	17,939	
Plus Group Relief	4291	
Total Amount Deducted		111,536
Net Trading Income after Losses, Charges and Group Relief		71,198
Passive Income (Rents, Foreign Dividends, Capital Gains)		15,626
Net Total Taxable Income		96,049

We saw earlier that Tørsløv and his colleagues estimated the amount of profits flowing untaxed through Ireland at €100 billion, and here we see the Revenue Commissioners give a slightly higher figure of €111 billion. Of this, multinationals shielded just short of €79 billion via the CAIA scheme in 2018, and a further €18 billion using loan manipulation through intergroup debt financing. They were also able to shield €10 billion using historic losses brought forward and current losses. Most tax codes accept the idea that a company can use a loss in one year to shield a profit in the next, but there are two reasons why this is an unusually generous tax break in the Irish context.

The first is the scale of the recent global crisis, coupled with the ability of companies to use Ireland as a worldwide tax system. Ireland allows companies that made a loss *anywhere in their group* to look for a tax deduction through Group Relief and this affords companies massive scope to use losses from the Great Recession to get future tax deductions in the Irish system.[72] To the extent that these tax credits are not used against trading income, moreover, they can also be used to offset the passive income in the immediate or preceding period. Secondly, the Irish tax code doesn't put time limits or upper caps on the amount of losses that can be brought forward. According to the Revenue Commissioners, there is still €213 billion worth of losses that can be used to write off corporate taxes – making this three times more expensive than the much more visible bailout of the Irish banks.[73] All of this makes it hardly surprising that the amount of profits running through the Irish tax code has increased massively over the last seven years.

Table 4.5   Corporation Tax Receipts 2011–18 (millions)

Year	2011	2012	2013	2014	2015	2016	2017	2018
Gross Trade Profit	54,022	74,775	80,672	95,374	143,926	158,788	159,025	182,734
Passive Income	5149	5936	6347	8307	12,379	12,667	14,590	15,626
Total Profits Overall	59,171	80,711	87,046	103,681	156,305	171,455	173,615	198,360
Total Taxable Income	40,062	43,242	40,462	50,703	65,076	71,475	79,654	96,049
Tax Payable	4173	4374	4078	4930	6248	7159	8104	10,211

Source: 'Summary of Corporation Tax Returns', Revenue Commissioners.

The implementation of the CAIA coincided with an economic recovery that has led to some genuine uplift in corporation taxes. By far the bigger portion has come from the CAIA programme, however, as revealed by parsing through the official statistics. Take the rise in passive income as an example. Under the 'Double Irish', passive income officially flowed to the owners of foreign assets in Bermuda, whereas with the shift to the CAIA system, these assets are now officially housed in the IFSC. This is surely one of the reasons why passive income tax suddenly jumped by 50 per cent in 2015.[74] In addition, the amount allowed for intergroup interest relief also shot up from €17 billion to €24 billion in the very year that Apple executed the biggest onshoring of IP in recorded history. But the strongest indication comes from the discounts for capital allowances themselves, which have grown from €16 billion in 2011 to

€79 billion in 2018, at the same time as the broader category of deductions went from €21 billion to around €110.[75] Taken directly from the state's official revenue service, these figures confirm that Ireland is now among the biggest tax havens on the planet. Our next task is to investigate the people who make this all happen.

5
The Fixers

Imagine life as a corporate executive, working in a plush office in Manhattan. Your annual bonus is tied to performance and you want to cut your company's tax bill. You consider moving the headquarters to Bermuda or the Cayman Islands, but your name might turn up on a CNN Investigates programme or appear on social media sites as a tax dodger. Then one of your directors suggests Dublin. It is a politically stable, outwardly respectable place that hasn't got the 'tax haven' label. It is inside the EU and, as an added bonus, is English speaking. This begins to sound like a good idea, but, as Shakespeare wrote, 'Thoughts are no subjects. Intents but merely thoughts'. To jump the chasm between thought and deed, you need some help. This is where Ireland's fixer network comes in. This ranges from corporate law and accountancy firms to corporate services providers who can give the appearance of Irish tax residency from the other side of the Atlantic. By reaching into the heart of the Irish state, this network will also provide you with direct channels to the political elite and the Revenue Commissioners. And as an added bonus, they will even ensure that Irish laws are continually updated to keep ahead of the Inland Revenue Service of America. Sounds good? Let's have a look inside the fixer network – without paying the exorbitant fees.

THE CORPORATE LAW FIRMS

Irish law firms used to occupy dusty offices where they met with clients appearing in a District Court or doing a conveyancing deal. These practices still exist, of course, but there is much more happening nowadays. On the south side of Dublin's river Liffey, opposite the National Convention Centre, is a legal quarter that houses major firms who specialise in corporate services. Companies like McCann Fitzgerald, Dillon Eustace and Beauchamp's sit in spanking, glass-filled offices, priding themselves on the architecture of their atriums. At the most easterly point of the quay, stands the office of Matheson – Ireland's largest tax practice. When you arrive at their door, a notice informs you that Matheson houses a number of other companies too. But if you ask for a print-out of this list, none is ever supplied. It turns out, however, that 125 US companies have registered several hundred subsidiaries or investment funds at 70 Sir John Rogerson's Quay.[1] These include, Airbnb, Dell, Honeywell International, LinkedIn and Pepsi. Solicitors working at Matheson serve as directors on the boards of hundreds of these companies. The law practice, is, in fact, a small global conglomerate, with 350 legal and tax-based professionals spread over offices in London, New York, Palo Alto and San Francisco. Its own rise parallels the growth of Tax Haven Ireland. Back in the late 1980s, legal and accountancy firms came up with a fantastical idea. They proposed a special provision in the Taxes Consolidation Act (1997) known as Section 110. This was part of Fianna Fáil's wider push to bring US corporates into Dublin and the particular provision dealt with what is known as Securitisation. Securitisation is a way of turning assets with a longer-term income stream into something that can be sold immediately. The assets can be anything from mortgages to student loans and the idea is to bundle these assets and sell them in tranches (of, say, 1000 mortgages) rather than waiting for the monthly repayments. This process was well established elsewhere, and the Irish rich thought they could get in on the action. To engage in this process, banks usually set up what are known as Special Purpose Vehicles (SPVs). SPVs help to separate a parent firm from financial risk by moving assets off balance sheet – meaning beyond the prying eyes of regulators. It is called 'off balance sheet' because it does not appear on the books of the company that owns it, which remains protected from bankruptcy if the SPV gets into trouble. The legal and accountancy lobbyists reckoned that thousands of SPVs could be housed in Dublin, if the city offered them a haven from taxes. The political elite were all ears and let the revenue officials know they were in favour too. The Irish Revenue Commissioners already had some experience in facilitating domestic-based tax dodging. The retail giant Dunnes Stores, for example, was allowed a unique arrangement, whereby ownership was vested in a Dunnes Settlement

Trust to minimise tax. A subsequent tribunal found that the head of Ireland's largest privately owned business made payments of more than £2
million to Charles Haughey when the latter was Taoiseach. In return,
Haughey asked the then head of the Revenue Commissioners, Seamus
Paircéir, to meet Ben Dunne, and the two men entered into negotiations
during which the chairman offered to settle a £38.8 million tax bill for
£16 million.[2]

Securitisation was an entirely new game, however. To make sure the
process got started successfully, Revenue provided the basic Section
110 framework and then left it up to the corporate lawyers to tell them
how it might need to be adjusted. A company would qualify if they
acquired assets of at least €10 million, notified Revenue and acquired
Irish tax residency. The necessary paperwork for the latter could
then be supplied by the law firms driving the process. The aim was to
protect investors from tax officials in the US and elsewhere, and this
required a continuous updating of Irish tax law to stay ahead of the
game. To do this, corporate lobbyists were embedded in several official
decision-making bodies. There was an IFSC Funds Industry Association, a grouping of fund managers and speculators, which boasts that
it has 'helped shape the development of Ireland's regulatory and legislative framework.'[3] There was an IFSC Clearing House Group which
linked the top legal, accountancy and financial firms with state officials
who met once a month in government buildings. The Department of
Finance and the Revenue Commissioners were also instructed to 'fully
engage and consult with the [Financial Services] industry to enhance
the tax framework, including through the annual Finance Bill process.'[4]
The Finance Bill is where seemingly technical changes are made in the
country's tax law. While the government introduces its annual budget
with great ceremony, they rarely talk about the technical finery of the
Finance Bill. But it is here that the serious moves are made every year to
create and maintain Ireland's tax haven infrastructure.

In the late 1980s a special channel was established whereby agents
working for the big corporations could contact Revenue officials to
'tweak' any suggested changes. In the official words of the Revenue Commissioners, 'technical implications of new legislative proposals during
the period from publication of a Finance Bill to its enactment may be

addressed to the relevant Policy & Legislation Division'.[5] To be even more helpful, they also provided a detailed list of which exact adviser an agent should contact. The official rhetoric is that Ireland has a tax rate of 12.5 per cent on trading profits and 25 per cent on non-trading profits or passive income – but the state writes a series of exemptions into the Finance Acts that guarantee 'tax neutrality' for those in the know. Meanwhile, the legal eagles work in 'partnership' with the Revenue Commissioners to update the exemptions. Here for example, is James Somerville, a partner in A&L Goodbody explaining the process, 'Representatives of the industry...raised problems being encountered in practice with the Department of Finance and Revenue Commissioners....There were ongoing consultations identifying these areas and proposing solutions. The product of this work is the revised Section 110 contained in the Finance Bill'.[6] Somerville was writing in 2003, but the same process is at work today.

ENTER THE LAW FIRMS

Matheson was one of those firms that had an inside track with state officials and it soon became a point of contact for US multinationals. Back in 2001, when it went by the name of Matheson Ormbsy Prentice, it devised a version of the 'Double Irish' whereby one of Microsoft's subsidiaries, Round Island One, was deemed to be incorporated in Dublin but not paying taxes there. This company was the holder of Microsoft's copyrighted software code and charged licence fees throughout Europe, the Middle East and Africa for its use. Although it apparently had assets valued at $16 billion, its address was listed as the Matheson Ormbsy Prentice office. The scheme brought – and continues to bring – Microsoft a tax saving of approximately $1 billion a year.

After reports about Round Island One appeared in the *Wall Street Journal*, Matheson's reputation increased rather than decreased in corporate circles – hence the large number of companies currently located in its office. Today, Matheson boasts the 'largest tax practice amongst Irish law firms' with more than half its efforts involving 'tax professionals who have the sole or lead role'.[7] As we have seen, one of their main roles is to act as lobbyists for their clients, by bringing specific 'problems' to the Revenue Commissioners and the government. When the government proposed introducing a 6.25 per cent tax on profits gleaned from a new 'Knowledge Development Box' (KDB) for example, Matheson issued a document advocating a 'wide definition of intellectual property' and a series of reliefs that might lower the rate even further.[8] It sent a specific letter to the Department of Finance with detailed proposals that needed to be included in the Finance Bill to make sure 'the effective tax rate should not exceed 2.5%'.[9] Not surprisingly, many of these proposals were taken on board. The second key role of the corporate lawyers is to devise very specific schemes to shield their clients from paying taxes. In the year that Matheson lobbied around the KDB, they also worked with state officials to introduce a new scheme known as an Irish Collective Asset-Management Vehicle. This was yet another tax dodging scheme as there was no Irish withholding tax and it allowed US investors to escape any taxes in their own country.

After its inauguration, Matheson boasted that its partners 'were extensively involved' in a 'joint government and industry project' to bring it about.[10] Matheson's lobbying efforts operate on a variety of fronts. It writes to specific officials; it hosts conferences and social events attended by government ministers; it works through a specially created vehicle, the Irish Debts Securities Association, to meet state officials; it gets on the 'inside track' to acquire tax changes for its corporate backers. Matheson then uses its detailed inside knowledge of Irish tax law to devise specific legal schemes for foreign multinationals. The most notorious of these schemes involved the use of charitable trusts to enable vulture funds to pay minimal tax on assets picked up after the property collapse. This was a new venture for Tax Haven Ireland as it involved shielding profits from Irish assets rather than moving foreign profits through the state. In order to pull it off, the Matheson Foundation operated three charities, Medb, Badb and Eurydice to hold the property assets in trust. This allowed companies controlled by Goldman Sachs, who had bought up distressed Irish properties, to pay little tax on their profits. One of its front companies, Beltany Property Finance, earned an income of €44 million from these acquisitions in 2014, but paid just €250 in tax. It was not the only one. Mars Capital is an affiliate of a big US hedge fund, Oaktree Capital Management, the largest purchaser of distressed assets in the world. It bought up the mortgages on Irish homes from the old Anglo Irish Bank at a discount price of 42 per cent of their value, but it then squeezed the mortgage holders for the full value of the loan. It took in revenue of €14 million – but paid just €250 in total corporation tax. Once again, a charitable trust was used, and by pure coincidence, it ended up with the very same tax bill. The same technique was also used by WLR Cardinal Mezzanine Fund, which is controlled by the former US Commerce Secretary, Wilbur Ross.[11] In 2015, it took in €3 million from its activities and paid €250 in corporation tax. Another company, BlueBay Ireland, took in €36 million in 2015 and 2016 but each year paid just €250 in tax. It was all starting to look like more than a coincidence. When this pattern became public knowledge, the revelations about Matheson's use of charitable trusts brought a howl of outrage from Irish politicians. One of their number, Stephen Donnelly, produced a detailed paper where he showed that about €1 billion a year was being lost in taxes to the Irish revenue.[12] Donnelly's primary concern was that Section 110 companies were getting an unfair advantage over Irish capitalists who might equally wish to buy up property. Within its own terms, this was an accurate point, but it missed the bigger picture.

The use of charitable trusts is a well-known technique of the Irish tax-planning industry. Charities provide a number of key advantages – they convey an image of philanthropy which the wealthy love to acquire. They cannot be declared bankrupt, so their investments are safe. They provide a residency location that keeps revenue officials in the US and elsewhere away. Most importantly of all, they acquire trust status, providing a 'thin veil of secrecy' that real owners can hide behind. The Irish securitisation industry has been built on this type of technique for tax avoidance. The Matheson charities did not just offer this technique to the vultures, moreover, it sheltered all sorts of global securities. Adam Lerrick, for example, is an investment banker and a member of the right-wing think-tank, the American Enterprise Institute. He was also involved in the Argentine Bond Restructuring Agency that bought up that country's bonds at a knock down price – and then squeezed the country for the return of the loans. To cut his tax bill, he linked up with one of Matheson's charitable trusts, just like the vulture funds who were buying Irish property. So too did Davidson Kemper, which is not a person but a giant US hedge fund. One of its subsidiaries, Burlington Loan Management, bought up the debts of a failed Icelandic bank, and although it controlled assets of €8 billion across Europe, it only paid €125 in tax in 2015. Once again, the trick was to link up with one of Matheson's charitable foundations in Dublin. While outrage against the vulture funds in Ireland is perfectly justified, it is also a case of the dog biting its owner. The techniques that were used to build up Ireland's financial sector are now being used to squeeze the revenue normally due to the Irish state itself. The irony is that it is occurring with the direct connivance of the Revenue Commissioners themselves.

This becomes evident when we look at the third function that law firms play within the fixer network. As well as lobbying and devising tax dodging scams, they act as intermediaries with the tax authorities for individual clients. They are the conduits for 'guidance notes', rulings and 'opinions' produced by the Revenue Commissioners. These notes are not supposed to be legal documents, but simply 'guidance' on how technical aspects of the Finance Acts will be interpreted. Yet they give a good idea about what corporations can get away with and what they cannot. Rulings about how income will be deemed taxable by the Revenue Commissioners, for example, can be obtained in advance to provide certainty to corporate clients. The whole ethos of the Irish Revenue Commissioners is to develop a harmonious, cooperative relationship with corporations and their tax advisors. Within the Revenue Commissioners there is a Large Cases Division (LCD) which deals with big companies. It states that it operates a 'Cooperative Compliance Framework as a mutually beneficial mechanism for managing the relationship between large businesses and Revenue'.[13] There is also provision for 'tax agents' to contact this division to get confirmation from Revenue that their analysis of the tax/duty consequences of a proposed course of action or in respect of a specific transaction is 'acceptable to Revenue'.[14] Solicitors working in this area need only obtain a Tax Advisory Identification Number to act as agents on behalf of their corporate clients. Through these mechanisms, the advice of legal firms plays a key role in corporate calculations. One example occurred over whether vulture funds might be required to pay a Capital Gains Tax on the disposal of their Irish assets. Should this apply – as it does to Irish people disposing of property – it might curtail their

profits. Maples and Calder, however, is a law firm that does this intermediary work for its corporate clients, describing this activity as 'making
protective claims to the Irish Revenue to protect a taxpayer's rights'.[15]
It informs interested parties that a Revenue Commissioners' guidance
note means that it 'should generally operate to exempt investors in Irish
regulated funds where they dispose of units in the funds'.[16] The word
'generally' is significant here, because it acts as a signal that corporations should book a meeting with Maples and Calder to do the necessary
paper work. Where there is any dispute, the legal firm will also act as
representatives of the firm in negotiating a settlement. Law firms are at
the centre of Ireland's network of tax fixers because they understand the
detailed legal clauses that give corporations an appearance of tax compliance – while also giving 'tax neutrality'. This is the common term used in
the trade for paying no tax.

THE BIG PLAYERS

Matheson is the main, go-to law firm for the bigger, better known US
multinationals, but it is still only the third biggest law firm in Ireland.
A&L Goodbody is the country's largest firm with 293 solicitors and
like Matheson it runs its own charity foundation, known as Arbutus
Homeless Person's Trust. Once again, however, the purpose is hardly
philanthropic. One of the global companies that used the trust for tax
purposes was the arms manufacturer BAE Systems. One of its subsidiaries, Trident Aviation Holdings, was supposedly based in Ireland through
shares in the homeless charity. The fact that a company that specialises in destroying homes through its cluster bombs was hiding behind a
homeless charity didn't seem to bother the authorities. A&L Goodbody
was also the advisor to the US vulture fund, Cerberus, when it bought
up property in Northern Ireland from the National Asset Management
Agency (NAMA). The Comptroller and Auditor General subsequently
estimated that Irish taxpayers lost out on €200 million in the Project
Eagle transaction largely because the property was undervalued. This
may account for the fact that Cerberus, through its subsidiary Promon-
toria Eagle, made a profit of €77 million in 2014. But with the help of
A&L Goodbody, it was able to use the Section 110 scheme to write off

interest payments against this profit, ending up with a tax payment of just €1900.

We have already encountered Arthur Cox, which is the second biggest law firm with 274 solicitors. It is not as focused on helping US firms as Matheson – but it still runs a substantial operation in this area. Its speciality has been helping US firms to engage in Irish inversions. This means that big US corporations buy the stock of, or merge with, a smaller Irish company, so that they appear to be headquartered primarily in the Republic. This accounts for the fact that 8 of the 13 biggest Irish companies, by revenue, are US companies who have used inversion to take advantage of the legal code. Arthur Cox boasts that it has helped global heavy hitters like Accenture, Covidien and Ingersol-Rand to migrate their tax residency to Ireland. It makes no bones about how this can be done, moreover, claiming that 'a flexible credit system usually eliminates any tax liability in Ireland'.[17] It also promotes its close links to the Irish state. One of its partners, Padraig O'Riordan, was appointed to the chair of the Dublin Airport Authority, a significant posting in view of the fact that Arthur Cox has a special unit to offer 'advice' to aviation companies. O'Riordan subsequently argued against a salary cap of €250,000 in the public sector because he claimed that chief executives were a 'rare commodity'.[18] But for those at the bottom of society, he suggested extra social welfare cuts.[19]

William Fry ranks fifth and employs 220 solicitors and another 100 or so tax professionals. It prides itself on helping not just international but also Irish businesses reduce their tax bills, and its best-known client is the Irish billionaire, Denis O'Brien. In 2015, William Fry set up an Irish Collective Assessment-Management Vehicle (ICAV) to reduce O'Brien's tax bill on the sale of a property in Dublin's Stephen's Green. The billionaire made €30 million on the sale of the LXV building, but because William Fry helped transfer the asset into an ICAV known as the Real Estate Development and Investment Fund, he avoided a €10 million tax bill. Strangely enough, William Fry was also appointed as the government's legal advisor for the Irish Bank Resolution Corporation (IBRC) Commission of Investigation. One of the purposes of this investigation was to examine the facts surrounding the sale by the former Anglo Irish

Bank of Siteserv to a company controlled by Denis O'Brien. The sale was followed by the write off of a €110 million IBRC loan to Siteserv.[20]

More broadly, there is an unusual relationship between the legal firms who facilitate tax avoidance and the Irish state. As we have seen, the legal firms have built up an extensive industry based on servicing SPVs to ensure tax neutrality. But the Irish state maintains a friendly relationship with the very firms that deprive it of tax revenue. The traditional argument was that even though multinationals paid very little tax, they established linkages to the rest of the economy that generated economic activity. But this is not the case with the securitisation industry that the law firms are helping. Here is how a research article in a *Central Bank Quarterly Bulletin* put it:

> the contribution from domestic SPVs to Irish GDP is very limited. They are generally designed to be tax neutral and most are established as companies with Irish directors but no dedicated employees. Their contribution arises indirectly through fees to resident professional services firms, primarily in the legal and financial sectors. Estimates by the Central Bank suggest that fees paid in Ireland were less than €100 million in 2015.[21]

This gets to the heart of the matter. If the main benefit to the Irish economy are fees to corporate fixers, why is the Irish state facilitating this tax avoidance when it could be collecting billions extra each year in tax – or at least a proportion of it?

To make matters worse, the Irish state is paying out vast sums to the very legal firms which are helping to deprive it of revenue. Each year, the Irish state pays out more than €200 million in fees to the legal professions. This is an underestimate, moreover, as it does not include fees paid out by commercial semi-state bodies, which are exempt from the Freedom of Information Act. The Department of Finance indicates that these fees typically range from €80 an hour for a trainee to €390 an hour for a senior partner.[22] And the biggest beneficiaries of these payments are the same legal firms that are engaged in schemes to generate 'tax neutrality' for their wealthy clients. Between 2011 and 2014, for example, Arthur Cox received €7.7 million in consultancy fees from NAMA and €4.6 million from the Department of Finance. The company also appeared to have a close relationship with the Health Service Executive as it became the main external legal advisor who fought patients looking for compensation in the courts. In 2011 and 2012, payments to Arthur Cox's Consultancy Services amounted to over €19 million. Its rival, Matheson, received over a million. But even more ironically, the very client which Matheson helped to minimise its tax bill, Goldman Sachs, received €9 million from the Irish government for its financial advice.

The most startling aspect of these state payments to legal firms is the role of the Revenue Commissioners. Mason Hayes Curran runs a major tax planning practice to help corporations use Ireland 'as part of their global tax strategy'. But it is also one of the largest recipients of payments from the Revenue Commissioners for legal advice. Matheson, which specialises in helping US corporations to minimise their tax bill, also receives substantial payments. Arthur Cox is primarily used by Revenue in their Human Resources functions and receives relatively small amounts. Overall, however, it would appear that a number of the legal firms which facilitate tax dodging can also work for the gamekeepers. The pay-outs from Revenue to legal firms illustrates this point.

Table 5.1 Payments by Revenue Commissioners to Law Firms 2012–17[23]

	2012	2013	2014	2015	2016	2017
Mason, Hayes Curran	€703,014	€894,981	€822,290	€799,628	€937,446	€919,730
Matheson	€816,473	€824,739	€623,421	€1,027,824	€162,526	N/A
Arthur Cox	N/A	€13,479	€6541	€28,379	€8000	N/A
William Fry	N/A	N/A	N/A	N/A	N/A	€614,159
Byrne Wallace	N/A	N/A	N/A	€144,320	€514,899	€591,663

A similar pattern emerges with NAMA, which was charged with raising as much money as possible for the Irish state after it took over the distressed assets of the banks. One strategy would have been to only sell property to corporations that were willing to pay taxes on their profits. Instead, NAMA sold much of its property portfolio to companies using SPVs to pay as few taxes as possible. Moreover, the lucrative contracts for

NAMA's legal advice were often given to the same law firms that helped the vulture funds to achieve this. Table 5.2 shows some of those who benefitted from NAMA fees.

Table 5.2   Payments (€) by NAMA to Law Firms 2012–17[24]

	2012	2013	2014	2015	2016	2017	Total
Arthur Cox	€519,911	€345,003	€381,150	€498,093	€431,734	€353,240	€2,291,418
A&L Goodbody	€300,976	€29,734	€115,935	€487,113	€198,599	€269,602	€1,401,960
Matheson	€402,647	€95,907	€128,734	€417,853	€14,931	€47,643	€1,107,715
William Fry	€7309	€77,716	€41,155	€90,729	€48,907	€1289	€267,105

No wonder some of the big law firms think they are on a gravy train. They are receiving big fees from the tax dodgers – and at the same time, lucrative contracts from a state that is reluctant to collect those taxes.

CORPORATE SERVICES PROVIDERS

Our Manhattan executive has met a Dublin legal firm and now understands Ireland's sophisticated tax system. He thinks it's a good offering and gives the go-ahead for investment. One of the most enticing prospects is his ability to use the state's 'command and control' test to claim tax residency in the Republic. He has been assured that the key decisions can still take place in the United States, so long as a number of board meetings are held each year in the Republic. This will mean periodically flying people across the Atlantic, however, unless he hires the services of the Trust and Corporate Services 'industry'. The use of the word 'industry' here is a misnomer to provide a bland, inoffensive aura. The real function of the corporate service providers is to find local directors who will run a shell company, a company secretary who will ensure compliance with existing rules and a small number of local administrators. There are two main companies in Dublin who provide these services – Structured Finance Management (SFM) and the TMF Group.

As an example of how it works, let's look at the previously mentioned Goldman Sachs subsidiary, Beltany Property Finance Limited. In 2016,

Beltany needed company directors to comply with the Companies Registration Office, so it went to Structured Finance Management. SFM were more than happy to oblige, assigning Karen McCrave, Jonathan Hanly, Fiona de Lacy Murphy and Rachel Martin to become directors. At the time, Karen McCrave was the managing director of SFM and she and her colleague, Jonathan Hanly, were both directors of 117 other companies. These included subsidiaries of Cerberus and other Goldman Sachs subsidiaries. Fiona de Lacy Murphy and Rachel Martin were fellow staff members at SFM and were on the boards of 24 companies and 100 companies respectively.[25] US hedge fund Oaktree chose Matheson for its tax strategy when it set up Mars Capital Ireland. However, it still needed the right paperwork to function as a company, so it went to the TMF Group. Like their rivals, TMF was more than happy to oblige, assigning two directors, John Hackett and Kevin Butler, who were not only directors of the TMF Group – they were also directors of 393 other Irish companies between them. In the past, these corporate services functions were provided by small, fairly secretive companies, but in recent years, there has been a major consolidation in the industry. Structured Finance Management was taken over by Intertrust a company, like TMF, that originated in the Netherlands. The Netherlands was traditionally a transit harbour not only for goods but also for capital. The country originally grew rich from maritime trade and today there are still echoes of this past in the fact that Holland is one of the biggest conduit tax havens on the planet.[26] The Netherlands also pioneered the double tax treaties that knit up the global avoidance system, and to this day, there are an estimated 23,000 letterbox companies managed by trust firms like Intertrust and TMF in the country. Rock stars like U2, football megastars, hedge funds and big corporations all go Dutch for tax shelters and discretion. Indeed, the tax industry became so notorious that the Dutch parliament was recently forced to hold an inquiry into the matter. Without naming any particular company, it found that they often ignored international laws and regulations, facilitated money laundering and corruption and regularly failed to identify the people behind capital flows as required by law.[27] With the wealthy hiding ever more of their money offshore, these corporate services firms were themselves snapped up by even bigger global conglomerates. Intertrust, for example, was taken over by Blackstone – one of the biggest US hedge funds, who then floated it on the stock market at a value of €1.32 billion. TMF was taken over by the London-based hedge fund, Doughty Hanson, and floated with a valuation of €1 billion. Intertrust's clients include six of the top ten Fortune Global 500 companies and 30 of the largest private equity funds.

Tax avoidance has evidently become big business – and Dublin's corporate firms have formed partnerships with the global companies to facilitate it. Beyond their role in sourcing local directors, corporate services firms also write the complex paperwork that facilitates tax scams like the Double Irish. Most of them have major offices in Bermuda and the Cayman Islands – as well as in the British Virgin Islands, Delaware and Luxembourg. Prior to 2015, they showed companies how to route money through the Netherlands on to places like the Bahamas in order to avoid withholding taxes on dividends, interest payments and royalties. This work continued until 2020 for companies that got into these schemes before 2015, and SFM and the TMF Group continue to provide paperwork necessary to satisfy the relevant tax authorities. With hundreds of so-called brass plate companies in the IFSC one might expect that the Irish state would take a dim view of these activities. Instead, when Intertrust held a ceremony to celebrate the expansion of its office in Dublin, the Minister for Business, Enterprise and Innovation, Heather Humphries, turned up as a guest of honour. An IDA executive, meanwhile, called the expansion 'a notable endorsement' of Ireland's financial services industry.[28] It certainly was – if you acknowledge its role as a facilitator of tax avoidance.

THE ACCOUNTANTS

Back to our Manhattan executive. The overall tax plan has been explained and he has learned that he doesn't have to spend too much time in Dublin, thanks to the corporate services providers. There is still a missing link, however – the numbers people. Let's say you want to use historic losses from a subsidiary in Germany to get a tax break in Ireland. A corporate lawyer can tell you whether this is legal or not, but you will still need the numbers specialists to make it happen. The same applies when firms want to engage in transfer pricing, inter-group financing and a range of other measures that must be accounted for. Whichever scheme you happen to choose, you need an accountant to make the figures balance. Accountancy is now one of the world's most profitable businesses, because every corporation must place a value on its assets, its expenditure and, crucially, its profit margins. There are currently four main firms who dominate the global accountancy profession – Deloitte, KPMG, Ernst and Young (EY) and PricewaterhouseCoopers (PwC). In the US, for example, the big four audit 99 per cent of all public companies if measured by sales.[29] Worldwide, they earn between $37 billion a year, in the case of Deloitte, to €26 billion, in the case of KPMG. One of the reasons for their staggering growth is that they have evolved from merely doing external audits to a host of diverse activities that range from risk assessment to aggressive tax planning. Audits were the original life blood of accountancy firms because companies are required by law to produce one each year. This was primarily a safeguard for shareholders with little relationship to company management, but in recent decades the big four have branched into all manner of corporate services – particularly tax avoidance. A 2013 House of Commons report into the role of the 'large accountancy firms in tax avoidance', found that PwC were involved in 'the promotion of tax avoidance on an industrial scale'.[30] But they were not alone. The report stated that all 'four firms have developed internal guidelines on where the line between tax planning and aggressive avoidance lies…selling schemes with as little as a 50% chance of succeeding if challenged in court'.[31] Indeed, in the case of PwC, they found that the company 'will approve a tax product if there is a 25% chance – a one-in-four chance – of it being upheld'. As Professor Prem Sikka has rightly pointed out, 'this effectively means the company offered schemes to its clients – knowingly marketing these schemes – where they judged there is a 75% risk of it then being deemed unlawful'.[32] A US Senate report similarly found that,

> Accounting firms…have been major participants in the development, mass marketing, and implementation of generic tax products sold to multiple clients…. [The] tax shelter industry was no longer focused primarily on providing individualized tax advice to persons who initiate contact with a tax advisor. Instead, the industry focus has

expanded to developing a steady supply of generic 'tax products' that can be aggressively marketed to multiple clients.[33]

The Senate investigation found, for example, that 'KPMG had an extensive organisational structure for developing and marketing tax avoidance schemes'. These included a 'Tax Innovation Centre' and an 'Ideas Bank' to think up new schemes. As in Europe, the committee also found that KPMG senior officials calculated that the revenue from tax scams would outweigh penalties and on this basis its Sales Opportunity Centre rang up corporations with a standard patter on how their schemes could save vast amounts of money.[34] This expansion of accountancy firms from their original function has led to considerable problems, moreover. In their role as auditors, accountants were supposed to be entirely independent of the corporations that hire them, in order to act as external examiners. But when the accountancy firms run a tax-planning department, they become agents of management, showing them how to avoid their social obligations. Audits are supposed to publicise the result of a year's commercial activity. But tax dodging involves a degree of secrecy and hiding real business activity behind a wall of appearances for 'tax purposes'. An accountant who acted as an auditor could pride himself on rigorous standards which might even take account of the public good. But now the public good never comes into it – the only question is 'how much can we get away with?' Of course, this type of crude, impolite conversation is only held in private, with a more coded language used for public consumption. Typically, the accountancy industry will advertise their ability to help corporations avoid tax by talking of 'risk assessment'. Here is how one tax partner from an Irish accountancy firm put it:

> If I was to talk to a client, I wouldn't use the words – 'ethically you have to pay tax'. I would be putting it to him, the risk he puts himself and his business and his family and his employees under, by not being tax compliant. If you start talking to a client about ethics, he thinks you are God and you have a Revenue Commissioner's stamp at the back of your head. Talk to them about risk and you are giving them good advice for which they will thank you.[35]

But behind this talk of 'risk' there are cold-blooded calculations that show no concern whatsoever about a need to contribute to society at large. Here is another tax partner from the same study:

> To a certain extent there is really no ethics in tax. There is no ethical dimension to taxation. I don't think that many tax people would feel that if I save my client's tax, patients die in hospital or anything like that. I think they don't think in those terms at all. I think they will always resist the view of that kind of relationship between the common good and what they do.[36]

These types of conversations are treated as perfectly normal within the accountancy profession. But there is, in fact, nothing normal about it. To put this in perspective, let's imagine there exists a profession to help the meat industry do a 'risk assessment' on avoiding food regulation. Or to assist the building industry to find new ways around health and safety standards. This is an absurdity because, of course, there is no 'profession' that advertises its ability to dodge food regulations or health and safety laws. But today's accountants think it is perfectly normal to dodge taxes. They will appear in pin-stripe suits and have an eminently respectable air that projects their 'professionalism'. They will even show you a 'code of conduct' to prove how professional they appear, but the reality is very different. Accountancy firms develop a symbiotic relationship with their corporate pay masters and, sometimes, both audit their accounts and help them hide taxable income. Their primary aim is to keep the lucrative contracts that boost their own profits, and this can lead them to turn a blind eye, often with disastrous consequences.

In a number of cases, they deliberately or accidently missed out on the most glaring forms of malpractice. Ernst and Young, for example, has had to pay $10 million to the New York Attorney General's Office – and distribute another $99 million to aggrieved investors – for covering up 'a massive accounting fraud' at Lehman Brothers. In the seven years before that firm collapsed, triggering the global crash of 2008, Ernst and Young had earned $150 million in fees.[37] A year before the giant British building firm, Carillion, collapsed, accountants from KPMG and Deloitte, signed off on accounts that painted a rosy picture, justifying a dividend payment of £79 million. In reality, Carillion was already massively in debt, but the two accountancy firms did not appear to notice as they had collected £40 million in fees from their long-standing relationship with the company. In the US, there are fines when investors are hit by accountancy fraud. In Britain, there was a parliamentary inquiry and talk of breaking up the big four after the Carillion scandal. But in Ireland, such is the reverence shown to the accountancy profession, there are no serious consequences.

Ernst and Young, for example, produced audited accounts for Anglo Irish Bank throughout the early 2000s, but it managed to miss the fact that there was a €7.2 billion fraudulent receipt of a temporary deposit from Irish Life and Permanent. The purpose of this transfer was to convey an impression that the bank was in a healthy financial state when clearly it was not. Ernst and Young earned €10.3 million in fees from 2000 to 2008 for this audit work but never warned about the bizarre practices that led to the bank's downfall. Yet, a decade later no punishment has been imposed. EY gets to keep its fees while the Irish taxpayer picked up a bill for €29 billion to bail out Anglo Irish Bank. The only gesture to alleviate public disquiet has been a call by the Director of Public Prosecution for the Standards Unit of the Chartered Accountants of Ireland to investigate the case. In other words, for an internal investigation within the 'profession' where the fines for malpractice are a measly €30,000. This leniency, shown to firms like Ernst and Young, is not accidental. The big four accountancy firms stand at the core of Ireland's fixer network for tax avoidance. The political elite meet with them regularly; they commission them to produce expert 'reports' which will give the desired results; they act as advisors in devising tax policy. They play a central role in maintaining Ireland's tax haven – and in doing consultancy work for a state which presides over it. In brief, they are the fixers' fixer.

At the top of these 'tax planning' operations stands Feargal O'Rourke, the managing partner of PwC. Before assuming leadership of the firm, O'Rourke ran the tax-planning side of the business for more than a decade. He has described himself as 'a business advisor whose speciality happened to be tax'.[38] He is unusual, however, in the degree to which his networks overlap with the key power structures in Irish society. Born into a Fianna Fáil dynasty, he is the son of a former Cabinet Minister and a cousin of a former Minister for Finance. When the state was looking for a Commission on Taxation in 2009, O'Rourke was also invited to participate – even as he advised his own clients about their 'tax neutrality'. This Commission advocated the extension of deductions for the cost of intangible assets, which, as we showed in the previous chapter, led to a major spike in tax dodging through the CAIA programme. Before this, however, he was also the architect of Ireland's most famous tax avoidance scheme – the 'Double Irish'. Under his guidance, the PwC tax planning department set up a structure through which the California-based Google routed its European sales via a subsidiary in Dublin. This unit in turn paid billions in royalties to another Irish company for the rights to Google's patents in Bermuda, saving the company about $2 billion in taxes per year.[39] The Irish state was forced to close down this scam in 2015, after an international outcry but, as we have seen, gave a 'grandfather clause' extension until December 2020 for those firms that had already enjoyed huge tax reducing privileges.

As part of a global chain that facilitates tax avoidance, PwC ensures its planning departments in different countries work together. A scheme devised for Glanbia illustrates this. Glanbia is one of the largest food companies in Ireland and had its early origins in the agricultural cooperative movement. But since at least the year 2000, it has been employing PwC as its main business advisor on tax. The Lux Leaks revelations show that PwC Luxembourg held a meeting with the local tax authorities about Glanbia on 6 August 2007, and then followed this up with a letter to summarise an Advanced Tax Agreement that both parties had reached.[40] Advanced Tax Agreements are a mechanism by which multinationals – through their tax advisors – meet the relevant tax authorities to propose tax-dodging schemes that they have devised. Essentially, it is a mechanism to guarantee certainty about legal tax dodging – to reduce the risk. PwC devised a scheme whereby Glanbia Commercial provided a Luxembourg subsidiary, Glanbia Luxinvest SA, with money to make a loan to another subsidiary, Glanbia Financial Services, at a high interest rate. These interest charges were then used to reduce the tax bill of the last-mentioned subsidiary. And even though Glanbia Luxinvest SA gained from the large interest payment, they only paid a tiny tax because PwC had found one of Luxembourg's many 'loopholes'. To make doubly sure, they met with Luxembourg officials to get the all clear. The accountancy firm was literally able to juggle the figures and boost the profits of its corporate client.

PwC also drew the ire of the British House of Commons because of the way it helped another Irish-based company. The word 'Irish' is a misnomer in this case, however, because Shire is a global pharmaceutical company with production facilities in Basingstoke in Britain, and Pennsylvania and Massachusetts in the US. It relocated its corporate headquarters from Britain to Ireland in 2008, but this was purely for tax purposes, designed to facilitate the same type of tax scheme that PwC devised for Glanbia. PwC held similar Advanced Tax Agreement meetings with the Luxembourg authorities and then wrote up their understanding of the deal.[41] Essentially, it meant that a Shire holding company in Ireland gave out loans to a Luxembourg subsidiary which then lent out money to other Shire subsidiaries at high interest rates. The Luxembourg subsidiary earned $1.9 billion from these interest payments but ended up paying a 0.0156 per cent tax rate on this money. The other subsidiaries outside Luxembourg also used the high interest bill to reduce their taxes. In the industry, this is called 'tax arbitrage' but a simpler way to put it is that they play one tax system off against the other.

PwC hit the limelight because of Lux Leaks, but other accountancy companies have displayed a similar enthusiasm to help their wealthy clients. KPMG, for example, devised a scheme whereby wealthy individuals did not have to pay the 20 per cent Capital Gains Tax on money they gained from selling shares. Take the case of Lorraine Kinsella and her husband, Shane Ryan, son of the founder of Ryanair, the late Tony Ryan, who wanted to sell shares but did not want to pay tax on the earnings. They went to KPMG who advised them that Ms Kinsella could take up residence in a 'tiny apartment' in Rome and register herself as living there. Soon afterwards she purchased Ryanair shares worth €18 million from her husband, using funds loaned to her by him. She then sold the shares on to a third party for more than €19 million, and paid tax in Italy of less than €40,000.[42] A few years later, the same scheme was repeated for the McCaughey family who owned Century Homes. Gerry McCaughey simply transferred his shares in the company to his wife, Sophie, who then took up residence in Italy. She sold the shares on to Kingspan and cut her Capital Gains Tax because of a 'loophole' in a double tax agreement between Ireland and Italy. KPMG produced a special report for Century Homes shareholders on how exactly this tax dodge scheme should be worked. But it added 'We would prefer to minimise dissemination of knowledge of the matters contained in this report as Revenue attack is more likely if this route was to be copied by others.'[43] This is the same company that is making money by liquidating the Irish branch of Debenhams UK, but which refuses to speak to the more than 1000 workers thrown out of work without any form of redundancy. It is revealing that workers who built the company for 20 years are entitled to less than the liquidators who come in to wind the company up. Ernst and Young, meanwhile, came up with a fairly simple scheme to help the rich avoid paying value added tax (VAT) on their private jets. Most people have no choice but to pay VAT on their clothes and their petrol, but if you are a billionaire buying a private jet, all you need to do is bring it in through the Isle of Man to save yourself €1 million in VAT. Despite these many activities, the accountancy firms enjoy a close and frictionless relationship with the very state from which they seek to deduct taxation. When 'loopholes' are seemingly discovered by clever accountants, state officials make it look like they just have to work a little harder to catch up. But even this cosy image is no more than a myth. The real game is a collaboration between the state and the tax-dodging industry to shift the burden away from corporations and onto the wider society. It operates at many levels and it is sometimes difficult to know where the boundary of state policy ends and the lobbying begins. Let's look at three specific areas where the accountancy firms industry interacts with the Irish state. The first is through consultancy fees. Accountancy firms, as we have seen, engage in both auditing and devising tax-dodging scams. But, ironically, they also establish consultancy services which win lucrative contracts from the same state they deprive of revenue. Here, for example, are the pay-outs from the Irish Central Bank to the big four accountancy firms. The figures cover a five-year period, but no details are provided for what exact services were provided, as this is categorised as 'commercially sensitive'.

Table 5.3   Total Fees from Central Bank to the Big Four Accountancy Firms
2012–17

Accountancy Firm	Consultancy Fee
Ernst Young	€27,028,090
KPMG	€13,605,009
Deloitte	€3,638,000
PwC	€2,947,009

These are quite large fees, but the poacher-gamekeeper contradiction is sharpened by the fact that Ernst and Young tops the list. This is the firm that missed out on the fraudulent transactions of Anglo Irish Bank and thus helped cover a looming disaster that eventually cost the Irish taxpayer €42 billion overall. Second, the Irish state hires the consultancy departments of accountancy firms to provide advice and produce reports. The reason for this is that it knows their recommendations will fit well with the mentality of its own officials and their political masters. The French sociologist, Pierre Bourdieu, has argued that 'the state nobility' – by which he means the high-ranking civil servants – have embraced a neoliberal outlook with the all gusto that old-style communists in Eastern Europe now believe in privatisation. The officials preach a gospel about a 'withering away of the state and the undivided reign of the market and the consumer, the commercial substitute for the citizen.'[44] In the past, Irish officials sometimes thought in terms of expanding state services as a mechanism for bolstering native capitalism. But the neoliberal revolution that has gathered pace since the 1970s changed all that so that, today, state officials are more likely to seek private, market-based, solutions. This shift is not presented in terms of ideology or political choice – but is legitimated through an emphasis on efficiency and productivity. However, the assumption that private equals more efficiency, is not a matter of empirical test but a right-wing dogma. The political elite, drawn primarily from Fine Gael and Fianna Fáil, share this approach but need to justify their actions to a wider public. One of the ways they do this is by preparing the ground for policy changes by commissioning apparently independent reports drawn from experts. In this way, they can 'depoliticise' political choices and present issues in terms of technical changes. Here is where the interests of the Irish state and the accountancy firms who deprive it of revenue really coincide. The accountancy firms are well paid by corporations to minimise tax obligations. They have no interest in social rights and have an extreme aversion to increasing taxes on corporations to improve public services. Yet, despite this, they appear as neutral experts in their guise as consultants to the state. The state officials hire them not just for their proficiency with numbers – but because they share similar attitudes to themselves. Two examples will suffice to illustrate this point.

When the Irish state sought to introduce water charges, they first went to PwC to produce a report. There was no possibility that PwC would ever conclude that the funding of a water service should come from general taxation. It was far more likely that they would propose measures which reduced state spending on water services and turned water into a commodity with a pricing structure. Not surprisingly, this is exactly what they proposed. They suggested that 'Irish Water could become a self-financing utility as early as 2018, depending on how quickly government wishes to cease funding and on the level of water charges imposed.'[45] It was a conclusion which suited both the political elite and the corporate sector who wished to further reduce the bills of their business clients. One year after its report on water charges in 2011, PwC produced another for the Department of Social Protection on pension charges. It made no recommendation about the need to regulate these charges or insist that the state limit the amount that pension providers could skim off people's savings. It simply called for more openness and transparency. The notion that the state might become a repository for pension savings and invest in housing, for example, was not even considered. Instead PwC proposed that workers be automatically enrolled into the private pension industry to 'overcome the problem of inertia.'[46] It was music to the ears of the financial sector and the neoliberal politicians who want to reduce state spending on pensions in the long term.

The third area where the state interacts with the accountancy industry blurs the line between private interest and public good even further. Partners and senior figures from the main accountancy firms are seconded to state departments to help write taxation policy. Officially, this is defined as 'pro-bono work' to convey the impression that the accountancy firms are engaged in an act of generosity. In reality, it means that accountancy firms shift from being outside lobbyists to inside policy makers who help devise Ireland's tax policy. Here is a list of some of the 'pro-bono work' undertaken by the accountancy firms for the Irish state between 2008 and 2015.

Table 5.4 Pro-bono Work Undertaken by the Main Accountancy Firms for the Department of Finance 2008–15[47]

Corporation	Subject area	Time spent
Deloitte	Assist with formation of Corporate Affairs Unit of Department of Finance	13 months
Deloitte	Advise on Common Consolidated Corporate Tax Base	9 Months
KPMG	'Technical Aspects' of International Tax Policy	11 months
KPMG	Mortgage Arrears	19 months
PwC	Advice on Financial Transaction Tax	12 months
Ernst Young	Research paper on Irish Corporate Tax System	(Fee of €6,150 paid)
PwC	Assistance with OECD BEPS Project	N/A
KPMG	Assistance with International Tax Policy	N/A
PwC	Assistance with International Tax Policy	N/A

It is perfectly clear that the type of pro-bono work undertaken is hardly accidental. The accountancy firms operate inside government departments to help devise policies which benefit clients from whom they collect lucrative fees. The involvement of tax partners and accountants at the very heart of the state also suggests that tax avoidance does not arise from the lucky discovery of loopholes, but rather from collusion between the neoliberal state and the tax-dodging industry. How else are we to explain why PwC, for example, sends one of its top officials to work on devising ways to oppose a Financial Transaction Tax? This was a modest proposal from the EU Commission for a 0.1 per cent tax on sales of shares and bonds and a 0.01 per cent on derivative contracts. In Tax Haven Ireland, the accountancy and legal firms get privileged access to the state they deprive of resources. They have become the guardians of corporate interests and form a social layer in the wider society that provides the activist core of Fianna Fáil and Fine Gael. Their cultural outlook – often caricatured as Dublin 4, the postcode of a wealthy suburb of Dublin – pervades the media, the economics departments of universities and the golf clubs. From it arises a message that is endlessly repeated – 'where would we be without foreign investment?; we need to keep our tax rates low to be "attractive"; Ireland needs to remain competitive'. What they rarely say, however, is that 'our fees and our own privileges are intimately tied up with this policy of competitiveness'.

6

The Irish Financial Services Centre

Larry Fink was once labelled 'the hub of the wheel of American capitalism'.[1] He is more generally regarded as a 'titan' of the world of finance, earning over $25 million dollars a year as CEO of the world's largest asset management company, BlackRock. This firm does not produce goods or services but scours the world for investment opportunities using the latest algorithms and thousands of computers. It deals in shares, commercial paper (short-term loans), bonds and a host of other activities associated with 'financial engineering'. Contrary to the myth about a free market, moreover, BlackRock also cosies up to governments to win contracts to manage bailouts. The company has no morality about where it invests but concerns itself only with the bottom line. Thus, BlackRock is the biggest owner of fossil fuels in the world, holding more oil, gas and coal reserves than any other investor. It is also the largest investor in Amazon rainforest destruction and the global arms industry. When two million Americans were evicted from their homes, after the 2008 crash, BlackRock went on a buying spree.[2]

It is now the largest private portfolio holder of single-family homes and is pulling in vast amounts of rental income. In the words of William Lazonick, BlackRock is a 'value extraction' company rather than a 'value creation' one.[3] Or, put more simply, it is a financial speculator. BlackRock also has an important interest in Ireland. In 2011, one of its subsidiaries, BlackRock Solutions, was given a contract by the Central Bank to stress test the six main private banks. There was no public tender and BlackRock gathered its share of the €20 million fee for the three companies who got the contract. Having examined the inner workings of the banks, it took a stake in Bank of Ireland before increasing it to 5 per cent. This was a shrewd move because Bank of Ireland began charging excess interest rates that were above the European average to bolster its profits. In 2018, it made €935 million in profit and the following year it made €758 million. BlackRock got its share, but, better still, these were tax-free profits. Under Irish legislation, companies can write off past losses to reduce their taxable income. As Bank of Ireland made considerable losses during the Celtic Tiger crash, it was guaranteed tax-free profits well into the future. This tells us something about BlackRock's wider modus operandi –and it could hardly have found a more hospitable place than the Irish Financial Services Centre (IFSC), where it now has billions of assets under management.

The IFSC was established in 1987 as a physical location in an area of Dublin's Docklands designated as a Special Economic Zone. The idea was to move Ireland into the tax-dodging big leagues and today there are two main ways that this is achieved. On the one hand, the IFSC functions as one of the world's major offshore shadow-banking systems. A recent report by the Financial Stability Board estimated that the IFSC currently hosts €4.5 trillion in gross assets – with €676 billion in the under-regulated offshore sector.[4] On the other hand, the IFSC is plugged into the wider Irish avoidance system through its links to transnational corporations. We saw in Chapter 5 that the fixer network operates out of the IFSC, where one of its primary jobs is to arrange the complex legal and corporate structures that allow transnationals to interpret the law and get around it. From a small hub on the river Liffey the IFSC now casts a dark shadow over all of Irish society. How did this come to be?

BACKGROUND TO THE IFSC

As early as 1967, Charles J. Haughey predicted that American capital would transform the domestic banking sector, but it would take another 20 years before his dream could be realised via the Irish Financial Services Centre. The external conditions for an Irish financial hub were created by the Single European Act (SEA) of 1986. This was designed to create a no-holds-barred Single Market across the continent in the wake of the big bang deregulation of the City of London. The European Commission also supported a more unified capital market, both in the interests of competing with the United States and to enforce neoliberalism within the Single Market. Their most important initiative was the introduction of the UCITS.[5] At its core, this agreement meant that financial services could be located in one part of the Single Market and sold into the rest of it. The UCITS was particularly advantageous to the Irish establishment who saw it as a golden opportunity to create a tax-free paradise that wasn't available to many traditional tax havens.

As the IFSC grew, they offered potential investors two important strategic advantages. Firstly, by locating in Dublin, global companies would have access to one the of biggest markets in the world via UCITS. Secondly, they could artificially declare their profits in the Republic via discrete deals with Revenue. The fact that the IFSC had light-touch regulation and extremely low levels of corporation tax made this prospect a virtual no-brainer. One man who understood this better than most was the Irish financier, Dermot Desmond. Desmond started his career with Citibank in Dublin during the 1960s, before moving to Pricewaterhouse-Coopers (PwC) and eventually into his own brokerage firm – National City Brokers (NCB) – in 1981. This gave him the perfect vantage point from which to recognise the potential for an Irish tax haven linked to the City of London.[6] He also understood the extraordinary support he could receive in a Republic steeped in the corporate corruption of Haughey. To plant the seed, Desmond's brokerage firm helped to finance a full-scale feasibility study on a financial services hub carried out by PwC. He also approached the future CEO of Allied Irish Bank, Michael Buckley, to collaborate on a proposal that was pitched to Haughey in 1987.[7] Haughey bought in to the idea more or less immediately, including the proposal in the Fianna Fáil manifesto for the upcoming general election.[8] He also put his chief political fixer, Padraig O'hUiginn, on to the project to make sure that it came to fruition. Given its colonial past and geographical location, Dublin was originally pitched as the perfect back office for the major investment firms in the City of London.[9] Irish banks already had relationships with their British counterparts and the costs of doing business in Dublin were at least 20 per cent cheaper than in London or Luxembourg.[10] Beyond this, Ireland was also the only other English-speaking country in the Single Market and was willing to do whatever it took to attract investors. Companies relocating to the IFSC could originally expect the following suite of generous incentives:

- 10 per cent corporate tax rate on trading income, guaranteed until 2005.
- A range of double taxation treaties, which included the US, Japan, Canada, Korea and Germany and was expanding.
- Double rent allowances for favoured IFSC tenants.
- Exemptions from local rates.
- Availability of tax-based financing.
- No withholding taxes on dividends and interest.[11]

Desmond was able to accrue these benefits for his own stockbroking company and he also owned some of the buildings in the area designated to house the IFSC. This made him a lot of money and he made sure that Haughey was similarly rewarded. According to the Tribunal set up to investigate corruption payments to politicians, Desmond gave Haughey £216,000 to buy a yacht, including payments to refurbish it between 1990 and 1991.[12] The Moriarty Tribunal also found that Desmond gave Haughey another £100,000 in September 1994, followed with a payment of £25,000 in October 1996.[13] The first payment was made via an account at Ansbacher & Company to an account at Cayman International Bank Trust Company, held exclusively for Haughey's benefit. If this sounds familiar, it is because the Ansbacher Cayman Trust was linked to the tax scam run by one of Haughey's most loyal lieutenants, Des Traynor. In 1987, Traynor approached Desmond and asked him if he could move his 'nominee shareholding accounts from Guinness and Mahon to NCB'.[14] The first account that was moved was that of Haughey, and so Desmond became the 'contact man for an investment account established for Haughey by...NCB and operated under instructions from the men most centrally involved in the Ansbacher scam, Des Traynor... and John Furze'.[15] Scarcely could there have been better conditions to shift into the tax-dodging business. Domestically, the IFSC was being pushed by two men with a stellar record of gift making and receiving, while externally there were the vast new opportunities to be exploited by those unscrupulous enough to create opportunities for global multinationals. From humble beginnings, the IFSC has grown to become one of Ireland's leading industries. The Irish Central Bank (ICB) estimates that the IFSC now has assets under management that are 25 times the size of

Ireland's Gross National Income – comprising different sets of specialities, including Investment and Money Market Funds, Financial Vehicle
Corporations and Insurance Corporations.[16] The IFSC also plays host
to the world's biggest aircraft-leasing industry with 14 of the world's 15
biggest firms operating out of Dublin.[17] Let's take a look inside, starting
with what are known as 'mutual funds'.

MUTUAL FUNDS

The funds industry is a broad category of financial activities that
involves wealthy people pooling their money and paying a manager to
scour the world for investment opportunities. Mutual funds buy and sell
any financial assets that are outside the regulated banking sector. These
can include shares, bonds or simply bets on indexes of different financial
assets. Traditionally, these funds operated out of Caribbean islands,
but over recent years Ireland has also become a major player. The IFSC
currently hosts 13,000 different funds with total assets amounting to
approximately €5.2 trillion.[18] These funds are typically organised through
a threefold division of labour. The big beasts are the fund managers who
usually charge 1 per cent or 2 per cent on assets under management,
plus a cut of the profits they secure. These brokers are normally based
on Wall Street or in the City of London, but they rely on promoters to
drum up business and administrators to carry out lower-level functions
such as auditing accounts and making payments. Fund administration
is less lucrative than managing or promoting, but it is often attractive
for financial centres looking to get started. Back-office jobs are relatively
easy to secure, and they provide a platform to diversify once financial
services have become established. This was exactly the thinking of the
Industrial Development Authority (IDA) during the late 1980s and their
strategy soon proved successful. One of the big fund managers in the
IFSC today is BlackRock, which has about €500 billion in assets under
management. Like all modern corporations, BlackRock is really a conglomerate of different companies, each one specialising in a different
area of financial speculation. One of these companies is known as Institutional Cash Series plc, which concentrates on speculation in money
markets. However, this is itself an umbrella company which advertises

different funds into which wealthy people can put their money. There are funds for buying public debts from European governments or from the British government or US treasury bonds or 'ultra-short bonds' which involves cash for different currencies. You take your pick and sit back while fund administrators in Dublin monitor the screens, keep accounts up to date and ensure there is no cheating.

The big decisions are made by investment managers based in London and Delaware. But BlackRock's different funds are still 'domiciled' in Ireland, meaning they are (somewhat) regulated by the Irish Central Bank and subject to Irish tax law. This also means that they are fronted up by some Irish residents and draw on Irish legal services for support. The chair of Institutional Cash Series plc, for example, is Paul McNaughton, who worked with the IDA for ten years and then switched over to the private sector, working initially for Deutsche Bank Offshore Funds business in Dublin and the Cayman Islands before joining BlackRock. The legal firm handling the paperwork is, you guessed it, Matheson. The various funds run by BlackRock are then promoted by means of a prospectus which potential investors examine carefully before buying any shares. After looking at where their money will be invested, they come to a key section which concerns taxation, because they don't want the Irish state skimming off any of their speculative gains. The prospectus is quite blunt on the advantages of locating in Ireland.

It states that,

> On the basis that the Company is Irish tax resident, the Company qualifies as an 'investment undertaking' for Irish tax purposes and, consequently, is exempt from Irish corporation tax on its income and gains.[19]

Gains made by participants do not have to be notified to the Revenue Commissioners if they come through a Recognised Clearing House. These entities include BNY Mellon and Deutsche Bank and, as we outline below, they operate a partnership with the highest levels of the Irish state. In addition to this, non-residents don't have to pay any capital gains taxes on the disposal of their shares, while for Irish residents there are so many exemptions that they generally don't pay either. There is no stamp duty tax on the issuing or transferring of shares, and for those concerned with their own mortality, there is no inheritance tax on their shares – provided they are non-residents. PIMCO is the second largest mutual fund in the IFSC, with €154 billion in assets under management. Their offering consists of edgier, riskier opportunities for those investors who want a higher rate of return. Thus, you can take your pick from mortgage backed securities, Russian equities, corporate debt, securities in distressed companies or commodities which can be affected by flood, drought or livestock disease. Possibly because it trades in these higher risks, moreover, PIMCO is fronted up by directors drawn from the most respectable elements in Irish society. Sitting on its Irish board are John Bruton, the former Fine Gael Taoiseach, David Kennedy, the former CEO of Aer Lingus and Francis Ruane, the former director of the Economic and Social Research Unit. To entice their clients, PIMCO point out that there will be no tax for non-Irish residents or those not ordinarily resident in Ireland for 'chargeable events'. These include turning your shares into cash, transferring your shares to another person or simply picking up your speculative gains at the close of the fund.[20] All that is required is that a Relevant Declaration about non-residency is made to the relevant authorities and there will be no withholding taxes on the way in to the Irish Haven and no taxes on the way back out again.

HEDGE FUNDS

Hedge funds are a sub-category of mutual fund with some key distinguishing features. They are normally restricted to 'sophisticated' institutional investors who can put up €100,000 to join. They are free of the normal regulations and can borrow up to double the amount of their investment money, giving speculators a bigger bang for their buck. The hedge fund manager also has greater freedom to invest as they are not tied down by rules which require greater diversification. Dublin has become a major centre for this form of riskier, high-stakes speculation, sometimes known as Alternative Investment Funds, and claims to administer 40 per cent of global hedge funds.

The lynchpin of the Irish offering to these speculators was the innocuous sounding Section 110 of the Taxes Consolidation Act (1997).

This allows hedge funds to achieve what one accountancy firm euphemistically describes as 'tax neutral status', by setting up Special Purpose Vehicles (SPVs) to manage their activities.[21] As we saw above, SPVs are legal entities designed to insulate parent companies from financial losses, but they also muddy the waters surrounding ownership and provide a range of tax advantages. One important benefit of Section 110 legislation is the ability of hedge funds to compute their taxes as if they were a trading company.[22] This means that the costs associated with issuing securities and bonds become tax deductible as far as the authorities are concerned. Since 2003, the cost of borrowing has also been included, making it extremely lucrative for hedge funds to decamp to Dublin before borrowing on the open market.[23] As if this wasn't generous enough, Section 110 companies also qualify for Ireland's Double Taxation Treaty network, allowing dividends to be sent to shareholders via Ireland without any withholding taxes.[24] To qualify for these advantages, hedge funds must be registered in Ireland for tax purposes and have at least €10 million under management. Initially, they had to acquire a relatively narrow range of shares and/or derivatives. However, since 2011, the range of qualifying assets has expanded to include commodities, plant and machinery and even carbon offsets.[25]

One particularly important group of SPVs are known as Financial Vehicle Corporations (FVCs).[26] These specialise in a process known as securitisation, which involves bundling longer-term income streams (mortgages, business loans, etc.) into marketable assets to be sold to investors more or less immediately. FVCs get particularly favourable treatment from the Revenue Commissioners, with 1049 located in Ireland, or 40 per cent of the Eurozone total.[27] To get a feel for how they work, consider a company known as Orpington Structured Finance I. In 2013, this company had assets of €1.7 billion on its balance sheet, making it appear to be one of the most valuable firms in Ireland. Despite this, however, Orpington had no physical buildings, no employees and no contribution to the Irish tax take.[28] Instead, it was a paper company using Ireland for a range of financial advantages at the behest of its beneficial owners – HSBC and Deutsche Bank.[29] In 2013, the company directors were David McGuiness and Eimir McGrath, both of whom were named as employees of a further company – Deutsche International Corporate Services. Corporate directors would ordinarily have strategic oversight, but this seems unlikely in the case of McGuiness or McGrath who were actually directors of more than 300 companies between them.[30] More importantly, although the company was registered in Ireland, the key investment decisions appeared to be taken in the United Kingdom.[31] Professor Jim Stewart has analysed more than 80 of these FVCs, highlighting some striking similarities between them. According to Stewart, all of the companies he investigated had (1) zero employees, (2) administrative services run from Ireland, and (3) management structures that lead back to financial centres such as London and New York.[32] Stewart also claims that FVCs were used to remove assets from the parent company and/or to escape the regulations that come with this, although there is no evidence that Orpington is guilty of this.

Despite their prospectuses being up to 200-pages long, a hedge fund can be authorised within 24 hours, provided the fund manager works with an Irish accredited administrator. With this level of regulatory support and the range of benefits outlined above, it is hardly surprising that hedge fund assets administered in the IFSC have increased from €129 billion 2008 to €732 billion in 2019.[33] However, the provisions of Section 110 were not 'flexible' enough for some investors, particularly as they involved a level of public reporting to the Companies Registration Office. Their unease increased when a major scandal erupted after it was revealed that vulture funds were buying up distressed Irish property and salting away their profits, tax free, in Section 110 vehicles.[34] Even before the scandal broke, a new legal regime known as Qualifying Investor Alternative Investment Funds had been set up in 2013, but no sooner was it established than the lobbying for greater 'flexibility' began again in earnest. The following year, yet another scheme emerged, known as an Irish Collective Asset-Management (ICAV) vehicle, which was designed to give an offering superior to that of the Cayman Islands. Walkers, one of main global legal promoters of tax avoidance, explains how it emerged:

> The ICAV is being created in response to both industry and investor demands for a fund specific vehicle that reduces the administrative

burden on investment funds and provides a tax effective structure for US investors.[35]

ICAVs quickly became the main vehicles for hedge fund speculation because they had some key advantages. First, they continued to be exempt from Irish taxation and did not have to impose a withholding tax on non-Irish residents. Second, they did not appear on any public register and did not have to register at the Companies Registration Office. They only had to fill in a form with the Central Bank. Third, these vehicles were specially designed to allow US investors to use 'check-the-box' provisions. In the words of Walkers, 'One of the main attractions of the ICAV is that it will be able to "check-the-box" to be treated as a transparent entity for US tax purposes, facilitating tax-efficient investment by US investors.'[36]

The sheer scale of the Irish involvement in offshore speculation can be gleaned from the annual 'Global Monitoring Report on Non-Bank Financial Intermediation'.[37] This is produced by the Swiss-based Financial Stability Board, to track financial assets held outside the supervisory systems of the world's central banks. Lending by these non-bank institutions currently stands at $184 trillion, meaning an amount twice the size of the global economy has been lent outside the regulated banking system. More troubling from an Irish perspective, is the fact that the IFSC holds 14 times Irish GDP in shadow banking assets including €417 billion that regulators know very little about.[38] The Republic of Ireland currently ranks 44th on the list of countries by size of economic activity (Gross Domestic Product), but it has the 4th largest shadow banking system on the planet.[39] Only the US ($13.8 trillion), the Cayman Islands ($4.3 trillion) and Japan ($3.2 trillion) come higher on the list, making Ireland an extreme outlier in terms of the influence of finance capital.[40] One obvious consequence of this is the potential for criminality. Research by Cillian Doyle seemed to confirm this fact, moreover, when he found that Russian firms are sending vast sums into the IFSC only for it to flow back to them again.[41] This process, known as Round Tripping, can be used to move illicit funds out of Russia in order for them to come back as what appears to be foreign direct investment.[42] Doyle's work also shows that the IFSC is being used to conceal corporate losses and money laundering, in the grey area between corporate tax dodging and outright criminality.[43]

Another sector that has grown rapidly in the last number of years is the market for insurance and reinsurance (insurance contracts sold on to secondary investors). According to a Central Bank study, Ireland recently had the second highest number of reinsurance companies in Europe with 40 per cent of them involved in captive insurance. This refers to a practice where a parent company sets up a subsidiary in order to minimise risk. As far back as 2004, the Dublin law firm, William Fry, highlighted the fact that 'reinsurers could establish in the IFSC without having to concern themselves about solvency margins, asset admissibility rules and authorisation delays'.[44] A joint brochure issued by Insurance Ireland and the IDA puts matters even more clearly, stating that 'In theory Ireland taxes foreign branch profits at 12.5%, but has a generous tax credit regime which can mean that no net Irish tax is paid on foreign branch profits of qualifying companies'.[45] This message must have been heeded, moreover, as half of the world's top 20 insurance companies currently have bases in the IFSC, including AIG, Barclays and HSBC.[46] According to the IFSC official website, 'over a quarter of the IFSC companies are involved in insurance-related operations, particularly captive insurance and reinsurance'.[47] Beyond the low tax and light-touch regulation they are likely to receive, the big draw is unfettered access to European markets. As part of the wider extension of European economic integration, the Insurance Framework Directive aims to create a unified market for insurance products throughout Europe. Once an insurance fund has been listed with the Irish Stock Exchange, it can be 'passported' throughout the EU with regulations applied exclusively at the point of origin. This allows Dublin-based firms to avoid the scrutiny of European regulators, particularly in the wake of more stringent requirements following the Great Recession. According to Financial Services Ireland, for example, 'companies and their products and services have only to be regulated once – in Ireland's case by the Central Bank of Ireland'.[48] But the Irish regulators have already shown themselves to be notoriously lax in applying rules to international insurance companies.

In 1999, an Australian insurance broker named John Houldsworth was involved in a major fraud created in the IFSC. While working for Cologne Re – the Dublin-based subsidiary of General Re – Houldsworth used reinsurance contracts to artificially inflate the balance sheet of an Australian company known as FAI.[49] This was done to make the latter company more attractive to investors, and it had the desired effect when a rival company, HIH Insurance, paid over the odds to acquire FAI. HIH duly collapsed under the weight of its disastrous acquisition, creating the biggest bankruptcy in Australian corporate history. As a result of the bankruptcy, the Australian authorities wanted to take criminal proceedings against Houldsworth, but they were unable to achieve this, as he refused to return home. Instead they had to content themselves with informing their counterparts in the Irish Republic and barring Houldsworth from the Australian Securities and Insurance industry for the rest of his life. Ordinarily, this would be expected to send up major red flags, but the Irish authorities did absolutely nothing. Two years later Houldsworth and his team were at it again – this time creating a fraud that involved the giant US insurer American Insurance Group (AIG).[50] Reinsurance companies specialise in buying and selling insurance from other insurance companies and AIG was General Re's biggest customer at the time. Under pressure from poor results, AIG approached General Re with a view to making it look like the latter was purchasing $500 million worth of insurance when in fact they were not. This improved the balance sheet of AIG, but it also led to major losses for unwitting investors. When the fraud was rumbled by the US authorities, Houldsworth only avoided prison by testifying against his co-conspirators.[51] Five people went to prison for the fraud in the United States. However, the Irish authorities didn't even launch an investigation, despite the fact that the IFSC was the scene of the crime. Fintan O'Toole takes up the story:

> After the Australian authorities banned Houldsworth…in 2004, the Irish regulator did nothing, even though [he] was still employed at Cologne Re in Dublin. In 2005, when the AIG scam came to light [the

regulator] publicly endorsed this state of affairs, claiming Cologne Re had taken [their own] corrective action.... The realisation that the IFSC had been involved in a spectacular tri-continental triple crown of dodgy dealing...meant that the Irish authorities surely had to react. They did – by bringing in more tax loopholes and corporate benefits and increasing their commitment to light touch regulation.[52]

Since these scandals broke, the Central Bank has issued a Corporate Governance Code for the Captive and Reinsurance sector. However, the IDA continues to repeat the boast that 'companies and their products only have to be regulated once...with no requirement for further regulation in the markets being sold into'.[53] With such tax-free benefits, and porous regulations, is it any wonder that Ireland is seen as a paradise for reinsurance companies?

AIRCRAFT LEASING

Ireland's aircraft-leasing 'industry' receives gushing praise from the business press as a spectacular IFSC success story. The common narrative is that one man, Tony Ryan, set up Guinness Peat Aviation during the 1980s and since then, Ireland has grown to attain the top position in aircraft leasing, accounting for half of all leased planes and a quarter of the global aircraft fleet. PwC have produced a special report to explain how vital the leasing business is to the Irish economy and universities facilitate their activities with special postgraduate courses on aviation finance.[54] One would be forgiven for thinking that there are thousands of planes at Irish airports available for leasing out, but the murky reality is very different.[55] There are a small number of highly paid Irish people who front up the Irish aircraft-leasing sector, but they are based in the IFSC, not in any of the country's airports. And for very good reason. Despite the myth making, Ireland's aircraft-leasing industry is really a platform for global tax avoidance on an industrial scale. In this ethereal, intangible world, executives drop in and out on a temporary basis while their sights are fixed on deals in Singapore, Dubai or New York. The few natives that oversee local operations are rewarded handsomely – as are the legal and accountancy firms that pick up lucrative contracts. Their role is to guide the corporations towards the 'loopholes' that have been deliberately created for them. And there are quite a few.

According to Professor Sheila Killian, aircraft leasing 'benefits from no withholding taxes on lease rental payments, wide exemptions from withholding tax on interest and dividend payments and no stamp duty or transfer taxes on the transfer of aircraft or aircraft parts'.[56] Ireland's depreciation regime, meanwhile, allows aircraft lessors to depreciate the cost of buying aircraft over only 8 years while the average lifespan is actually around 26 years. This is a technical point that increases the amount that can be written off against taxes by up to three times. Finally, since 2011, designated aircraft and aircraft engines can be used as qualifying assets in Section 110 SPVs – effectively allowing the companies in question to pay little or no tax.[57] As one tax consultant put it, 'in reality most aircraft lessors could significantly reduce or cancel out their Irish taxable profits by use of allowable tax deductions and structuring'.[58] As usual, this suite of benefits has had the desired effect, with most of the world's major players now working out of Dublin. Companies like GE Aviation Capital Services, which is an offspring of GE Capital, the financial wing of General Electric; AerCap, which is owned by Cerberus, the notorious US fund which bought up NAMA properties on the cheap; and Avalon, which is owned by a Chinese and Japanese investment company. Any Irish companies that still exist mainly *manage* the transfer of aircraft rather than physically holding or maintaining aircraft in Ireland. The Irish Maintenance, Repair and Overhaul sector is actually quite small, yet this is an area that once provided decent jobs and apprenticeships. At one stage, for example, hundreds were employed in the state-owned Team Aer Lingus plant at Dublin airport before it was privatised. Today, aircraft leasing employs well-paid company executives and a small number of clerical staff to support them. The Department of Transport estimates that only 1500 people work in aircraft leasing but that their average salary was €165,000 in 2016.[59]

This is an eye watering average that reflects a phenomenal level of income being earned by the Irish executives who front up these financial operations. In 2014, for example, seven executives at Avalon collected a pay pot of €10 million between them, while in 2017, five executives of AerCap shared out €9.3 million. These amazing levels of pay can only be explained by supernormal profits partly derived from dodging taxes. Although the leasing corporations are not household names, they are among the most profitable in Ireland. In 2017, for example, GE Capital Aviation Services turned a pre-tax profit of $733 million, while AerCap reported an after-tax profit of $544.1 million for the first six months of the year.[60] According to the IDA, the industry held assets of €100 billion in 2017 and was expected to generate returns in the region of €5 billion annually. Taxed at 12.5 per cent this would have brought in €600 million but in the five years from 2010 to 2015, the average level of corporation tax from the whole industry was less than €20 million per year.[61]

Despite this, many of these high-flying aviation executives maintain an extreme sense of personal entitlement. For those coming to Ireland to take up lucrative posts there is a Special Assignee Relief Programme which exempts 30 per cent of their income above €75,000 from PAYE tax and a 'cost of return home allowance' for executives, their spouses and children. There is even a special tax allowance for private school fees up to €5,000 – but there is still a sense of embarrassment among the Irish natives that everything is not fully in place for the global elite. Here is Aengus Kelly, the CEO of Aercap, making some complaints about the Irish education system:

> The biggest problem is no one knows what the Leaving Cert is, and no one cares. You've got to remember, when you're selling this country globally, you've got to make it appeal to global talent. You need a baccalaureate system. In Amsterdam, there are three international schools and here's a statistic; the average fee for those international schools is €18,000 per child…. [T]hey're full and employers pay them. So, the employers don't pay this money for kids who are sons and daughters of someone who isn't making big bucks. You've got to create the ecosystem that's friendly….[62]

He did not have to wait long. A special private school, the Nord Anglia International School has been set up in Sandyford, Dublin with an annual admission fee of €24,000. And sitting on its board is none other than the former Finance Minister and Labour Party leader, Ruairi Quinn. It is a small testimony to the cosy relationship between the political and corporate elites.

BANKING AND INTERNAL GROUP FINANCING

Banking is the other big area in the IFSC, with about 10,000 people employed in corporate and wholesale banking; securitisation; treasury management; and corporate and structured finance. On their official website, the IFSC claims to have attracted 50 per cent of the world's top 50 investment banks.[63] Major US brands such as Citi Bank, JP Morgan and BNY Mellon now have offices in Dublin, as have important European banks such as BNP Paribas, Credit Suisse and HSBC. In the main, these banks focus on administration of financial services for their non-bank corporate clients, but they also provide 'multi-million-euro loans to corporates and governments and finance large-scale items such as airplanes and power plants'.[64] Within the range of services provided, treasury management is particularly important as a link into Ireland's wider tax haven network. Treasury management (TM) firms are subsidiaries of wider multinational groups, set up to manage internal flows across the corporation. Crucial tasks include hedging against currency and interest rate changes, making sure the various entities are properly financed, booking sales and making loans between the various arms of the corporation. According to Jim Stewart, this makes treasury management firms essential 'conduits for the global movement on intra-firm financial flows...forming part of a complex organisational structure whose immediate parent may be located in a tax haven'.[65]

In 2002, Stewart investigated 41 of these firms in the IFSC, finding that their 'median size in terms of gross assets was $379 million, their median profits were $6.3 million ($9.6 if those reporting losses are excluded) but the median number employed was zero'.[66] He also found that all, but one, was audited by one of the big four accountancy firms and 31 were CFCs with parents in known tax havens.[67] Given their roles within the corporate group, TM operations tend to be volatile in terms of the direction of their flows (to/from subsidiaries; to/from parent) and the forms of finance being used (dividends, capital increase/reduction or changes in intra-firm assets or liabilities).[68] When the US government passed the American Jobs Creation Act 2004 for example, Stewart found it was likely that major US corporations used their IFSC TM operations to move €21.78 billion back to the States to avail of a tax amnesty rate of just 5.25 per cent.[69] He also found evidence that global companies establish treasury management operations in the IFSC to avoid taxes in other jurisdictions. Here the example given was two rulings by the European Court of Justice (ECJ) in a case taken under UK anti-avoidance legislation against Cadbury Schweppes. The UK authorities claimed that Cadbury had set up two controlled foreign companies without any genuine activity in order to avoid taxes in the UK. The ECJ actually ruled against them in this matter, but the nature of the judgement is particularly revealing: 'the fact that Cadbury decided to establish its subsidiaries in Ireland solely so that those subsidiaries are subject to the very favourable tax regime applicable in the International Financial Services Centre does not, in itself, constitute an abuse of the right of establishment' (par. 50).[70] Another key link between the IFSC and the wider offshore network is created by non-securitisation Special Purpose Vehicles. That is, SPVs that are not set up to bundle assets into liquid forms but are formed by non-bank financial multinationals for other purposes such as creating holding companies or engaging in intra-group financing.[71] Information on these entities is both sparse and recent, with the Irish Central Bank only collecting statistics since 2015. Using granular information from 2170 SPVs, the ICB found that there were 1121 with assets under management of €269 billion, but this figure is deemed an underestimate by the Irish Revenue who estimate that there are more than 3000 SPVs in the IFSC.[72] Either way, it is clear that the number of non-securitisation SPVs has increased significantly over the last few years, up from 750 in 2015 to at least 1150 in 2018. This is likely to be important, moreover, as 43 per cent of all non-securitisation SPVs are involved in External Financing (22.9 per cent), Intra-Group Financing (16.9 per cent) or Loan Origination (3.6 per cent) – three ways for companies to move funds between the parent company and its subsidiaries.[73] In Chapter 4, we highlighted the nature of the CAIA BEPS tool which uses IP valued from within the corporate group and intra-group loans to generate deductions on effective tax rates. This tool is likely to be correlated with the strong growth in non-securitisation SPVs vehicles, particularly as the ICB note that SPVs 'sponsored by non-financial corporations held €16 billion in SPVs engaged in intra-group financing and €7 billion in external financing'.[74] According to the Revenue Commissioners, meanwhile, corporations claimed €16 billion in Trade Interest Changes in 2017, making it very likely that IFSC SPVs are being used to move money between the arms of corporations to be used as deductions against Irish taxes.

A CAPTURED STATE

In his book *Treasure Islands: Tax Havens and the Men Who Stole the World*, Nicholas Shaxson develops the concept of a 'captured state'.[75] The idea is that major banking and financial interests gain so much power that they effectively begin to control the state. Shaxson applies his concept to Delaware and the Channel Islands, but it is no less applicable to the Republic of Ireland.[76] With success in the IFSC initially uncertain, key arms of the Irish state were deployed to secure a number of flagship financial enterprises. Overtures were made to major firms in the US and Asia in particular, with provisions in the Finance Act (1995) specifically designed to lure Merrill Lynch to Dublin for example.[77] This worked, with a team of 80 staff moving from London to Dublin to service their non-euro-dollar market operations.[78] Explaining their reason for relocating to Ireland, another flagship firm, Mitsubishi, stated 'we have always been on the lookout for places with as little regulation and as much tax incentives as possible...and Ireland is more profitable in terms of tax and reserve costs'.[79] This candour was matched by their counterparts in the Japanese investment house, Daiwa Securities, who told the Guardian that 'Ireland levies no tax on investment trusts so we decided to try it instead of Luxembourg which is usually used as a tax haven'.[80] One senior civil servant described the thinking from the government perspective:

> The IFSC was a success in my view primarily because of the excellent working arrangements between the private and public sector. The IFSC product was clearly defined around the favourable taxation benefits and the capability of an educated workforce. These factors combined with the *willingness of the authorities to meet and discuss the*

specific requirements of prospective corporations made for a competitive product offering [our emphasis].[81]

One of the initiatives most welcomed by the industry was the 'holding company regime' introduced in the Finance Act of 2004. This included a tax exemption on profits made by Irish registered holding companies when they buy and sell overseas subsidiaries. Even more welcome was the tax relief on dividend payments from overseas operations in what the *Irish Times* described as 'a whole new set of cogs and teeth to the Dublin tax-cutting machine'.[82] To make sure that the proper links are developed and maintained, the Department of the Taoiseach explicitly requires both the Department of Finance and the Revenue Commissioners to 'fully engage and consult the [Financial Services] Industry including through the annual Finance Bill Process'.[83] The Central Bank – nominally the regulator of the financial services centre – was also tasked with promoting the industry from 2003–10, in what was an obvious conflict of interest.[84] The workings of the relatively unknown Clearing House Group (CHG) are even more important, however. Most countries foster links with global financiers, but very few have embedded the industry within the Department of the Prime Minister. Yet this is precisely what the Irish state once offered financiers. This group, which used to meet monthly, included heavyweight representatives from Merrill Lynch, Citi Bank, KPMG and State Street International. Overseen by the Department of the Taoiseach, the Clearing House Group also included representatives from the IDA, the Revenue Commissioners and senior government officials.[85] The CHG was much more than a powerful lobby group – it was an integral part of the Department of the Taoiseach, participating fully in the drafting and tweaking of government policy.

Consider their influence on annual budgets as an example. In 2011, the government proposed austerity measures totalling €3.8 billion as part of a series of budgets overseen by the International Monetary Fund, the European Central Bank and the European Commission (Troika).[86] Yet, hidden in the small print of this austerity budget, was a series of reliefs for foreign executives, including €5,000 a year in private school fees and 30 per cent off taxes on income accruing to foreign executives up to €500,000.[87] This represented a potential saving of up to €52,275 per executive, at a time when the Troika and the Irish elite were hammering the general population. A Freedom of Information request made by an Irish MEP, Nessa Childers, revealed that 21 such measures had been hammered out privately by the CHG and inserted into the budget for 2012.[88]

In the case of the executive perks referenced above, the heavy lifting was done by two international accountancy firms, Deloitte and KPMG, backed up by Citi Bank and the American Chamber of Commerce. In March 2011, John Bradley, a tax partner at KPMG, sent a letter to Gary Tobin who was head of the business tax team at the Department of Finance. By December, the changes proposed by Bradley were duly incorporated into the budget, but instead of expressing the slightest gratitude, KPMG complained about the cap of €500,000 per year. Their ungrateful response read 'do we want the important people to come here, but not the really, really important people'.[89] Similar lobbying took place for the 2014 budget with tax breaks for Research and Development (R&D), beneficial changes for the treatment of investment funds and exemptions to capital acquisitions tax for foreign executives proposed by the CHG before going into the budget.[90] Tax breaks on R&D currently represent corporate welfare of more than €700 million annually, showing just how important this arrangement has become.[91] Since 2016, the industry has received even more featherbedding with the Special Assignment Relief Programme (SARP) lifting the previous earnings cap of €500,000 for top executives coming to Ireland. Small wonder Nicholas Shaxson has lambasted Ireland for its 'deliberate removal of democratic checks and balances and [for giving] *carte blanche* to financial...interests to write laws in secret'.[92] The revelations contained in Nessa Childers' Freedom of Information request provoked some outrage and as a result the Irish state had to refurbish its cosy relationship with the financial sector. The Clearing House Group was officially abolished but was replaced with an Industry Advisory Committee which consists of representatives of BNY Mellon, State Street, BlackRock, Sumitomo, Mitsui Banking Corporation, Aviation Capital as well as accountancy and legal firms such as PwC and McCann Fitzgerald.

These get to 'advise' a High-Level Implementation Committee consisting of the top civil servants in various government departments and the IDA. To ensure there is no breakdown in communication, a Junior Minister has also been appointed with special responsibility to promote the financial sector. Lest there is any doubt about the access granted to financial corporations, moreover, one has only to check the lobby register. Between 2016 and 2020, representatives of BlackRock met with public officials on 20 separate occasions to lobby for legislation at an Irish and EU level.[93] The latter is quite significant because it indicates that BlackRock regards the Irish state as a key conduit into EU institutions. Another aspect of the 'captured state' is the ease with which members of the elite move from positions in the regulatory system to major financial companies. From 2017 until 2019, former Fine Gael TD, Michael D'Arcy was Junior Minister for Financial Services – participating in policy formation and launching a new strategy for the industry in April 2019.[94] Then, in September 2020, having lost his Dail seat, D'Arcy was appointed as the next Chief Executive of the Irish Association of Investment Management (IAIM) in a conflict of interest that may have broken ethical rules. When he takes up the role, D'Arcy will work alongside IAIM chairman John Corrigan, who himself was previously head of the National Treasury Management Agency.[95] D'Arcy also follows in the footsteps of another former Fine Gael TD, Brian Hayes, who in November 2018 gave up politics to become CEO of Banking and Payments Federation Ireland.[96] Then there is the case of Liam O'Reilly, the former Chief Executive of the Irish Financial Services Regulatory Authority, who became a member of the boards of Merrill Lynch International Bank and Irish Life and Permanent.[97] There is also former General Secretary to the Department of the Taoiseach, Paddy Teahan, who became a director at Merrill Lynch's IFSC operation and Treasury Holdings – one of the companies at the centre of the property collapse.[98] But the case of William Slattery is the most emblematic of them all. Slattery joined the Central Bank in the late 1970s and was responsible for supervision of the IFSC from its inception in 1987 until 1995. Just one year later, Slattery moved to Deutsche Bank International before taking up a role with State Street International. More remarkable still is the fact that Slattery went on to chair the bankers' lobby group – Financial Services Ireland from 2002–6. There could hardly be a clearer case of a gamekeeper turning poacher as the man once tasked with regulating the bankers then taking charge of tearing down these same regulations.[99] In 2007, Patrick Neary summed up the attitude in supervisory circles when admitting that as the Irish regulator, he was not required to police the activities of SPVs run by companies such as Merrill Lynch and State Street International. Speaking to the Banking and Payments Federation Ireland, Neary boasted that 'financial services firms are…generally regarded as having adequate professional expertise available to them when undertaking…investments [and] internationally, the approach has therefore been that these vehicles do not require regulatory oversight'.[100] A year later, the global financial architecture almost collapsed, with major investment funds in the IFSC caught in the middle. One of the biggest firms to go under, Bear Stearns, had two investment funds and six debt securities listed on the Irish Stock Exchange. Hedge funds in the IFSC were also responsible for billions in losses at four German investment banks (Saches Bank, WestLB, IKB and Depfa/HypoVereinsbank). Depfa Bank eventually cost the German taxpayer €100 billion, an amount that may have been borne by Irish taxpayers had the lender not been bought up by the German Hypo Real estate in 2007.[101]

Even after this near miss, the Irish state remains at the forefront of protecting the interests of the financial elites. In 2014, the government rejected the introduction of a Financial Transaction Tax (0.1 per cent tax on shares and bonds and 0.01 per cent on derivatives) proposed by the European Commission. This initiative was supported by eleven countries – including France, Germany and Italy – as a deterrent against some of the worst speculative practices behind the Great Recession. It was also expected to raise in the region of €500 million for the Irish exchequer, but it was blocked by Dublin with support from the financial lobby.[102] The Irish state also zealously protects the identities of those doing business in the IFSC. In September 2017, the Financial Action Task Force criticised Ireland for its lack of transparency around corporate ownership structures. Their key concern centred on the contribution of tax havens to money laundering, with Ireland criticised for failing to put the proper safeguards in place to guard against this practice.[103] In public, the state lauds the importance of proper financial supervision, but, in private, they work hard to protect the privacy of financial elites. In November 2017, for example, Ireland was fined by the European Commission for failing to transpose the Money Laundering Directive 4 into law.[104] Ireland is also among a number of EU states that dragged its heels on creating a register to identify the beneficial owners of Irish-based companies.[105] Public information about who owns companies listed in Ireland should be a basic minimum in a democratic state. But the elites are committed to protecting corporate privacy, even at the cost of allowing money laundering to go undetected. Taken together, these measures reveal the extent to which Ireland has become one of the best small countries in the world in which to dodge taxes – the very epitome of a captured state.

7
Foreign Direct Avoiders

Apple Inc. is one of the largest companies in the world, valued at around $1 trillion. One route to its success was to create a special cult around one of its founders, Steve Jobs, as the icon of hipster capitalism. Gone is the image of the nasty, cigar-smoking capitalist of Henry Ford's generation. Instead we have an entrepreneur whose personality is embodied in a product that can supposedly transform your life. The legendary elements of the Jobs' storyline are well known – the invention of the first Mac in a garage; his embrace of Zen Buddhism; his showman act to unveil the latest iPhone. All of this is designed to create an emotional connection between the customer and the product. You are not just buying a phone. You are buying a piece of the Jobs personality, because, as his gushing biographer put it, 'the passion, intensity, and extreme emotionalism he brought to everyday life were things he also poured into the products he made.'[1] The real story is very different, however. Jobs was a miserable character who denied the fatherhood of his daughter for years, while her mother lived on welfare. When confronted with a paternity test, he initially responded by saying that '28% of the male population of the United States could be the father'.[2] When he finally relented, he agreed to pay a mere $500 a month in maintenance – even though he was a millionaire soon to be worth $200 million. Lisa Brennan-Jobs summed up her experience of her legendary father in the following way: 'For him, I was a blot on a spectacular ascent, as our story did not fit with the narrative of greatness and virtue he might have wanted for himself. My existence ruined his streak.'[3]

This personal miserliness reflected Apple's ruthless ambition to make a profit. The corporation's success arose from two primary ingredients – super-exploitation of workers and world-class tax dodging. The first occurred at places like the Foxconn facility in Zhengzhou, China, which made half of the world's iPhones and where 400,000 workers are currently employed. These workers often have to work in freezing temperatures six days a week, wearing only thin uniforms, and are forced to sleep on buses or in dormitories. Conditions were so appalling that twelve workers committed suicide in 2010, prompting the company to install nets around its building lest others jump off. True to form, Jobs continued with the fantasy image of how his products were being made. 'You go in this place, and it's a factory but, my gosh, they've got restaurants and movie theatres and hospitals and swimming pools. For a factory, it's pretty nice.'⁴

Apple's tax-dodging operation was primarily organised from Ireland, although other opportunities were taken elsewhere too. The company was offered tax-free profits for five years in Zhengzhou while its hedge fund arm was located in Reno, Nevada – to avoid taxes. But the really big scam to eliminate taxes on its non-US profits was organised in connivance with the Irish Revenue authorities. The story of how this came about would never have been told were it not for the efforts of one man, Carl Levin. Levin was a middle-of-the-road Democratic Senator with an unusual sense of social justice. Trained as a Harvard lawyer, he won his Senate seat almost by accident in 1978 and before that had worked briefly in a car factory and as a cab driver. From his family background he inherited a simple notion: that it was a citizen's duty to pay their fair share of taxes. He often recounted how his father-in-law, an immigrant, voluntarily left €10,000 in his will to the US government as a debt of gratitude. That story was repeatedly told when rich people complained about their tax 'burden'.⁵ By 2012, Levin had become chair of the Senate Permanent Sub-Committee of Investigations. He had already established a reputation for challenging big companies like Microsoft and Goldman Sachs when he opened a new investigation into Apple. By piecing together the results of this inquiry with a subsequent EU Commission investigation, we get a sense of how Ireland's tax haven really works. Apple's Irish operation was established in 1980 in Hollyhill, Cork, as a manufacturing facility. It was one of the last companies to benefit from the Export Sales Tax Relief Scheme which guaranteed zero tax to companies making manufactured products for export. As a result of EU pressure, this scheme was abolished the following year, but companies who arrived before the 1981 cut-off date got a tax holiday for the following decade. Apple arrived just in time to avail of this tax-free holiday. A decade later, the company had become so used to not paying profit tax that it approached the Revenue Commissioners with a new scheme to ensure this continued.

Their proposed method was quite simple. Apple would use two front companies, Apple Sales International (ASI) and Apple Operations Europe (AOE) to funnel vast amounts of profits from its non-US sales into Ireland. Both were supposed to have joint ownership of Apple's intellectual property with the parent company in the US – even though hardly any research was conducted in Ireland. ASI was supposed to be organising the sales of computers manufactured by Foxconn in China to other parts of the world – even though it never took physical possession of these products. It even claimed to have sold computers made in China to other Apple companies in Asia – at 'a substantial profit', without them ever passing anywhere near Ireland.[6] The whole point was to make it look like huge profits could be attributed to ASI and AOE. The figures involved were quite astounding. Between 2009 and 2011, for example, AOE had a net income of $30 billion but paid no tax to any government.[7] ASI took in $74 billion in sales income over four years but had no tax residency anywhere in the world.[8]

The tax scam was organised in direct collusion with the Irish Revenue authorities. Essentially, Apple hired a tax advisor who wrote three letters, with the first sent in October 1990, proposing a scheme to avoid taxes. On 23 May 2007 the Irish Revenue confirmed its endorsement of the method for determining the profits to be allocated to the Irish branches of ASI and Apple Operations Europe (AOE), as explained in the letter from Apple's tax advisor.[9] At the US Senate Inquiry, Apple was quite blatant about what happened when its tax advisor met with the Irish Revenue Commissioners because its top executives were giving evidence under oath. An official memo from Apple stated that

> Since the early nineties, the Government of Ireland has calculated Apple's taxable income in such a way as to produce an effective rate

in low single digits…. The rate has varied from year to year, but since 2003 it has been 2% or less.[10]

The EU Commission subsequently got hold of the minutes of the meetings between Apple's tax advisor and the Revenue Commissioners. The tax advisor started the meeting by outlining how many employees worked at Apple in Ireland before stating that 'the company is at present reviewing its worldwide operations and wishes to establish a profit margin on its Irish operations'.[11] It was a clear hint that Apple would move if its tax-free status was not respected. He then proposed a figure for the amount of taxable income that would be attributed to the manufacturing operation in Cork. This was crucial because a key mechanism for tax dodging in Ireland is establishing a low base line of 'taxable' income from which calculations are made. This is not an objective measure of profit, but rather a figure that a company declares to the Revenue Commissioners. If they can start with a relatively low level of 'taxable' profits, they can then use a host of write-offs and loopholes to cut the bill to miniscule levels.

The advisor proposed a notional figure of between $30 million and $40 million as a 'ceiling' for the maximum amount of profit to be declared taxable. When asked how this figure was arrived at, he simply 'confessed that there was no scientific basis for the figure'.[12] In other words, he was making it up and suggesting that the Revenue Commissioners would simply work off that figure to create a tax rate that would amount to less than 2 per cent. Bizarrely, the Revenue Commissioners immediately accepted this piece of fiction. Once this principle was accepted, moreover, it was simply a matter of dressing up the accounts to arrive at the agreed figure of less than 2 per cent. To cover itself, the Revenue Commissions wanted Apple to supply it with operating costs to justify the figure, but no separate accounts for its Irish branches were ever provided. Yet the Revenue accepted this practice for more than two decades.[13] Apple returned again to the Revenue Commissioners in 2007 for a new ruling, but this time it took only two weeks to confirm its endorsement of the method for determining the profits to be allocated to the Irish branches of ASI and AOE, as explained in the letter from Apple's tax advisor.[14] The purpose of the second interaction between Apple and the Revenue was to reduce even further the miniscule tax take from the company's Irish income. Beyond securing minimal taxes on its Irish manufacturing plant, Apple also used a difference in law between Ireland and the US to establish its tax-free status on worldwide sales. We noted in Chapter 4 that until 2015 a company could be incorporated in Ireland but not be tax resident if it was controlled from outside the country. Outside control meant that board of directors' meetings occurred in a different country – even if they were not required to pay tax there. By contrast, according to US law, a company is only taxed if it is incorporated in a particular jurisdiction. By playing these tax regimes off against each other, *Apple effectively declared itself stateless for tax purposes.*

However, the EU Commission investigation found that the ASI board consisted only of three directors and a secretary while AOE's board had just two directors and a secretary. The directors were employees of the parent Apple Inc and, in the case of ASI, received no renumeration for being directors. Crucially, these boards never even discussed the agreements concluded with the Irish Revenue Commissioners in 1991 and 2007. The whole set up was an elaborate scam to enable the parent company, Apple Inc, to avoid tax.

Discussions between big corporations and national tax-gathering agencies are not unusual. Officially, these often result in Advance Pricing Agreements where the pretext is giving corporations certainty over how much tax they may be required to pay over two or three years. In reality, there is a degree of negotiation between local states and big corporations. The Irish case, however, is unusual in two key respects. First, Apple made up a deal which the Irish Revenue just accepted – even though they knew there was no real basis to the figures. Second, the deal lasted for decades rather than the normal two or three years. Apple was allowed to get away with paying virtually no tax from 1980 to 2015 – for a total of 35 years. This, in turn, gave the company a major comparative advantage on its ascent to becoming one of the world's biggest corporations. The EU Commission could only investigate a ten-year period, from 2004 to 2014, rather than the whole 35 years, and so its figure for missing taxes is an underestimate. Nevertheless, it concluded that 'selective treatment allowed Apple to pay an effective corporate tax rate of 1 per cent on its European profits in 2003 declining downwards to

0.005 per cent in 2014'.[15] It ruled that the company must pay €13 billion in back taxes or between €14 and €19 billion when interest is included – and that was only for ten years of its 35-year tax holiday.[16]

In July 2020, the General Court of the European Union overturned the original ruling, stating that the Commission had not proved its primary case of state aid to Apple or the fact that the vast sums flowing through ASI and AOE were entitled to be taxed in the Republic.[17] Although the court did accept that the contested tax rulings were 'incomplete and occasionally inconsistent' they insisted that this didn't reach the standard of legal proof that Apple had received an unfair advantage.[18] These inconsistencies presumably refer to the obvious contradiction that European Judges were now ruling that Ireland was not entitled to tax profits that were not created in the state *without thereby explaining why profits that had nothing to do with Ireland were being routed through the country in the first place.* The details of the legal case are taken up in more detail in Chapter 9, but it is worth noting that the European Commission has launched an appeal on the basis that they 'respectfully consider that in its judgement the General Court has made a number of errors in law'.[19] It is also worth noting that as the case was playing out, Apple was busy setting up another tax scam – this time even more effective than the one it replaced.

THE GREEN JERSEY

Apple's tax reorganisation actually began as early as March 2014, just after the explosive revelations of the US Senate Sub-Committee. They hired one of the top US law firms, Baker McKenzie, who linked up with another law firm, Appleby, an expert facilitator on offshore tax evasion. Appleby sent out a questionnaire to its offices in six major tax havens, including the Cayman Islands, Bermuda and Jersey, a tiny island in the English Channel. One of the questions asked of its local offices was to 'confirm that an Irish company can conduct management activities without being subject to taxation in your jurisdiction.' Another asked for assurance that there were no 'developments suggesting that the law may change in an unfavourable way in the foreseeable future'.[20] In the end, Apple settled on Jersey, a British Crown Dependency that had no tax charges on corporate profits. Management and control of ASI was transferred to Jersey, while AOE was relocated to Ireland for taxation purposes.

This might seem an unusual move for Apple to make, but, in fact, it was choreographed with the Irish state. Faced with the growing scandal over its policies, the Minister for Finance, Michael Noonan, announced the ending of the 'Double Irish' tax scam in October 2014. However, Noonan gave a two-month grace period to allow companies incorporated in Ireland before 1 January 2015 to use the 'Double Irish' trick until 2020. Apple used this grace period to relocate control of its Irish subsidiaries to Jersey. Then in another sleight of hand, Noonan also announced a new, special reduced 6.25 per cent tax rate on profits derived from a Knowledge Box, in other words, mainly from intellectual property. This headline rate was, again, only a teaser for big corporations to look at the loopholes behind it, because Noonan also increased the capital allowances for purchasing nebulous, intangible forms of intellectual property from 80 per cent to 100 per cent.[21] If an Irish subsidiary decided to fork out €50 or €100 million on purchasing a brand logo or the right to use a piece of software for example, it could now cut its already small tax bill by this amount. It is virtually impossible to put an exact value on intangibles, particularly when purchased from within the same company. So, it was almost a fool-proof way of cutting their tax bill.

This was the move that Apple had been waiting for. They simply got the newly tax resident Irish company, AOE to 'purchase' intellectual property from the Jersey-based ASI for hundreds of billions of euros. That way, the Irish-based company could use the cost of buying the IP to legitimately write down its tax bill for decades to come. And the lucky recipient, ASI, which had been paid for this over-priced intellectual property, would pay no tax because it was based in Jersey. Moreover, AOE had to borrow from yet another Apple subsidiary and, apparently, paid a huge rate of interest to itself in Jersey. Hence the name coined for this new tax dodge – the Green Jersey.[22] This interest charge was also used to write down its Irish taxes in an elaborate game of smoke and mirrors that produced one of the greatest tax dodges on earth.[23] Apple continued to pay virtually the same tiny rate of tax as it did before the EU

Commission ruling, even as the Irish state was pretending to make sure its tax code was fit for purpose.[24] According to one study, Apple should probably owe an additional €21.5 billion to the Irish Revenue for the period 2015–17 – if the same reasoning used in the original EU Commission ruling was applied.[25] Moreover, even though the maximum cap on capital allowances for purchasing intellectual property was eventually reduced back to 80 per cent in 2017, this did not apply to Apple because it only affects companies who are established after that date. This is all very convenient and suggests that the changes made by the Irish state were neatly choreographed with Apple to allow it to onshore a vast amount of its intellectual property to Ireland – and then get a massive write down on its tax bill. The material benefit has been enormous, moreover, with a Congressional Services Report showing that Apple is now the world's biggest hoarder of offshore cash with an estimated $246 billion in 2017.[26]

There has been an embarrassing side-effect for the Irish state, however. In 2015, the Irish economy apparently grew by 26 per cent, an 'achievement' never rivalled in the whole of human history.[27] A great economic engine like China, which had set the previous record growth rate of 14 per cent in 2007 was, supposedly, put in the shade by such a performance. This transpired to be entirely fictional, however, mainly arising from the fact that Apple transferred its intellectual property into Ireland. Officially, Ireland's net stock of productive assets rose from €500 billion at the end of 2014 to €800 billion in 2017 but these included intangible forms of intellectual property. As a result of these accountancy changes, Irish economic data has become permanently distorted, with one IMF report stating that a quarter of Ireland's economic growth in 2017 was attributed to the iPhone – even though none is actually made in the country. More importantly, Ireland has to pay an extra contribution to the EU budget as a result of the inflated figures, which in 2015 amounted to an estimated €400 million.[28]

INVERSIONS AND BIG PHARMA

Apple is unusual in having faced two investigations into its tax-dodging affairs – both conducted by powerful agencies from outside Ireland.[29] However, the negligible rate of tax that the company paid is by no means the exception. When the Irish government was challenged by the EU Commission to prove that Apple did not receive special treatment by supplying an 'illustrative list of at least five comparable tax rulings', it actually produced nine other cases.[30] Since the Apple case, the Irish Revenue Commissioners have drawn up guidelines on Advance Pricing Agreements that must be shared with other EU states. However, the Revenue continue with a less official mechanism for interacting with corporations known as Advance Opinions. These have grown significantly from 99 in 2010 to 316 in 2017 in an indication that tax dodging has become more informal.

Further evidence of the unusual pattern of US investment into Ireland can be garnered from a process known as inversion. Most of the Base Erosion and Profit Shifting (BEPS) tools we have discussed previously, involve US companies using Ireland as a conduit to shift their *non-US profits* to and through. Inversion takes this process one step further by moving the legal headquarters of a corporation from the US into Ireland.[31] This is done by buying, or merging with, an Irish rival so that the current parent becomes a subsidiary of their new Irish 'owner'. The US company can maintain its effective headquarters, management team and majority shareholders in the US, while its legal status shifts to Ireland for paying taxes. This is a dramatic move that has the potential to deprive the US of vast profit taxes, particularly if there are no rules to stop what are known as naked inversions – companies moving nothing but their legal address for tax purposes. The first US inversion took place in 1983 when construction company, McDermott, moved its legal residency from Texas to Panama. This was followed by a wave of naked inversions from the US into the Caribbean islands from 1996 until 2004, when Ingersoll-Rand, Accenture, Seagate, Cooper and Tyco all moved their headquarters to offshore centres where they had no other business interests.[32] In response, the Inland Revenue Service (IRS) introduced Section 7874 of the American Jobs Creation Act 2004, which requires any inverted company to be at least 20 per cent owned by new shareholders.[33]

This effectively ended the possibility of naked inversions to the Caribbean and opened the door to Irish ones. Since the 1980s, Ireland had attracted a wave of US multinationals that meant it was often possible to buy or merge with an Irish-based company that met the 20 per cent foreign shareholder threshold. To make sure that Ireland was noticed as a destination of choice, moreover, the tax authorities also introduced a very attractive holding company regime that allowed US inverted companies to gain full tax relief on withholding taxes and payments of dividends from Ireland to the US.[34] From 2009 to 2012, a number of US companies relocated their corporate headquarters from the Caribbean to Ireland, including the five mentioned above, but also a number of US insurance and reinsurance companies. Everest Insurance and Willis shifted their domicile to Bermuda and then to Ireland for example, while the XL Group moved their domicile from the US to the Cayman Islands and then onto Ireland.[35] Once these firms are domiciled in Ireland they can use the BEPS tools already in place to move US profits into Ireland, in a process known as earnings stripping.[36] From 2012 to 2016, a series of US companies moved their legal headquarters directly into Ireland in deals that were much bigger than before. These included the largest corporate tax inversion in history when the US medical devices company, Medtronic, merged with its rival, Covidien, in a deal worth $49.2 billion.[37] Covidien recently hit the headlines when it was partly responsible for the global lack of ventilators to deal with the Covid-19 pandemic. The radical US academic and activist, Noam Chomsky, takes up the story:

> The depth of the pathology is revealed by one of the most dramatic – and murderous – failures: the lack of ventilators that is one of the major bottlenecks in confronting the pandemic. The Department of Health and Human Sciences foresaw the problem, and contracted with a small firm to produce inexpensive, easy to use ventilators. But then capitalist logic intervened. The firm was bought up by a major corporation, Covidien, which sidelined the project, and 'in 2014, with no ventilators having been delivered to the government, Covidien executives told officials at the [federal] biomedical research agency that they wanted out of the contract, according to three former federal officials'. The executives complained it was not sufficiently profitable for the company.[38]

Ireland also hosted the third biggest inversion in history when the industrial goods manufacturer, Jonson Controls, merged with recently inverted Irish firm Tyco, in a deal worth $30 billion; the fourth biggest between US power management company, Eaton, and Irish electrical suppliers company Cooper Industries in a deal worth $21.5 billion; and the sixth biggest when US life sciences company Perrigo bought Irish biotechnology company Elan, for $8.6 billion.[39] Indeed, life sciences companies were responsible for 9 of the 16 inversions since 2009, helping to make the pharmaceutical industry one of the biggest in Ireland and Ireland the leading nation for inversions on the planet.[40] In 2016, two of the largest life sciences companies, Pfizer and Allergan, planned to execute another Irish inversion that would have been worth a staggering $160 billion. Pfizer is currently the world's biggest drug maker, and, after Apple, it is the company with the biggest offshore cash pile – standing at $198.9 billion in 2017.[41] Had this deal come off, it would have saved Pfizer $40 billion in US taxes, but the deal was aborted after tighter rules around inversions were introduced by the Obama Administration.[42] Allergan was subsequently purchased by another major US life sciences company, AbbVie for $63 billion, but the latter company kept its headquarters in the US.[43]

Pfizer may have lost out of that particular deal, but this hasn't stopped them using Ireland for more traditional BEPS operations. A recent report by Oxfam found that 'four of the world's largest pharmaceutical companies – Abbott, Johnson & Johnson, Merck and Pfizer … avoid large amounts of tax by shifting profits to and through Ireland'.[44] None of these companies used Irish inversions, but it is likely that they are all abusing patent-based royalties to declare high rates of profit in the Republic. In 2015, Johnson and Johnson's Thai-based subsidiaries posted an 8 per cent profit for example, while its Irish operation posted a profit of 38 per cent. Over the same period, Abbott made just 8 per cent in Thailand, 4 per cent in Chile and a 36 per cent loss in India (with an average tax rate of 34.2 per cent), while they made 75 per cent profit in the Irish Republic.[45] Yet despite these high levels of profitability, none of the companies appeared to be paying even the nominal rate of 12.5 per cent in corporation tax. In 2015, Abbott declared €1.2 billion in profits in Ireland but paid nothing in tax.[46] Johnson and Johnson only paid 6 per cent on profits of €4.31 billion, moreover, meaning that for just these two companies for just one year, the Irish Revenue lost out on €405 million.[47] The idea that these companies were abusing intellectual property tallies with a European Union Review which stated that the amount of royalties being sent out of Ireland in 2015 were equivalent to 26 per cent of GDP. This was more than were sent out of the rest of the EU combined, making Ireland the world's number one royalties' provider globally and indicating a high level of aggressive tax planning. Oxfam estimated the upfront costs of this activity to be in the region of €2 billion for the US, €1.2 billion for other developed nations and €100 million for seven developing countries.[48] Yet as the author of the paper goes on to stress, the human costs are often far greater.

In 2017, 1317 children died at the Baba Raghav Das Memorial Medical College and Hospital (BRD) due to acute encephalitis syndrome, a mosquito-borne disease that is usually contracted through proximity to livestock, poor sanitation and a lack of preventative public health services. Had the Indian government received the estimated €63.8 million the four companies may have underpaid in their corporation profit taxes, 'it could have allocated these funds to fighting encephalitis and still have had enough money left to buy Japanese encephalitis vaccines and bed nets for every child born each year in the whole of India'.[49] This would have saved at least 95 per cent of these children, but instead, pharmaceutical companies that make their money through fighting illness allowed an easily preventable disease to kill some of the world's poorest children.

PROFIT SHIFTING AND OFFSHORE ENTITIES

One of the biggest challenges in exposing the nature and scale of the offshore system is the lack of public information. A recent study by the US Institute on Taxation Policy and the US Public Interest Research Group (PIRG) found that US Fortune 500 companies had approximately 95,000 tax haven subsidiaries in 2017, instead of the 9755 they actually disclosed.[50] To reach this shocking figure, the authors noted a major discrepancy in the way that figures are reported to the Securities and Exchange Commission (SEC) versus the Federal Reserve.[51] The data used in *Offshore Shell Games: The Use of Offshore Tax Havens by*

Fortune 500 Companies came from publicly available data reported by companies in their SEC filings, but these only include 'significant' subsidiaries based on the share of company assets held by a given entity. This allows multinationals to structure their affairs so that the vast majority of their subsidiaries do not meet this criterion and the evidence suggests that this is what has been occurring. A sample of 25 of the Fortune 500 showed that they reported 1328 subsidiaries and 139 in tax havens to the SEC, when they declared 14,714 to the Federal Reserve with 2390 in tax havens. On the basis of this discrepancy, the authors estimated that 'these companies are allowed to omit 91 per cent of the subsidiaries they reported to the Federal Reserve in their SEC filings'.[52] This means any figures reported here are likely to be a drastic underestimation, but this doesn't mean that they are negligible. On the basis of the available information, the authors showed that at least 366 of the Fortune 500 have offshore operations in tax haven jurisdictions, with Ireland coming 6th overall, after other major global conduits – the Netherlands, Singapore, Hong Kong, Luxembourg and Switzerland.[53] Ireland also featured prominently in the list of companies with the most tax haven subsidiaries, with 19 of the top 20 having at least one operation in the Republic. Table 7.1 gives the detail.

Irish Gross National Income is roughly 0.25 per cent of the global total, but nearly 10 per cent of the tax haven subsidiaries of the major US corporations had a base there in 2017. It is theoretically possible that this anomaly is not significant, but the authors of the paper go on to estimate that multinationals reported 43 per cent of their foreign earnings in Ireland, Luxembourg, the Netherlands, Switzerland and Bermuda, despite the fact that these countries accounted for just 4 per cent of their global workforce and 7 per cent of their foreign investments.[54] In other words, there is a very strong correlation between countries that house offshore entities and those in which foreign profits are declared, and a very weak correspondence with real activity and the level of employment. In 2012 for example, US firms declared profits of $625 billion in the top ten tax havens, as against $428 billion in the rest of the world. This equated to 27 per cent of GDP in the former versus just 1 per cent in the latter, strongly indicating a level of mismatch between where profits are being made and where they are being declared. With reported profits of $135 billion, moreover, Ireland was actually the second most profitable destination for US corporates after the Netherlands, indicating the relative efficiency of the country's BEPS tools when benchmarked against their rivals. This also tallies with our analysis in Chapter 4 which indicated that US companies are responsible for the vast majority of the gross profits being declared in Ireland above what would be expected given the number of their workers. A second indication of profit shifting into Ireland can be found in the US Bureau of Economic data in Table 7.2.

Table 7.1   US Multinational Tax Haven Subsidiaries

Company	Number of Tax Haven Subsidiaries	Number of Subsidiaries in Ireland
Goldman Sachs Group	905	57
Morgan Stanley	619	39
Thermo Fisher Scientific	199	8
Bank of New York Mellon	177	52
AES	174	2
J.P. Morgan	170	9
Pfizer	157	27
Marriott International	147	7
Citigroup	137	10
Marsh and McLennan	137	17
Pepsi Co.	133	9
Merck	115	23
Abbott Laboratories	111	13
Stanley Black and Decker	103	22
Occidental Petroleum	99	0
Dow Chemical	98	3
Flour	96	2
Jones Lang Lasalle	92	7
Bank of America	91	7
Wells Fargo	88	3
Total	3848	317

Source: 'Offshore Shell Games: The Use of Offshore Tax Havens by Fortune 500 Companies'.[55]

Table 7.2 US Direct Investment into Ireland for 2009–19

	2009	2010	2011	2012	2013	2014	2015	2016	2017	2018	2019
Direct Investment (Millions $)	129,829	158,851	184,804	212,411	220,670	273,247	337,811	391,264	446,383	410,636	354,940
Employment (Thousands)	99.7	98.0	98.3	106.6	106.6	123.6	119.3	123.0	130	134	N/A
Corporate Income/ Profit (Millions $)	69,580	95,344	119,203	119,624	106,789	115,282	133,960	149.403	157,058	217,351	N/A

Source: Bureau of Economic Analysis.[55]

According to the statistics, US investment into Ireland grew more than threefold in the years between 2009 and 2018, but the number of employees only rose by 34 per cent. Despite this, however, the amount of profit being declared has also increased dramatically. The US Bureau of Economic Statistics labels profit as 'corporate income', which more than tripled from $69,580 million in 2009 to $217,351 million in 2018. To put this in context, it suggests that each Irish worker was making $1.6 million profit for their US employers when the average German worker was making only $25,676. These are astounding figures which indicate that something strange or 'intangible' is occurring. Not even Karl Marx could have dreamt that an Irish worker could be so exploited as to produce this much 'surplus value' compared to that extracted from his or her German counterpart. There are only two possible explanations for this conundrum. Either US corporations have invested so much productive capital that Irish workers vastly outcompete their rivals – or some strange form of accountancy tricks are occurring. There is no evidence that US companies have invested more physical capital in Ireland than in Germany. But there is yet another indicator of the exceptional nature of US investment in Ireland which comes from the European Intellectual Property Office (EIPO). A recent report by the EIPO showed that 'patent intensive industries' or corporations that rely on high levels of intellectual property account for 49 per cent of GDP in Ireland compared to 13 per cent for the EU as a whole. The number of workers in such industries is estimated at 23 per cent of the Irish workforce compared to 13 per cent for the EU as a whole. But how could nearly a quarter of the workforce be employed in 'patent intensive industries' when Ireland spends just 1.1 per cent of its GDP on R&D compared to an EU average of 2 per cent? If only a modest level of research is occurring in Ireland, how does it manage to outstrip its competitors in terms of intellectual property? The answer to this question takes us back into the heart of the Irish tax haven.

In the past, US investment into Ireland concentrated in three main sectors – computers, pharmaceuticals and medical devices. This helped to create employment during the dark days of the 1980s, and helped to create a deference towards FDI that is highly unusual. Establishment politicians still encourage the population to bow down in front of the sacred cow of foreign investment, but, by 2017, employment in

Dublin when they were really made abroad. Take one of Ireland's recently inverted companies, Eaton Capital Global Holdings Unlimited Company as an example. Eaton is currently ranked as the eighth biggest Irish company according to the *Irish Times*, yet few people have ever heard of it.[58] It also holds shares for a network of subsidiaries of the parent corporation in its Irish holding company, but it only employs 50 workers at its headquarters in Pembroke Road, Dublin. The company is a manufacturer of electrical power tools, but it is hard to imagine these being made in the leafy suburbs of Ballsbridge. The real reason Eaton inverted to Ireland is for tax purposes and, as an added bonus, it can do its work in secret, because it incorporates itself as an unlimited company, meaning that it does not have to produce public accounts. The Irish government has delayed implementing an EU Accounting Directive that would have required companies like Eaton to issue public accounts. When it was finally transposed into Irish law in May 2017, moreover, there was an exemption for holding companies until 2022 – so Eaton's secrets remain secure for the time being at least. The dividends paid from foreign subsidiaries to the Irish holding company are officially taxed at 12.5 per cent, but, as usual, big write downs are available.

These include:

- A generous and flexible foreign tax credit system which usually eliminates or reduces any Irish tax liability on the receipt of dividends.[59]
- Controlled foreign company legislation that ignores all forms of tax avoidance on passive income except that which has actually been proved.[60]
- An ability to sell off shares in subsidiary companies with only minimal exit taxes.
- Distributions to foreign beneficial owners without giving rise to Irish Dividend Withholding Tax (DWT), as long as certain conditions are fulfilled.[61]

The growing pattern of US investment in holding companies is yet another indication that tax dodging rather than 'job creation' is its primary purpose. Instead of factories and offices hiring job-starved workers, there is an increasing tendency to artificially shift profits into Ireland by means of creative accountancy.

THE HIGH-TECH AVOIDERS

There is one sector in which US investment is leading to increased employment, namely social media and internet-platform companies. Many of the biggest US tech companies, such as Facebook, Google, Twitter, Yahoo and Amazon, now have their European bases in Ireland. Figures from the US Bureau of Economic Statistics indicate that employment in this 'information' sector has grown from 6100 in 2008 to 17,000 in 2018. The stereotypical image of the US factory making computers or pharmaceuticals is being replaced by offices, call centres and data centres. Today, there are as many workers employed in 'processing information,' as there are in any manufacturing sectors. Significantly, like other US companies in the state, these firms place a huge emphasis on their intellectual property and 'intangibles'. Back in the 1990s, the arrival of social media was hailed as a new utopia. Early writers like Daniel Bell thought computers would usher in a new 'information age' where those who possessed knowledge would replace money-grabbing capitalists. From California, writers emerged around *Wired* magazine and Howard Rheingold who spoke of the internet creating 'virtual communities' which would flatten hierarchies and bypass the power of the state. It was all a libertarian fantasy, of course, and very little of it came to pass. Today, big corporations use the internet to turn consumers into commodities, while our habits and identities are packaged into large chunks of data that are sold to advertisers. The most basic elements of personal privacy are stripped away to allow businesses to target us for all manner of consumer desirables. And far from bypassing the power of the state, the social media companies rely on states to actively promote their interests.

The Irish state is second to none in its enthusiasm for this project. It operates a 'light touch' approach to regulation and maintains an open-door policy for corporate lobbyists. The former German Information Commissioner, Peter Schaar recently stated, 'Of course Facebook would go to a country with the lowest levels of data protection. It's natural they would choose Ireland'.[62] Until recently, Ireland's Data Protection Commission operated out of a small office in Portlaoise and turned a blind eye to some of the activities of the social media companies. Despite being warned in 2011 that an app on people's phones allowed Facebook to harvest information from their friends without their knowledge or consent, the Irish Data Protection Commission did nothing. This type of 'loophole' was subsequently used by Cambridge Analytica to send personalised political messages to voters. When an Austrian student, Max Schrems, complained that Facebook was transferring data from EU citizens to US security authorities, the Data Protection Commission dismissed his case as 'frivolous and vexatious'.[63]

After its laxity was exposed, the Irish Commissioner has made some effort to regulate the companies – but it is hardly stringent. Less well known is the support that the Irish state is giving to data centres. These are often large buildings where a very few employees keep guard of huge computer mainframes for the world's biggest tech companies. Amazon's proposed data centre in Mulhuddart in Dublin, for example, will occupy 223,000 square foot and employ just 32 people. According to a Wikileaks report, Amazon has seven data centres in Dublin – and that was before a centre in Tallaght or the one in Mulhuddart. The problem with this is that they consume huge amounts of electricity, with the Mulhuddart centre expected to use the equivalent of the town of Drogheda. This constant demand for electricity can create problems for the national grid at peak times. Data centres state that they prefer to get their electricity from renewable sources, but one estimate put their consumption from these sources at just 22 per cent.[64] One result is that the Electricity Supply Board (ESB) has been forced to upgrade its national grid, spending somewhere between €110 and €180 million.

The main support which the Irish state provides to the social media corporations, however, is to facilitate tax dodging on an enormous scale. The original 'Double Irish' scheme allowed Google to route huge profits to Bermuda via an intermediary company in the Netherlands. The company simply exploited Ireland's bizarre law which allowed companies who were incorporated here to be tax resident elsewhere. Bermuda was the ideal location to be tax resident as it had a zero-tax rate on corporate profits. In 2017, Google Ireland Holdings made $14.5 billion – and paid no tax using a 'Double Irish' scheme that was meant to be closed two years earlier. The company has no staff and even though it registered in Ireland, its tax residency is still Bermuda. If tax dodging were a victimless game, Google could still claim to live by its motto of 'Don't be Evil'. However, when you take €14 billion which could have been used to provide public services in Ireland or the developing world, there is something very wrong afoot. Google's tax affairs became a headline story after the revelations about the 'Double Irish' scam. But the focus on a single company missed the wider story about Ireland's role in the tax-dodging operations of the social media giants. Essentially, Ireland plays two key roles in allowing companies to pocket profits that might otherwise have been used to redistribute some wealth. One is through the use of a notorious loophole concerning 'administrative expenses' which helps to create costs that can be used to write down gross profits. Table 7.4 illustrates the fictional nature of pre-tax profits of social media companies declared in Ireland.

Table 7.4 Gross Profits, Pre-Tax Profits and Percentage of Taxation on US Social Media Corporations in Ireland 2017[65]

Corporation	Gross Profit	Pre-Tax Profit	Percentage of Pre-Tax Profit to Gross (%)	Tax as a Percentage of Gross Profits (%)
Amazon Data Services	€1,110,912,891	€30,226,115	2.7	1
Twitter International	€141,067,901	€11,643,498	8.2	2.7
Google Ireland Ltd	€23,132,522,000	€1,334,552,000	5.7	0.7
Facebook	€18,134,627,789	€251,777,633	1.3	0.2
Uber	€13,324,223	€607,203	4.5	1.1
Oath (EMEA)	€55,490,751	€5,760,411	10.3	4.8

The figures in the table reveal that although Google and Facebook are the most profitable of the social media corporations, they share a similar pattern with other smaller ones. Namely, that there is an extraordinary discrepancy between gross profit declared and pre-tax profits. The gap between the two figures is mainly explained by the use of 'administrative expenses' usually paid to another subsidiary company in the overall group. These expenses are typically a cover name for licence fees or royalties paid to a parent or holding company for use of intellectual property. But what exactly is this property? As usual, it can be a brand name, a piece of software, a commercial idea or anything 'intangible'. By its very nature, moreover, a notional figure can be placed on it – particularly when it arises from internal trade within a large corporation. The sheer scale of the outflow of such fees from Ireland is having a major impact on the Irish economy. In the years from 1995 until 2017 this form of admin payment rose from 11 to 21 per cent of GDP.

The other way that Ireland facilitates tax dodging is by denying geography. Although Facebook and Google are located in Dublin, the vast majority of their consumers are located elsewhere. Google, for example, has over 70 million users in Germany, 60 million in the UK and a relatively small number in Ireland because of lower population figures. Nevertheless, there is an official fiction that the sales are 'booked' in Ireland. Google, Facebook or Airbnb offices abroad merely provide 'marketing services' to the Irish-based headquarters of these companies and fees are paid accordingly. This has clearly irritated the governments where Google and Facebook are actually obtaining their revenue, spearheading the European Commission to propose a new Digital Tax with the following characteristics. Firstly, the tax would try to limit base erosion by linking profits to the levels of business activity, number of employees and customers in a country rather than a legal address in a tax haven. In the words of the Commission, profit taxes would be levied 'where businesses have significant interaction with users through digital channels'.[66] Secondly, they want to tackle profit shifting by imposing, on an interim basis, a tax of 3 per cent on all revenue from digital activities by the major high-tech corporations. This would only be levied on companies with worldwide revenues of €750 million and would help to end the fiction of made-up prices for intangible assets.[67] Both proposals are sensible given the nature of the modern digital economy, but they have been strongly opposed by the Irish government.

Despite being formally against the base erosion and profit shifting that currently exists, Ireland joined with three other European countries to formally oppose the EU Digital Tax in October 2018 on the basis that it would contravene bilateral tax treaties, undermine the sovereignty of member states and risk double taxation.[68] But the head of taxation at PwC, Joe Tynan, was more honest when he warned readers of the *Irish Times* that a tax on sales across Europe could see companies reducing the profits they declare for taxes in the Republic.[69] In other words, far from facing double taxation, these companies would actually have to pay their taxes for once and this would leave Ireland out in the cold. For now, Ireland has managed to block these proposals, but the pressure is growing, particularly in the wake of the major recession that will come in the train of Covid-19. Originally, the state warned its EU partners that any digital tax would see tech companies moving their headquarters to the UK after Brexit, but this argument was undermined when the British government itself announced it was bringing in a digital tax.[70] Facebook has also begun to accept that more of its digital sales should be booked in countries where they operate, in a move that gets to the fragility at the heart of Ireland's strategy for economic development.[71] Global companies are called *multi*national for a reason. They have no loyalty to Ireland beyond its ability to shelter their profits, and they will find new locations if this service is no longer available.

8
The Vultures Have Landed

A prevalent myth in Irish society is that everyone loves property. This desire is meant to derive from a post-colonial complex that has rooted home ownership deep in the national psyche. As part of their evidence, the myth makers point to the fact that, until recently, two thirds of Irish adults owned their own homes. This is high by western standards but is not entirely unusual. It equals the Netherlands, for example, and is much lower than the ownership rate in France – but regardless of what the statistics suggest, home ownership did not arise from collective trauma, but from deliberate state policy over many decades. From the 1930s until the early 1950s, more than half of new builds came from local authorities, but this changed dramatically once the country was opened up to foreign capital.[1] We noted in Chapter 3 that, as part of a dual strategy to support accumulation, the state set about attracting foreign investment *and* expanding opportunities for domestic capital, with construction often deemed the sector of choice. Fianna Fáil duly spent the 1950s and 1960s winding down the provision of social housing, while giving tax breaks for private mortgages.[2] They also passed a Housing Act in 1966 that allowed local authority tenants to purchase their own houses. But if state policy created this love affair with home ownership, Tax Haven Ireland is ripping it apart again.

To understand why, we need to return to an important truth contained in the original myth. Namely, that the Irish *rich* have a love affair with hoarding property as the safest way to make their money. You get a sense of this by looking at their pattern of borrowing during the Celtic Tiger years when bank lending for real estate initiatives grew from €5.5 billion in 1999 to €96.2 billion in 2007 – an increase of 1730 per cent.[3] More houses were built per head of population than any other country in Europe, but the speculators still pulled off a 'miracle' by maintaining high prices until the very end. Their secret lay in monopoly control of building land and an endless supply of cheap credit provided by the banks. The cost of land was less than 15 per cent of a new build before the property boom but rose to between 40 per cent and 50 per cent at the height of the Celtic Tiger. In just one year, this translated into a super-normal profit in excess of €6 billion for the small group of speculators who controlled the bulk of Irish land.[4] Construction and property speculation offer other important attractions for the Irish rich too. These sectors are better protected than many others, because it is difficult to import cement and other bulky items. There is also the possibility of shorter-term profits, as loans can be repaid after every project, meaning capital need not be tied up in machinery or marketing for a long period. Crucially, the property market can also be shaped by state intervention.

The Irish state currently spends €100 million annually leasing property from the private sector, with Larry Goodman and Ryanair among the main beneficiaries. Decisions on land use can also bring easy financial gains, with land re-zoned from agricultural to residential almost literally turning muck into gold. Similarly, if the state holds back its own land from public housing then it helps to inflate house prices for developers. Currently, the Irish state controls 17 per cent of land zoned for residential housing but has failed to use it for a major public house-building programme.[5] All of this helps to explain why there are such close ties between property speculators and the political elite. Sometimes the relationship shades into outright corruption as the Mahon Tribunal indicated. However, there is a broader basis for the relationship that goes well beyond a few crooked individuals or a nexus between the builders and Fianna Fáil. The weakness of native Irish capitalism has made it reliant on state support – and property is the easiest and safest way to harness that support. Of all the factors which helped forge the relationship between the political elite and the construction sector, the most important was taxation. Tax policies can either stimulate or obstruct the creation of property bubbles, and these, in turn, can create or lose great fortunes.

TAX DODGING AND THE CELTIC TIGER

During the recession of the 1980s, governments provided tax incentives to get the construction industry moving. The most important of these was

Section 23 tax relief – introduced in the Finance Act of 1981 – allowing investors to 'write off all but the site costs of an apartment or town house against their total rental income in the first year including rents from other properties owned, with any unused tax relief carried forward indefinitely'.[6] This was a boon for developers who could suddenly attain tax-free income from qualifying assets alongside any other property they happened to own. The scheme also allowed interest on loans raised to purchase Section 23 properties to become tax deductible. In 1986, the government went a step further with an Urban Renewal Scheme that bypassed existing planning laws in areas designated for development. This gave tax breaks for commercial ventures such as office blocks and hotels, at the same time as it created demand for building work in the capital. As usual, there was more than a hint of corruption involved, as the Planning Tribunal investigated links between decisions on urban renewal and money flowing to Fianna Fáil. With the party in financial difficulty, several property developers reported receiving phone calls from associates of Bertie Ahern indicating that a visit to the party fund-raiser, Des Richardson, 'would help them end up on the right side of the line'.[7] Files relating to urban renewal even went missing from government buildings and ended up with Richardson at the Berkeley Court.[8]

But, in the end, this plethora of incentives seemed to do the trick, as the Irish economy became one of the fastest growing in the world during the mid-1990s. This should have heralded increased taxes on sectors that had been featherbedded, but FF continued to heap largesse on their friends in construction. In 1997, they cut Capital Gains Tax (CGT) from 40 per cent to 20 per cent. A year later, Fianna Fáil extended the Urban Renewal Scheme to rural areas, creating an explosion of building in underpopulated places for no other reason than to avoid tax. This prompted the normally conservative Department of Finance to question the logic of the project as 'the majority of the beneficiaries of property tax relief schemes are high net worth individuals or corporate investors'.[9] They also worried that 'further tax cuts in times of economic growth would contribute to the emergence of asset price inflation and potentially destabilise the wider economy'.[10] They were to be proved right on both counts.

Mainstream analysis of the Celtic Tiger presents it as an export-led boom followed by an unsustainable housing bubble, but tax breaks for the construction sector were a feature of the process right the way through. According to the Revenue Commissioners for example, the combined cost of the various tax reliefs by 2004 was €8.4 billion, or nearly a quarter of the total tax take.[11] This is a truly remarkable figure, showing just how important tax avoidance became in the so-called miracle economy. Indeed, former FF councillor, Bernard McNamara, admitted as much when he stated baldly that his move into property 'largely came about from the capacity to use tax breaks'.[12] But the major developers also benefitted from the game of 'heads we win, tails you lose' the banks were playing with mortgage holders. Most businesses face lower prices as they supply more of their product, but banks are in the unique position of actually increasing the price level as they lend out credit. The more they lend, the more people have to pay, creating a positive feedback mechanism for the bankers and developers. In Chapter 3, we noted that house prices rose by 250 per cent across the country and by 551 per cent in Dublin during the decade from 1996 to 2006.[13] This equated to four times the rise in building costs, five times the rise in average industrial earnings and seven times faster than the consumer price index.[14] Prices went up year on year, and, despite this, the state maintained lucrative tax incentives that should have been withdrawn at least a decade earlier. By 2012, more than half of all Irish wealth was tied up in property assets – making the collapse so dangerous for the Irish elite when it eventually came. Their response was therefore utterly ruthless.

Within a month, the Irish state had saved the money-men at the centre of the crash through a blanket bank guarantee scheme. Contrary to the rules of the 'free market', this provided cover for junior as well as senior bondholders who had speculated, lost and still won. The Scheme also opened the door to the European Central Bank (ECB), which insisted that French and German banks, who were among the main lenders to Irish banks, get the same level of universal cover. The ECB President, Jean Claude Trichet, even threatened that a financial bomb would go off in Dublin if European bondholders were not repaid.[15] He wasn't to be disappointed. In December 2010, the government borrowed €67.5 billion from the European Central Bank, the European Commission and the International Monetary Fund, to be paid back using taxpayers' money. They also raided the Pension Reserve Fund of €17.5 billion creating the total 'bailout' of €85 billion. Of this, €35 billion was immediately ring-fenced to support what seemed like endless capital injections into the banks.[16] Two years earlier, Brian Lenihan had boasted that his bank guarantee scheme was the 'cheapest bailout in the world so far', but by 2010 it had cost the Irish people their political sovereignty and shouldered them with 42 per cent of all European banking debt.[17] This amounted to €9000 per person versus €192 for an average European citizen and excluded the billions taken from the state pension fund.[18]

The third key decision was to establish a National Asset Management Agency (NAMA) with the express aim of stabilising – and eventually reflating – the Irish property sector. The first task of the new agency was to relieve the domestic banks of €78 billion worth of non-performing loans, by moving them onto taxpayers' shoulders. This was to prove a godsend for the country's biggest property developers, who were suddenly relieved of their need to sell assets in a collapsing economy.[19] Without the state's intervention, billions worth of property would have been dumped onto the capitalist market, depressing prices and decimating a key group of FF supporters. It was to guard against this outcome that NAMA took on the debts of any borrower with loans of at least €5 million – with 180 cases owing more than €100 million each. These were mainly property and construction-based loans representing €62 of the €78 billion in par value assets.[20] NAMA hired its own experts to work with these debts, creating conflicts of interest for people who often went back into property companies when the market recovered. But the agency also hired 134 builders and developers who were quietly put onto the public payroll. In evidence to the Public Accounts Committee (PAC) in 2014, the Chief Executive of NAMA, Brendan McDonagh, admitted that his agency was paying €11 million annually to developers for help in working through their property portfolios. In a time of widespread austerity for the general public, failed property moguls were receiving average salaries of between €70,000 and €100,000 – with the top three earning €200,000 annually.[21] This stuck in the craw of many commentators, but it was the less obvious benefits that really mattered. Although NAMA was dealing with assets with a face value of €78 billion, its commercial mandate was to turn a profit on the €32 billion it had actually paid out. This meant that, in principle, the agency could write down billions in developer loans, while still fulfilling its official obligations. Having bought the loans at a 58 per cent discount, NAMA had plenty of room to offer bargains to those lucky enough to still have cash in a busted market. This created ideal conditions for corruption to flourish, particularly as NAMA was kept out of the Freedom of Information system due to the supposed importance of commercial sensitivity.[22]

BRINGING IN THE WALL OF CASH

Collectively, these measures helped to stabilise Irish capitalism. Speculators in banking and construction were saved, while the bricklayers and electricians who built the houses were forced to emigrate to Australia or Canada. This, however, was only a prelude to a further revival based on industrial-scale tax dodging. To understand this aspect of the recovery, we need to take account of changes that were occurring in the world economy. After the crash of 2008, there was a flight to safety among the wealthy and the large corporations. Their sophisticated 'risk assessment' systems had completely failed and, to revive their 'animal spirits', the monetary authorities in many countries inaugurated a regime of cheap credit. In the US, this was known as the Troubled Asset Relief Programme (TARP), which enabled the government to purchase debt-laden assets and pump credit into the banks. In the Eurozone, the European Central Bank purchased bonds to the tune of €80 billion a month, supplying cheap credit to the banks and finance houses. In the past, governments would establish a public works programme or increase public spending to kickstart an economy. But in the neoliberal age, state money was only made available to the private sector. These programmes eventually helped the global economy to recover, but there was an important side-effect. Although the banks could profit from the Eurozone scheme, the levels of cheap credit in the system pushed interest rates and bond yields to historically low levels. This made life easier for capitalists who were borrowing money, but, for investment bankers and hedge fund managers, the pressure was on to find new avenues for reliable returns on their investment. One option was to put the money into blue-chip assets like gold or oil, but a more lucrative option was to shift into property. Leilani Farha, the UN Special Rapporteur on housing, takes up the story:

> Housing and commercial real estate have become the 'commodity of choice' for corporate finance and the pace at which financial corporations and funds are taking over housing and real estate in many cities is staggering. The value of global real estate is about US$217 trillion, nearly 60 per cent of the value of all global assets, with residential real estate comprising 75 per cent of the total. In the course of one year, from mid-2013 to mid-2014, corporate buying of larger properties in the top 100 recipient global cities rose from US$600 billion to US$1 trillion. Housing is at the centre of an historic structural transformation in global investment and the economies of the industrialized world, with profound consequences for those in need of adequate housing.[23]

But if there was a 'wall of cash' seeking opportunities in real estate, which cities would they settle on? And what type of property was most likely to secure steady returns? Soon after the crash, there emerged a series of so-called 'hedge cities', which appeared to guarantee rising property prices for the global rich. These included London, New York, Hong Kong, Sydney, Tokyo and Shanghai, into which cross border investments flowed. They came to resemble each other in a pattern of rising rents, high house prices, gentrification of inner-city areas and astronomical prices for land. They were also known as 'global cities' because it appeared that the money flowing into them knew no boundaries. After 2009, London topped the list and its then Mayor, Boris Johnson, joked that the city was to billionaires 'what the jungles of Sumatra are to the orang-utan. It is their natural habitat'.[24] There was nothing natural about the way these cities were being reshaped, however. The enormous flow of foreign credit into London exacerbated a tendency to separate the *use value* of a property from its *market value*. Use value implies that it is viewed as a shelter for domestic residence or commercial use. Market value views it as an asset that enables unearned capital gains or high rent extraction.[25] By flooding a city with foreign credit, market values rise as they are no longer restricted by consumer demand, but by the expectation of future gains when they are sold. The linkage between the price of a home and average income was totally shattered. In the 1990s, the median price of a house in London was twice or three times the annual median wage. By 2014, it was ten times as much and even that was not the most expensive. In Sydney, the ratio was 12 times while in Hong Kong it was a staggering 19 times.[26]

The strategists within the Irish state who were looking at these developments must have thought: 'how can we get a piece of the action?' After all, an influx of this 'wall of cash' could help restore Ireland's property market and complete the salvage of its entrepreneurs. But how to attract it into Ireland, or more precisely, into Dublin? For all its character and charm, Dublin did not have the same economic cachet as Paris, London or Shanghai. There were few high-end streets that trigger an 'Oh Yes' moment at the dinner parties of the world elite, and very few of the high-end amenities that characterise other European cities. With the establishment of NAMA, however, the state could offer the rich something that they always enjoyed – making money. The original idea was to offer Irish property to global moguls at bargain basement prices, but this was soon accompanied with a domestic tax haven to shelter their profits. Private equity funds, particularly those from the US, became the focus of the state's efforts to turn Dublin into a global city, as they have become awash with cash in recent years. Between 2014 and 2018, for example, $3.7 trillion was raised by private equity funds which is more than the annual wealth of every country, bar the four or five largest.[27] Private equity funds are essentially collective asset management vehicles that offer a steady flow of income and a handsome profit once an asset has been sold. Large asset management corporations agree to invest these funds for a defined fee which is usually 2 per cent of the total pot of cash and a performance fee based on the rate of return. This fee can be up to 20 per cent on the profits that a fund makes, particularly if they have a good track record. Funds normally operate on a four- to seven-year cycle and there are periodic calls on investors to join after the completion of each cycle. The corporations which have established such funds include Blackstone, Apollo Global Management, the Carlyle Group and Oaktree Capital Management. Before the crash of 2008, these funds normally bought and sold shares in other companies. They appeared in different guises – sometimes, for example, as venture capital, offering to help companies start or expand in return for a generous cut, or, on other occasions, as more hostile raiders seeking to buy out a company and gain control of its assets on the cheap.

However, after the crash, some of these funds shifted into buying non-performing loans at a big discount, particularly property bargains. Oaktree Capital Management provides a good example of this trend. Its overall portfolio currently holds just 20 per cent in shares while credit and property make up the other 80 per cent. Within the category of credit, moreover, distressed debt plays the biggest role. Soon after the crash, the Irish state began to forge strong links with Oaktree Capital when the National Pension Reserve Fund invested €103 million in Oaktree's Opportunities Fund V11, which was then the largest purchaser of distressed debt globally. No doubt some of the debt was in Ireland. In 2011, a Fine Gael–Labour government came to power promising to clean up the mess left behind by Fianna Fáil and rid the country of corruption. During the election campaign, Leo Varadkar, a prominent Fine Gael politician, claimed that there would 'not be another cent' given to the banks to pay off their creditors. But this soon changed. The seed for a new strategy was planted when a Texan vulture fund called Lone Star offered to buy NAMA outright at the World Economic Forum in 2013. Fine Gael declined their proposal, but over the next 24 months, officials from the Department of Finance began to scour the earth touting Ireland as a distressed market that was open for business. As their name implies, vulture funds operate in distressed markets primed for those with deep pockets and liquid capital. They typically acquire assets at rock-bottom prices before flipping them and moving on to their next target. Blackstone say they only invest 'when there is blood on the streets' and when they looked at Ireland, the vultures saw a bloodbath.[28]

No less importantly, they discovered a state that was willing to roll out the red carpet through special deals and tax incentives. Key to this was the appointment of John Moran as Secretary General in the Department of Finance. Moran was an unusual appointment in 2012 because he came from the financial sector. Prior to taking up his role as the second most important civil servant in the state, Moran worked as Chief Executive Officer (CEO) for Zurich Capital Markets. He also worked with GE

Capital Aviation Services and as an associate attorney with the corporate law firm, Sullivan and Cromwell. During his tenure as CEO of Zurich, the firm was fined $16 million by the US Securities and Exchange Commission for aiding and abetting four hedge funds in illegal activity. As a board member, Moran also 'lobbied for, and achieved, a significant change to Irish banking rules, which for the first time allowed a bank to operate within an insurance group and to engage in very lucrative hedge fund lending in Dublin'.[29] Moran subsequently went back to the private sector as a consultant for Japanese Bank Nomura – one of the backers on a notorious Project Eagle deal where property in Northern Ireland was sold by NAMA to the US vulture fund, Cerberus, at a huge discount rate. He was also found lobbying the government for state contracts after his departure.[30] This was exactly the type of character needed to attract the world's investment funds at a time when the Irish property market was on its knees.[31] Moran didn't disappoint.

After his appointment, contact with the vulture funds increased dramatically. The Minister for Finance, Michael Noonan, met with Lone Star Capital three times and Apollo Global Management twice in 2013 and 2014. Meanwhile, officials from his department met with representatives of the private equity funds no less than 65 times between 2013 and 2014. This was a staggering level of contact and in sharp contrast to a tiny number of meetings – five – held with groups advocating for mortgage holders. One can only conclude from the subsequent evidence that they were guaranteeing tax-free bargains.

TAX DODGING COMES HOME

The cornerstone of the tax-free pass into Irish property was the infamous Section 110 of the Taxes Consolidation Act 1997. Section 110 companies were initially set up to hold non-Irish assets in ways that made them 'tax neutral'. Such tax-free structures were originally denied to Irish companies, but after 2012, they became the vehicles for US vulture funds to warehouse their Irish property in the IFSC. The rules were really quite simple, moreover. Any private fund could register a Section 110 company if it was resident in Ireland and had qualifying assets of at least €10 million. These assets could be shares, securities, bonds – whatever instruments a vulture fund used to hold its distressed loans or portfolio of mortgages. Once it had set up a Section 110 Special Purpose Vehicle (SPV) tax planners in the IFSC could get to work. Their job was to create artificial loans from a subsidiary of the parent company to the SPV that was buying up the Irish property. These are known as Profit Participation Notes (PPNs) and they allowed the Irish SPV to pay interest out of the profits they were making on their Irish assets. From the outside it looked like the Irish-registered SPV was paying substantial interest to a third party, when in fact the money was going back to the parent company. And for good measure, the interest rates were always high enough to eat up all the domestic profit.

Lone Star is a good example. Thanks to its acquisition of billions worth of distressed assets, the US fund had an income of €1.24 billion in 2014. This would ordinarily be expected to bring in more than a hundred million for the Irish state, but Lone Star was able to escape with a tax-bill of just €1 million – or less than 0.1 per cent tax. This was because the company had a second operation based in Luxembourg called LSF Lendings SARL, which 'loaned' large amounts of money to its Irish counterpart. The Irish wing then used the interest it paid to itself in Luxembourg as a way of writing down its Irish taxes.[32] This kind of behaviour was also available to other major vulture funds, including Oaktree Capital Management, Cerberus Capital Management and Goldman Sachs. Even worse, Cardinal Capital and Blue Bay Capital, two companies specialising in mezzanine finance for junior bond holders, used Section 110 legislation to reduce their tax bills to just €250, at the same time as they were co-investors with the state backed Irish Strategic Investment Fund.[33] To keep its own borrowing off the state balance sheet, NAMA also set up a SPV with 51 per cent of the funding coming from the private sector. This meant that an agency set up to recover money for taxpayers was potentially now avoiding taxes in the state it was meant to serve.[34]

Analysis of the company filings of 15 subsidiaries of global funds by the University College Dublin School of Social Policy found that they each paid around €250 in tax annually despite controlling loans worth €10.3 billion in Ireland. In total, these companies paid just €8000 in tax with a loss to the exchequer estimated to be around €500 million in just two years.[35] A related study in the *Sunday Business Post* came up with similar findings, as 24 Irish subsidiaries of international investment funds paid less than €20,000 in tax over two years despite controlling €20 billion worth of assets.[36] Cerberus, meanwhile, made €77 million on its Northern Irish loan book in 2015, but paid just €1900.[37] The laxity displayed by the Irish state towards these vultures is also evident in the fact that the Revenue Commissioners never launched a single investigation or audit into their activities before 2017. There was, however, one snag. To achieve white-listing by the OECD, Section 110 companies had to file company accounts with the Companies Registration Office (CRO). This increased the transparency of their operations allowing many of the tax abuses by Section 110 companies to come to light. In 2016, a scandal emerged when it was revealed that some of Ireland's biggest legal firms were using charities as orphan accounts for SPVs using the Section 110 scam. Under pressure from the public, the Irish government was forced to close some of the tax-dodging loopholes. But like much else in their game of smoke and mirrors, they quickly opened another 'loophole' to make up for the one that was closed. This was an upgraded Qualifying Investor Alternative Investment Fund (QIAIF) vehicle to give the same tax-free structure on Irish assets without having to file public accounts with the CRO. Qualified Investor Funds (QIFs) can be set up in 24 hours in such a way that they can avoid taxes on income and gains for all investors and ensure that there are no withholding taxes made to foreign investors.[38] There are five varieties of these funds, but the most popular are Irish Collective Asset-Management Vehicles (ICAVs) which were designed to give shelter from US tax laws and Loan Originating-Qualifying Investor Alternative Investment Funds, or L-QIAIFs, which are specially designed for holding debt instruments. Kennedy Wilson Europe Real Estate is one example of a global property company availing of these new QIAIF structures. In 2016, the company earned €26 million in rent from its Irish assets but paid nothing in tax thanks to its use of two QIF structures.[39] Overall, the tax yield from vehicles such as ICAVs are minimal. The Revenue Commissioners have reported that although Irish property worth €8 billion is held in this type of fund – yielding €700 million in distributions – the tax was just €9 million or an effective rate of 1.3 per cent.[40]

The generosity of the state towards the property sector was expressed in other ways too. For example, Budget 2011 cut the rate of commercial stamp duty to just 2 per cent having been 9 per cent during the Celtic Tiger. This was designed to get the commercial office market 'moving again' and it certainly facilitated a subsequent round of speculation. Budget 2012 provided complete relief from Capital Gains Tax if a property was acquired between 7 December 2011 and 31 December 2014 and held for seven years. There was also a proportional reduction in CGT if the property was held for at least four years. This proved a particular bonus for private equity funds who were buying up distressed property with a view to selling them off on a seven-year cycle. Without this exemption, they would have to pay 30 per cent of their gains to the Irish exchequer. Budget 2015 contained a special bonus for those who speculated on hoarding land – namely the abolition of an 80 per cent windfall tax on gains made from re-zoned land. This had been introduced in 2009 after revelations about local councillors and planning officials being bribed by developers. After its abolition, builders who bought land had only to apply for planning permission on a number of occasions in the hope of getting it through. Once they were successful, they could sit on the land and wait for it to increase in price as they applied for re-zoning.

One of the most far-reaching tax changes came in Budget 2013, however, when a special exemption was introduced for Real Estate Investment Trusts (REITs). These are investment vehicles that focus on property assets to gain rental income over a longer period. The Fine Gael–Labour government gave them an exemption from corporation tax, provided that (1) 75 per cent of their income came from property rental, (2) they agreed to distribute at least 85 per cent of their property related income to shareholders, and (3) keep their loan-to-value ratio to less than 50 per cent.[41] Deirdre Donaghy from the Business Tax Team in the Department of Finance, offered a rationale for REITs which removed 'the double layer of taxation that otherwise applies to property investment via corporate vehicles'.[42] By this she meant that REITs would no longer be taxed on their corporate profits because shareholders would pay a withholding tax on their dividends. However, Deloitte, the accountancy firm, baldly stated that 'for non-resident shareholders, treaty relief should be available to mitigate "these withholding taxes". In other words, they wouldn't pay them.[43]

The combination of property sales at knockdown prices and tax-free profits unleashed a wave of speculative activity after 2013 that has had long-term consequences for Irish society. For three years, NAMA became the largest seller of distressed loans in the whole of Europe. In 2014, it sold off €17 billion of loans; in 2015 it sold €23 billion and in 2016, it sold a further €12 billion. When the NAMA sales and those of the former Anglo Irish Bank are combined, Irish distressed loans accounted for 37 per cent of such sales in Europe in 2013 and 2014. The majority of the sales were for property in Dublin and 90 per cent were sold to US equity funds. Some of the largest conglomerates in the financial world swooped on Dublin, buying up property on the cheap and getting away with tax-free gains. They included Blackstone, Starwood Capital Group, Lone Star Funds, Oaktree Capital Management and, the largest purchaser, Cerberus. NAMA's policy was to package up a variety of distressed loans into multimillion-dollar portfolios containing a mixture of commercial, retail and residential property. This, in turn, made it inevitable that only a small number of giant private equity funds would dominate the purchases. Such funds focused on a limited number of areas where they hoped to make the largest killings. The first was the commercial office market, where Dublin was giving the highest rate of return in the world, according to the MSCI's Investment Property DataBank Global Annual Property Index in 2014.[44] Driven by cheap purchases and high rental income, the rate of return was double that of London, for example. The vulture funds were able to access this property in different ways. They could buy it outright from NAMA at a discounted price or else take over the loans and pressurise the creditors to sell. In many cases, the US fund bought the property on the cheap and flipped it shortly after for a much higher price. Blackstone bought the Platinum portfolio from NAMA for a reputed €100 million in 2013 which consisted of three main office developments. But they sold just one of these, the Bloodstone building on the Liffey, for around €130 million two years later.[45] A German fund,

AM-Alpha bought an office building, Riverside 11, on Sir John Roger-son's Quay for €35.6 million in 2012 and then flipped it 18 months later for €50 million.[46] Starwood Capital Group bought the Elm Park complex of offices and apartments in 2015 for €184.3 million. But shortly afterwards, it began to flip parts of the complex, selling off one office block for a reputed profit of €5 million.[47] All of this using tax-dodging SPVs.

A second major activity for the equity funds was buying up land, sometimes in conjunction with Irish front companies. Land prices have risen dramatically as a proportion of house and office sales because unlike other commodities there is a limited supply in 'prime areas'. When this is combined with a huge deluge of credit from abroad, the purchasing of prime sites and hoarding of land banks becomes an easy path to profit making. Cairn Homes and Glenveagh are among the best-known Irish building firms, but both are backed by foreign financiers who have helped them accumulate large land banks around the cities. In the case of Cairns, a British investor from Sun Capital Investment, Alan McIntosh, helped them exit NAMA by refinancing their loan. The company then went on to buy land banks that could accommodate 15,000 housing units across 32 residential sites in Dublin. The relative importance of land ownership as against construction is neatly illustrated in their annual accounts. In the 2018 report, Cairns claimed to have €751 million invested in land while there was only €181 million in construction work in progress.[48] Oaktree Capital Management has backed another building firm, Glenveagh, which has invested €404 million acquiring a land bank suitable for 10,120 units.[49] While much of this land is being acquired through NAMA, there is little evidence that it is being used for a rapid house-building programme. NAMA's chief executive, Brendan McDonagh, has acknowledged that while the agency had disposed of land sites with the capacity to build 50,000 housing units, just 3700 units were built or even under construction.[50]

The third area where the funds are active is in properties that give long-term rental income. Some of this comes from the three REITs which have bought up both commercial and residential property. In 2018, Green Reit, Hibernia Reit and Ires Reit paid out €92.77 million to their shareholders, while their board members earned massive salaries.[51] This is largely because rents in Dublin have been at an astronomical level

– thanks in part to the land hoarding mentioned above. David Ehrlich, former CEO of Ireland's largest landlord, Ires Reit, admitted that 'We've never seen rental increases like this in any jurisdiction that we're aware of' adding, 'I truly feel badly for the Irish people'.[52] Presumably he didn't feel too bad for himself, though, as Ehrlich made around €7 million in the three years from 2014, due to these rent increases. However, it would be wrong to think that there is a strong dividing line between living off rental income and property speculation. Green Reit, for example, which is Ireland's most profitable REIT and includes among its sharehold-ers the beef baron Larry Goodman, as well as the Kuwaiti Investment Authority, was put up for sale after its stock market value reached €1.2 billion.[53] On the other hand, property speculators such as Kennedy Wilson are gaining a higher return from their 'income producing prop-erties' in Ireland than any other country bar the USA. The main reason is that the annual rent per square foot stood at $38 versus just $20 per square foot in the company's other European markets.[54] In this orgy of speculation, a number of former heavyweights of Irish capitalism have become front men providing 'local knowledge' to the world's financial giants. Brian Goggin used to earn an annual salary of €2 million as CEO of Bank of Ireland. But after the bank's near collapse from reckless lending, he became an advisor to Apollo Global Management while it was buying up distressed property in Ireland. Johnny Ronan, a poster boy for high living in the Celtic Tiger, works with Colony Capital, the giant US private equity, run by Tom Barrack, an avid supporter of both Donald Trump and the Saudi regime. The *Irish Times* describes the rela-tionship as follows:

> Colony, a source says, seeks high double-digit returns on its property investments, but Ronan is heavily incentivised to achieve higher returns. The higher he goes over it, the bigger his percentage of the spoils: his 'sweat equity'. Ronan also picks up chunky development fees as Colony's partner on the ground, identifying sites, planning schemes, ensuring quality and finding prestigious tenants.[55]

Joe O'Reilly ran up debts of €2 billion during the Celtic Tiger, but his company Chartered Land is now backed by the Abu Dhabi Investment

Authority. It was able to buy a site from NAMA in Ashton, Dublin, for €22 million even though another of his companies, Castlethorn, had sold it for €77 million in 2006.[56] Nothing better sums up the deep irony that lies behind Ireland's economic recovery, and the pattern of providing local knowledge to global financial companies even reaches into NAMA itself. Former key employees have reappeared in private sector investment firms, earning big fees for themselves. The CEO of Hibernia Reit, for example, is Kevin Nolan. He is a former senior portfolio manager at NAMA, and now earns a salary of €450,000.[57] John Mulcahy was former Chief Executive of Jones Lang LaSalle who was seconded to work on the establishment of NAMA in 2009, before becoming its head of asset management and eventually ending up on the board. Once he left the agency he became chairman of the Irish Property Investment Trust (IPUT), a major commercial property owner with €1.8 billion of assets in Ireland.[58] Like so many other property vehicles, moreover, IPUT is structured as a Qualifying Investor Alternative Investment Fund, allowing it to become 'tax neutral'. Targeted Investment Opportunities subsequently invited him on to their board of Directors, this time to advise on major development of the City Quay alongside the US Vulture Fund, Oaktree and NAMA itself.[59] This led to the establishment of the aforementioned, Glenveagh Properties, with Justin Bickle from Oaktree as CEO and Mulcahy in the chair. According to the *Irish Times*, Mulcahy's salary is now €300,000 per annum, but he also has just short of €20 million worth of share options and a bonus of between 50 to 75 per cent of his take home salary.[60] The orgy of speculation that was triggered by a state offering tax-free profits on property has thus benefitted a small layer of Irish society. But for many it has been a disaster with intense and immediate consequences for their lives. Nothing better illustrates how tax dodging is not a victimless practice than the way it has helped produce a housing crisis in a country that was once building too many houses. The most visible sign of that crisis is the number of homeless people sleeping outdoors in many Irish cities. But for every homeless person on the streets there are many more who live in overcrowded conditions in the homes of family and friends. If they do get to move into rented accommodation, they face a regime of insecurity as landlords use well-trodden loopholes to push up rents. Tenants are often evicted because the landlord claims to be moving 'a family member back into the dwelling' or because they 'are carrying out substantial renovations'. Once these 'reno-victions' take place, the rents are jacked up again for the latest tenant.

Behind this misery, state policy continues to create initiatives for global funds to reshape Dublin as another 'hedge city'. Social housing has been cut to the barest minimum, both because the state is starved of revenue and because its officials want to help the property market to keep roaring. In 2018, for example, Dublin City Council built just five normal social housing units and a further 69 modular, rapid built units, even though there are 17,000 on its waiting list.[61] Instead of providing housing as a social need, it has become an opportunity to strengthen the rental market. The target of *Rebuilding Ireland*, the government's housing strategy document, is to put nearly 100,000 households into privately owned properties that are subsidised by the state for leases ranging from two years to ten years. Nearly a third of rental tenancies are already social housing tenants who were subsidised to the tune of €640 million in 2018.[62] In order to incentivise private apartment owners, planning laws have also been changed to allow for even smaller units to be squeezed into the 'build to rent projects'. They can build high, have fewer lift or stair cores and provide less costly basement space so that higher yields are guaranteed. Even before these changes, moreover, space standards in Irish housing were among the lowest in Europe.[63] Now they can squeeze tiny units into high rent, high-storey, apartment complexes where rent is among the highest in Europe – and where tax on the big landlord companies is low to zero.

All of this has produced a 'generation rent'. Today a young person will stay in their family home far longer, maybe into their thirties. Or they may emigrate to save some money. But whichever way they are forced to cope, it has become far harder to buy a home than ever before. The various incentives offered to foreign funds has also directed money towards commercial office property and various forms of apartment, co-living and student accommodation. The money-men know there are safe and secure returns to be made from high density builds, high rents and low taxes. They have done the figures and know that land hoarding is driving up the costs of house building in 'prime sites'. Some money can be made in the outer suburbs, but it hardly competes with a rate of return to be found in other forms of property. In brief, Dublin has joined the long list of global hedge cities where homeownership is increasingly out of reach for many. The average house price in Dublin is now 9 times that of average annual earnings – and 14 times in areas like Dun Laoghaire.[64] The dream of home ownership is becoming a nightmare for the next generation – thanks to a state policy that has encouraged tax dodging to fuel a speculative market.

9

The Case for the Defence

At the end of January each year, 3000 of the world's politicians, business leaders and economists descend on the Swiss mountain resort of Graubünden for the World Economic Forum. Pitched as a conference to 'improve the state of the world', the forum is really an opportunity for the global elite to network and strategize for the coming twelve months. The Irish telecoms billionaire, Denis O'Brien, is a regular attendee, as are Fine Gael (FG) ministers who jet in to sell Ireland to potential investors. Traditionally, this has been a hospitable place for establishment politicians, but questions surrounding Ireland's tax policies have made life increasingly uncomfortable for FG ministers in recent years. During a heated debate in 2018 for example, Nobel Prize-winning economist Joseph Stiglitz accused Ireland of 'stealing revenue from other countries through its tax code'.[1] Referencing the Apple decision by the European Commission, Stiglitz subsequently made the same accusation on Ireland's most popular radio station – making sure that nearly half a million people heard what was going on.[2]

Speaking on the same panel, Davide Serra, the CEO of global asset management firm Algebris Investments, labelled Ireland's corporation tax system 'a joke', following a report from the Comptroller and Auditor General which revealed that 13 corporations headquartered in Ireland paid less than 1 per cent tax in 2015.[3] Minister for Finance Paschal Donohoe tried to deflect these criticisms with claims that Ireland does not do special deals with any individual corporation, but the wider perception from commentators was that significant damage had been done. In 2019, Donohoe was once again on the back foot when the General Secretary of the OECD, Angel Gurria, accused Ireland of 'gaming and abusing the international taxation system' with 'a sweetheart deal to reduce Apple's tax to 0.05%'.[4] The OECD has historically been one of Ireland's strongest defenders, making Gurria's accusation particularly damaging. But it wasn't the only one. Since the early 1990s, all of the best academic research into tax havens has included Ireland on their lists, as have the three most important non-governmental tax advocacy groups – the Tax Justice Network, the Institute on Taxation and Economic Policy and Oxfam.[5] Taken collectively, this body of research has done significant damage to Ireland's international reputation, particularly a 2018 paper that labelled Ireland the biggest tax haven in the world for 2015.[6]

As we explained in Chapter 7, a US Senate Committee also labelled Ireland a tax haven on the basis of its dealings with Apple, while two US congressional hearings – in 2008 and 2015 – came to the same conclusion.[7] This, in turn, helped to unleash the European Commission investigation that found Ireland guilty of illegal state aid in 2016, and helped to convince the majority of European MEPs to support a report that likened Ireland to a tax haven in 2019.[8] For the last four years, Ireland has also been labelled a tax haven by the Brazilian government, despite repeated efforts by the Irish authorities to reverse this decision. Beyond the reputational damage that this has created, Irish companies now face higher taxes when they trade in Brazil – up from 15 per cent to 25 per cent.[9] This is one example of the practical difficulties that are mounting for the Irish establishment, and the wider climate is not looking any more favourable. Years of austerity following the Great Recession were already moving tax avoidance up the international political agenda, when three major leaks focused public anger on tax-dodging corporations and their national partners. Between them, the Panama Papers, the Paradise Papers and Lux Leaks contained millions of documents that revealed how the richest corporations were squirrelling away resources at a time when governments were forcing the rest of us to pay the costs of failed banks and broken economies.[10] This anger is likely to once again increase as governments pile debt onto their balance sheets to fight the Covid-19 pandemic.

Operating in this environment of growing anger and accusations, the Irish establishment has had to create a sophisticated strategy to defend their position – particularly as successful offshore activity relies on the illusion of total compliance with international regulations. In order to achieve this, the state has constructed three layers of inter-locking arguments, perpetuated via a division of labour made up of government ministers, the Department of Finance, the Revenue Commissioners, tax haven insiders and establishment economists. The first layer of arguments flatly deny that Ireland is a tax haven on the basis that significant real activity takes place in the state, and that, unlike many of its rivals, Ireland's official tax rate is equal to the rate that is actually collected. Ireland's 12.5 per cent trading profit rate is pivotal to these arguments, which are designed to make it look like Ireland is more successful than other countries at attracting genuine investment through legitimate, tax-based competition. The second set of arguments, generally reserved for moments of crisis, accept that Ireland is occasionally used for international tax avoidance without conceding that the country is in any way responsible for these practices. Here, the trick is to argue that although a piece of evidence – for example the 'Double Irish' being exposed – cannot be denied, the culprits are not the Irish tax authorities, but the international tax specialists and accountants who find differences in national tax codes and exploit them. This argument hinges on the idea that international rules must be harmonised in collective fora, with Ireland presenting itself as anxious to close existing loopholes and stopping new ones from being developed.

This leads us to the final layer of arguments which present Ireland as an early adapter and enthusiastic participant in every international initiative to reduce what the OECD terms 'harmful tax competition'. As mentioned above, Ireland relies heavily on the perception of compliance with the OECD Base Erosion and Profit Shifting (BEPS) process, and it consistently talks up its role in driving this forward. Yet, it also understands when to avoid measures that would impact the corporations (ab) using Ireland. Sometimes it attempts to delay implementation until alternative arrangements can be found. On other occasions, it waters them down as much as possible. Collectively, these arguments have allowed Tax Haven Ireland to function on the basis of a plausible deniability, but they have also left enough room to expose the state on the basis of gaps and slippages in the official narrative. This is our aim in the penultimate chapter.

CLAIM 1 – IRELAND IS NOT A TAX HAVEN

1.1 Ireland Is a Real Economy

In 2018, Paschal Donohoe had to defend Ireland's international reputation following an unusually high-profile claim by Gabriel Zucman and his colleagues that Ireland was the number one profit-shifting destination globally in 2015.[11] Responding in the *Irish Times*, Donohoe insisted that global corporations declared more profits in Ireland than in all of the Caribbean Islands put together, 'because we have an economy that across that period has also attracted more jobs and more investment.'[12] Indeed, he continued, 'if you look…at the report that came out of the IDA [Industrial Development Authority], they showed that across that recent period we've seen the number of jobs in IDA-sponsored companies growing from 140,000 to in excess of 200,000.'[13] The Department of Finance provided a second layer of cover, highlighting what they claimed was the 'overly simplistic methodology' used by Zucman et al. in their investigation.[14] Instead of looking at 'where the value is being created', the academics focused on the 'ratio of employees to profits' in a way that supposedly distorted the true picture.[15] Here again, the argument was that genuine value is created in the Republic in contrast with tax havens that house shell companies and brass plate operations.[16] A similar argument also features in an article produced by two tax specialists working for the state. In 2013, Gary Tobin from the Department of Finance and Keith Walsh from the Revenue Commissioners wrote a joint paper that was published in the *Economic and Social Review*.[17] In it, they noted that the country was occasionally listed as a tax haven because of the 'perceived interaction of Ireland's 12.5% corporation tax rate and the tax planning behaviour of multinational companies, in particular the potential to abuse international transfer pricing regulations.'[18] But, say the authors, in a globalised economy with multinationals operating across many jurisdictions, it is far more likely that companies are rationally locating their most profitable operations in low tax economies like Ireland to avail of legitimate international tax competition. The crux of their argument is laid out below:

The underlying assumption that varying levels of profitability across locations are explained by transfer pricing is questionable…. Multinational companies spread their operations across multiple locations…. Some functions are likely to be highly skilled and capital intensive while others will be low skilled…. *Some activities will be more profitable, and companies are likely to seek to locate them in lower tax countries* [our emphasis].[19]

To back up their argument, Tobin and Walsh claim that Ireland has historically attracted disproportionate levels of inward investment due to a range of factors including 'access to European markets, membership of the Euro, agglomeration effects, an English-speaking population and an institutional structure that adjusts rapidly'.[20] Unlike many of its rivals, moreover, Ireland maintains a low headline corporate tax rate by having an unusually wide base which is administered equally to every company in the state.[21] Beyond these theoretical arguments, the establishment can also point to empirical data showing significant multinational activity occurring in the state. In 2018 for example, the IDA estimated that 229,000 Irish workers were employed by multinational companies, collectively earning €11.7 billion or just over €50,000 per employee.[22] This equates to one in ten workers employed in the state, adding further weight to the argument that Ireland gets misrepresented as a tax haven by commentators who – sometimes deliberately – misunderstand the legitimate ways the country successfully competes for international business.

As a rule, the best arguments are simple to explain, appeal to wide layers of people and have some basis in reality. These are precisely the hallmarks of the arguments laid out above, but they are also deliberately misleading. Although Ireland began to offer tax advantages in the 1950s, it was the creation of the Single European Market and the Irish Financial Services Centre (IFSC), during the late 1980s, that began to move Ireland into the tax avoidance big leagues.[23] The strategy that developed involved a twin package of access to European markets for genuine economic activity alongside legal instruments to reduce taxes and regulations. This worked for both parties in ways that were to prove mutually reinforcing, moreover. From the Irish establishment perspective, the economy received thousands of high-paid jobs in accounting and corporate law firms and in the pharmaceutical and information technology sectors, which typically exploit high levels of intellectual property. This, in turn, created higher levels of Gross Domestic Product, higher tax revenues and an ability to create high levels of legitimacy for FDI within the wider public. For their part, US multinationals gained access to European markets from a relatively low-cost economy, low levels of industrial conflict via social partnership and an extremely favourable business environment, both in terms of official legislation and through some of the world's most effective BEPS tools. They also gained the legitimacy of moving operations into areas with genuine economic activity, making it look like these companies were fully compliant with international tax regulations. Although they still have important uses, the most obvious tax havens are becoming relatively less attractive in an era of increased scrutiny from an austerity-weary public. Recall, for example, the importance of an existing pharmaceutical industry in Ireland for the major inversions carried out by US pharma companies after 2004. These were only possible because Ireland was already engaged in pharmaceutical exports into Europe – allowing US companies to set up their legal headquarters in a way that was no longer possible in traditional havens like Bermuda and the Cayman Islands. Episodes like this make Ireland relatively more attractive than the latter destinations so long as real activity is carried out alongside tax avoidance and regulatory arbitrage. Recall also, that any conception of tax havens as sunny places for shady dealing is dangerously misleading.

The offshore network is completely integral to the capitalist economy with financial districts in London and New York directing vast flows through conduits like Singapore, Ireland and the Netherlands.[24] Indeed, as Richard Murphy has recently shown, 'there is a trend for the significance of [these] larger countries, not generally thought of as tax havens or secrecy jurisdictions to increase over time'.[25] In Chapter 4, we highlighted the importance of tax treaties for connecting these capital flows across the system – with Ireland only able to sign such treaties by hosting an amount of genuine multinational activity. Far from showing the impossibility of Ireland being involved in tax avoidance, this suggests that genuine activity is a prerequisite for Tax Haven Ireland to function successfully. That said, it is also important not to overstate the amount of real activity that is occurring. When Minister Donohoe suggests that the €100 billion identified by Zucman et al. can be explained by an increase of 60,000 workers in the multinational sector, he is effectively suggesting that each of these workers was responsible for more than €1.5 million profit in 2015. Meanwhile, the assertion by the Department of Finance that real value creation is behind Zucman's figures is equally incredible, given the negligible amounts of Research and Development (R&D) actually being registered through Ireland's Knowledge Development Box (KDB). Set up in 2015, the KDB was meant to encourage domestically created intellectual property, and is touted by the Irish government as the first of its kind to be fully OECD BEPS compliant.[26] Yet, just ten companies claimed tax deductions via the KBD in 2017, with a cost to the exchequer of just €14 million.[27] Contrast this with the nearly €40 billion that the state allowed as deductions for expenditure incurred on the *acquisition* of intangible assets – 98 per cent of which was claimed by foreign multinationals.[28] In other words, the state allowed foreign firms almost 3000 times as many deductions for acquired IP as against IP created in the state. There is a second set of allowances for domestic R&D that came to €448 million in 2017, but even this is just over 1 per cent of the amount claimed through bought-in IP by the multinational sector.[29] Rather than operating as an unusually high technology hub, this suggests that Ireland offers a deal to US companies that have high levels of IP to (ab)use – you give us jobs and investment; we'll give you access to European markets, international cover and some of the best BEPS tools currently available.

1.2 Ireland Has a Transparent Regime

A second argument to deny Tax Haven Ireland focuses on the transparency of the regime versus many of its rivals. Because capitalism pits nation-states against each other in the race for investment, it creates international tax competition on two separate fronts. Countries compete on the official rates they offer corporations, but also through hidden exemptions that drive a wedge between the headline rate and the effective rates they actually collect. Ireland is often singled out for its usually low headline rate, but defenders of the Irish system imply that this is done by countries who prefer to compete in more underhand ways. When the Taoiseach was asked why 31 Irish-registered multinationals had paid just 2.2 per cent tax in 2012 for example, Enda Kenny quoted a World Bank–PwC report that put the effective rate at 11.9 per cent versus 8.2 per cent in France.[30] This implied that the gap between the Irish headline and effective rates was just 0.6 per cent – versus a gap of 25.1 per cent in France – making it look like every country competes on tax, with some preferring low headline rates, while others prefer hidden loopholes and exemptions.[31] It also gave the impression that the Irish regime was particularly transparent, when this was far from being accurate.

The original investigation by Trinity College Dublin Professor Jim Stewart calculated the effective rate for IP-intensive US multinationals using detailed financial information filed with the American Bureau of Economic Analysis.[32] It also used accounts filed with the Companies Registration Office in Ireland to identify information on revenues, profits and tax payments for US companies incorporated in the state.[33] This made it possible to pick up any profit shifting that was occurring by showing the gaps between the profits being reported and the level of taxes being paid. In contrast, the World Bank–PwC report concluded that Irish companies pay close to the official rate of 12.5 per cent on the basis of a *made-up ceramics company with just 60 employees and no imports or exports*. In other words, it projected a close fit between the headline rate and the effective rate by creating a fantasy company that looks nothing like the ones actually paying taxes in the Republic. With 80 per cent of Irish corporation tax paid by companies in the Large Corporates Division, the annual World Bank–PwC Report is completely useless when it comes to explaining the nature of taxes being paid in the state, but it is extremely useful as an ideological tool when needed for reporters. That said, a far more serious attempt to defend Ireland's 'effective tax rate' has been made by University College Cork economist Seamus Coffey and senior civil servant Kate Levey. In April 2014, they co-authored a paper published by the Department of Finance entitled 'Effective Rates of Corporation Tax in Ireland'.[34] This outlined eight different measures of the effective tax rate in Ireland, using three different methodologies. These were:

1. Model Company Approaches, preferred by the World Bank–PwC and Eurostat.
2. National Statistics, published by the Central Statistics Office and the Revenue Commissioners.
3. Reported Firm Level Data, such as that used by Professor Stewart and the *Irish Times*.

Measures for the effective tax rate for 2012 ranging from 2.2 per cent to 15.5 per cent are reproduced in Table 9.1.

Table 9.1   Measures for the Effective Tax Rate for 2012 Ranging from 2.2 per cent to 15.5 per cent

Approaches 1–8	Year	Current Estimate (%)	Average since 2003 (%)
(1) Model Company Approach			
1.European Commission/ZEW	2012	14.3	N/A
2.WorldBank–PwC	2012	12.3	N/A
(2) Aggregates Approach			
(2.1) National Income Approach			
3.Effective Tax Rate on 'Net Operating Surplus'	2012	8.4	10.9
4.Eurostat Implicit Tax Rate on Corporate Income	2012	5.9	8.3
(2.2) Corporation Tax Distribution Statistics			
5. Tax Due as Portion of Taxable Income	2011	10.4	10.7
6. Tax Burden as a Portion of Taxable Income	2011	11.8	11.9
(3) Combined Company Approach			
Average Tax Rate of Irish Times Top 1000 Companies	2012	15.5	N/A
Average Tax Rate of Irish Incorporated Companies in US BEA Data	2011	2.2	N/A

Source: 'Effective Rates of Corporation Tax in Ireland Technical Paper'. 2014, p. 3.[35]

The value closest to the headline rate for 2012 was 12.3 per cent, but, according to the authors, the artificial nature of the World Bank–PwC approach, meant it was 'not appropriate to determine the effective rate of Corporation Tax' using this method.[36] This also ruled out the model company approach used by the European Commission as it failed to mirror companies operating in the state.[37] Data from real companies might seem better in this regard – particularly those Irish-incorporated US firms most likely to use BEPS techniques. However, this approach was similarly rejected as not being an accurate reflection of *Ireland's* effective tax regime. With foreign profits for Irish-registered US companies standing at €147 billion and taxes at just €3.1 billion, the authors accepted that an effective rate of 2.2 per cent *for these companies* was correct. However, in the absence of available country-by-country reporting (CBCR), they insisted that it could not be concluded that this was a result of 'the interaction of the companies' profits with the Irish System of Corporation Taxes'.[38] In other words, US companies registered in Ireland were definitely avoiding their taxes, but the authors couldn't decide who was helping them to achieve this or what it meant for the effective rate in Ireland itself.

Their commentary at this point is extremely telling and worth outlining:

> [US Bureau Data] gives an income statement for Irish incorporated companies and is not necessarily reflective of their operating activities in Ireland, if indeed, they have any at all. In many cases, the companies concerned are Irish registered and tax resident in a zero-tax location – they have an Irish name that is disguising their true location.... It is also the case that some of these companies are not resident in Ireland for tax purposes. If these companies were tax resident in Ireland, their pre-tax profits would be subject to Ireland's 12.5% corporation tax on the amount of Taxable Income with little facility to reduce their effective rate below the headline rate.[39]

As noted earlier, most BEPS flows prior to 2015 involved moving profits through Irish-incorporated entities that were registered for tax in the Caribbean. The authors seem to accept that this was allowing US companies to reduce their tax bills, without thereby accepting that the Irish tax authorities were in any way responsible. If this information had been included, it would have driven a significant wedge between the profits moving through Ireland and those being taxed. But instead, Coffey and Levey focused exclusively on the effective tax rates of those *companies actually paying taxes in the state*. This allowed the authors to reject approaches based on company data, leaving them free to select Ireland's national statistics as the most accurate measures of the effective tax rate – knowing that these statistics completely missed the avoidance methods that their report, at least formally, was meant to identify.

This sleight of hand was then further compounded by arguing that if companies were tax resident in Ireland they would have 'little facility to reduce their effective rate below the headline rate'.[40] This assertion is not true, as we will show in a moment. However, in this context it served to allow the authors to argue that the national statistics produced by the Central Statistics Office (CSO) and the Revenue Commissioners are honest and reliable. Specifically, they argued that the figure for Net Operating Surplus produced by the CSO and the figure for Total Taxable Income produced by the Revenue Commissioners are 'the most appropriate measure of the effective corporate income tax rate applying to the total of corporate profits in Ireland'.[41] At 10.9 per cent and 10.7 per cent, these give rolling averages close to the headline rate of 12.5 per cent, allowing tax haven insiders to quote the Coffey-Levey figures as rigorous independent analysis. When the People Before Profit TD Richard Boyd Barrett asked about plans for an effective minimum corporation tax rate in May 2018, for example, the Minister for Finance responded,

In April 2014, my Department prepared and presented a report to the Finance Committee to explain figures which are quoted and attributed to Ireland on this matter. This technical paper, available on the Department website, provides clarity on the matter and to ensure this piece of work was as objective as possible, my Department commissioned an external and independent academic to co-author the paper. Based on Data from the Central Statistics Office and Revenue, the report highlighted that since 2003 the effective corporate tax rates on Net Operating Surplus and Taxable Income averaged 10.9% and 10.7% respectively.[42]

Deloitte referenced the same report in an article entitled 'Ireland Is Not a Tax Haven', noting that, 'As part of debates on the Finance Bill 2017 last November…. Minister Donohoe referred to a paper produced in 2014 which highlighted that since 2003 the effective corporate tax rate has averaged 10.9% and 10.7% respectively'.[43] An original report that included reference to 'companies [that] are Irish registered and tax resident in a zero-tax location' was now being used by a government minister to prove that the Irish tax regime is transparent, and by a major accountancy firm as independent proof that Ireland is not a tax haven. The fact that Ireland has since been forced to (formally) close the Double Irish proves it was always possible to conclude the state was responsible for the avoidance effectively being white washed by Coffey and Levey. However, this hasn't stopped the establishment from continuing to refer to their paper as authoritative. Indeed, it is precisely because the authors used technical language and a seemingly balanced assessment that their clean bill of health has become so useful. To confirm this, notice that even when corporations actually did start to declare billions in extra profits in the state, it was possible to use the Coffey–Levey methodology to argue for the legitimacy of the national statistics. In Chapter 4, we noted that since formally closing the Double Irish, Ireland has shifted its primary BEPS tools towards Capital Allowances for Intangible Assets. This has meant that the amount of gross profits being declared in the state has more than doubled over the last five years, which, in turn, should have made it easier to detect the gap between the headline rate and the effective rate being paid by corporations. As we also explained in Chapter 4, however, there is roughly a hundred billion in foreign profits being shielded annually, using capital allowances, losses brought forward and interest payments that make their way back to the parent company. To put this slightly differently, Ireland's BEPS tools are now applied by the Revenue Commissioners rather than being used to bypass the Irish system – as in the Double Irish. Despite this, however, the effective tax rate is still estimated to be around 10 per cent simply by benchmarking it against a taxable income *that has already been reduced by the Irish BEPS tools referenced above.* Table 9.2 explains the process.

Table 9.2 Calculation of Total Taxable Income Figure

	2018 (€ millions)	2018 (€ millions)
Gross Trade Profits		182,734
Less Deductible Amounts as Follows		
Trade Capital Allowances	79,019	
Trade Loss Forward (and Current Trade Losses)	10,287	
Group Interest Charges	17,939	
Plus Group Relief	4291	
Total Amount Deducted		111,536
Net Trading Income After Losses, Charges and Group Relief		71,198
Passive Income (Rents, Foreign Dividends, Capital Gains)		15,626
Net Total Taxable Income		96,049
Total Tax Paid		10,211
Effective Rate on Taxable Income		10.63%

Source: Revenue Commissioners. 'Summary of Corporation Tax Returns'.[44]

If the effective rate is benchmarked against Gross Profits being shifted into Ireland, the rate is only 5.5 per cent. However, this jumps to the far more respectable 10.63 per cent when the figure is benchmarked against taxable income *that has already excluded billions in profits.*

CLAIM 2 – TAX AVOIDANCE IS NOT OUR FAULT

The beneficiaries of Tax Haven Ireland would obviously like to remain anonymous. Sheltering profits works much better in the shadows, but the scale of avoidance in the Irish haven means there must also be strategies for moments of crisis. These are times when the weight of evidence becomes so overwhelming that outright denial becomes impossible. Times, that is, when the state has to hold its hands up in a way that avoids taking any direct responsibility while protecting the wider offshore network. Scandals surrounding the Apple ruling and the use of Section 110 companies by US vulture funds are two such cases. This section will look at how Fine Gael-led governments dealt with these issues as further evidence for Tax Haven Ireland.

2.1 The Apple Ruling

In August 2016, the European Competition Commissioner, Margarethe Vestager, announced that Ireland had granted illegal state aid to Apple which had saved the company €13 billion.[45] This threatened to bring down the coalition government when a number of independent ministers initially opposed fighting the case through the European courts.[46] Partly to placate them, the government initiated a 'Review of Ireland's Corporation Tax Code' by their favourite independent expert, Seamus Coffey.[47] In line with his previous analysis, Coffey produced an extremely long and technical document that made a number of recommendations, but which ultimately gave the tax code a clean bill of health. The terms of reference failed to mention the European Commission judgement, for example, or the fact the government was going to fight the case on behalf of Apple. That said, Coffey's analysis did touch on the government's real response to the Apple ruling – albeit in a way that didn't reveal it. In a section on the 'Sustainability of Corporation Tax Receipts', Coffey noted that Ireland's Gross Capital Stock had increased by an amazing €332 billion in early 2015 and that the Revenue Commissioners had covered up the source of this increase by *redacting their accounts*. Reflecting on this unusual practice, Coffey had this to say

> Changes in the capital stock are usually driven by investment [but] nearly 85% of the €332 billion increase...cannot be explained [this way]. In the 2015 data, two categories have been *supressed for confidentiality reasons*; transport equipment and research and development. The categories for which data is provided recorded an increase of €42 billion in 2015 so the remaining €289 billion is accounted for by the *missing categories* of transport and intangibles. *It is probable that the bulk of this was due to intangibles* [our emphasis].[48]

Coffey also noted that the amount of tax breaks for these intangibles had increased from €2.65 billion in 2014 to €28.8 billion in 2015 thanks to a government scheme – the Capital Allowances for Intangible Assets – that was allowing companies to write off the cost of bought-in IP against their Irish taxes. The latter scheme was initially proposed during the depths of the banking crisis by a Commission on Taxation, which included Feargal O'Rourke.[49] The Finance Bill for 2009 duly included a range of new IP assets eligible for capital allowances that were initially capped at 80 per cent.[50] In their Budget Submission for 2015, the American Chamber of Commerce called on the Irish government to further increase the allowance to 90 per cent, but the state 'went a step further and introduced a 100% cap on capital allowances that could be claimed for IP expenditure'.[51] In 2017, meanwhile, it was revealed that Apple has been the primary driver of the increase in the CAIA tax deductions identified by Coffey when they used the widow at the end of the Double Irish to move most of their non-US IP into Ireland.[52] *In other words, Apple were the primary beneficiaries of the state's new tax avoidance scheme during the years that Ireland was being investigated for granting Apple illegal state aid through the older one – while paying millions to fight Apple's original case in the European courts.* None of this came out in the Coffey report of course, but what we now know is that, despite the fanfare that surrounded the announcement of the 'Review of Ireland's Corporation Tax Code', the state had spent the previous two years quietly replacing the Double Irish with the CAIA while doctoring the national statistics to hide this fact.

The grounds on which they are fighting the Apple case are equally revealing. Speaking to the EU General Court in September 2019, the former attorney general, Paul Gallagher SC, argued that the bulk of Apple's *real activity* happened outside the state and therefore neither Apple Sales Ireland or Apple Operations Europe were entitled to tax it.[53] Specifically, he argued the Commission ruling 'is astonishing' given the fact that only routine activities were carried out in Cork and that the Irish offices carried out no R&D and held no intellectual property.[54] The General Court of the European Union seemed to accept this line of argumentation when it found in favour of both Ireland and Apple in its 2020 ruling. Overturning the original Commission decision, the Court accepted that Apple Sales International and Apple Operations Europe were incorporated in Ireland but not registered there for taxation.[55] This being so, the Court disputed the claim that Ireland was entitled to tax these profits, stating that 'the Commission should have shown that that income represented the value of the activities actually carried out by the Irish branches themselves'.[56] This brings us to the nub of the case, however, as it appears that the Irish government, Apple Inc. and the EU courts all accept that the profits were not being produced in Ireland but that Apple were still moving them through Ireland for no apparent reason. The obvious reason was to reduce Apple's non-US taxes, and so while the Court argued that the bar of legal evidence hadn't been reached, it left the most important questions hanging in the air. Namely, why did Ireland allow Apple to move profits out of countries where this value was created – via Irish-incorporated companies – to be taxed nowhere?[57] And if no R&D or intellectual property is created in their Irish operations, why are Apple IP assets that are worth billions still allowed to shelter in the Irish state to avail of tax breaks? Accepting that Ireland is not entitled to profits created in other countries is proof that these profits should never have been routed through Ireland in the first place, while using the lack of IP activity as the state's defence in the Apple case, exposes the artificial nature of the CAIA scheme they set up in 2015. Far from working hard to close loopholes that make Ireland a victim of international tax avoidance, the evidence suggests that Ireland helps to create these loopholes and adjusts them when they come under pressure.

2.2 Section 110 Companies

Tax Haven Ireland faced a further, home-grown controversy in 2016, when it was revealed that US vulture funds had bought €300 billion worth of distressed property assets, but were paying virtually no taxes on their profits.[58] The vehicles used on this occasion were created under Section 110 of the Irish Taxes Consolidation Act 1997, and the issue came to light when a number of these vehicles filed public accounts with the Companies Registration Office. Chapter 6 explained the genesis of these companies in the attempt by the Irish Financial Services Centre to compete in the global securitisation market. Section 110 companies were originally designed to offer 'tax neutrality' on foreign assets and there were no reported cases of them being used to avoid Irish taxes prior to the Great Recession of 2008. This changed dramatically, however, when vulture funds were invited into the Irish property market by the Department of Finance and the National Assets Management Agency (NAMA). A Freedom of Information request revealed that 'officials in the Department of Finance met private equity vulture funds 65 times in 2013 and 2014 [with] Mr Noonan attend[ing] eight of these meetings'.[59] NAMA chairman Frank Daly meanwhile participated in a seminar organised by Mason Hayes and Curran, which explained the tax benefits of the Irish system to distressed debt funds in London.[60] Vulture funds were encouraged to purchase Irish property assets at knock down prices and chose Section 110 SPVs to structure their activity in such a way that their taxes were eliminated. A Freedom of Information request confirmed that the Revenue Commissioners were aware of vulture funds using Section 110 Companies in January of 2016, several months before the issue was raised in the Dáil.[61] Indeed, the public only became aware of the scam when the *Sunday Business Post* revealed it more than half a year later.[62]

The ensuing scandal ensured Fine Gael had to act, and, in September 2016, the Minister for Finance, Michael Noonan, announced he would end 'the possible use of aggressive tax practices by some section 110 companies to avoid paying tax on Irish property transactions'.[63] Such a definitive response was designed to placate an angry public, but the state's own Budgetary Oversight Committee soon criticised the effectiveness of the government measure.

Their own words are insightful on the matter:

Having noted that an amendment to Section 110…will be introduced in the Finance Bill 2016…[t]he Committee remains concerned that the amendment will not have an impact as:

1. It allows the assets to be marked to current market value; 2. Vulture funds will continue to use arm's length loan notes which can be set against profits made; and 3. the amendment only applies to property.[64]

In other words, an Oireachtas Committee, chaired by a Fine Gael TD, remained unconvinced that the measures would be effective, because vulture funds could continue to use the artificial loans that had shielded their profits so successfully in the first place. A week after the announcement, Independent TD Stephen Donnelly more or less confirmed this when he claimed that large accounting and legal firms were already telling their clients how to get around the Section 110 amendment.[65] Despite the acknowledged losses to the exchequer, moreover, the Revenue Commissioners never pursued the money lost through avoidance or sanctioned those companies who had stolen from the state. Instead, vulture funds were offered an alternative way to avoid their taxes, when the Irish Central Bank upgraded the Loan Originating-Qualifying Investor Alternative Investment Fund (L-QIAIF) with the same tax features as the Section 110 SPV, but without the burden of filing public accounts.[66] With this added layer of secrecy, the L-QIAIF quickly became the vehicle of choice for US vulture funds who, by June 2018, had moved €55 billion out of Section 110 SPVs.[67] Meanwhile, all of the companies that had helped to facilitate the original evasion escaped without so much as a slap on the wrist. To successfully abuse Section 110 companies in the Irish property market, accountancy firms had to create successful avoidance structures; legal firms had to create the fiction of charitable status and corporate service firms had to supply Irish-resident company directors. All of this aided and abetted US companies evading their Irish taxes, yet none of the firms working out of the IFSC were ever punished by the state. Instead, those running Tax Haven Ireland made it look like they were taking decisive action to close a loophole, when in fact they were closing down public scrutiny of their offshore activity.

CLAIM 3 – IRELAND IS A RESPONSIBLE PARTNER

The final layer of Ireland's defence involves what the OECD defines as 'harmful tax competition'.[68] Here the objective is to present Ireland as an enthusiastic supporter of international regulation at the same time as the IFSC constantly evolves new ways to get around these measures. Ireland is a rogue nation that relies on other nations accepting that it isn't. This might seem like an impossible dilemma, but the question of international taxation is never as straightforward as it appears. On the one hand, every country wants to protect its own tax base, leading to pressure from non-havens to reduce the effectiveness of BEPS techniques. This is increasingly true inside the European Union, for example, where Germany, Spain and Italy are losing out on billions annually.[69] On the other hand, tax havens help to drive down wages and workers' conditions across the capitalist economy. This helps the ruling classes in every country by shielding profits and undermining the forces of democratic accountability. In this contradictory environment, the name of the game up to now has been *plausible deniability*. No state can openly declare itself a tax haven, but neither must it unilaterally close down its part of the offshore network. So long as the world's most powerful states and corporations are behind this system, Ireland can create the illusion of compliance with international standards that deliberately leave enough room to be ineffective. This is particularly true of the OECD BEPS process, which is lauded by the Irish establishment for this very reason.

3.1 The BEPS Process

The OECD's BEPS process is widely regarded as the gold standard in international tax regulation. Running from September 2013 to October 2015, it was meant to end regulatory mismatches that facilitate profit shifting into low tax jurisdictions and the erosion of tax bases via artificial corporate structures. The project was initially supported by 60 countries and now has more than 135 signatories.[70] Collectively, these countries have agreed 15 Actions in three broad policy areas – reducing the scale of tax avoidance and evasion, improving the coherence of international tax rules and ensuring a more transparent tax environment. These, in turn, address key issues facing global regulators including:

- The digitisation of the global economy;
- Abuse of intellectual property flows via transfer pricing;
- Abuse of tax treaties and bogus residency rules;
- Abuse of artificial structures that route profits into more favourable locations;
- Abuse of artificial structures that create illegitimate interest and royalty deductions; and,

- A lack of information sharing between tax planners, national regulators and international organisations.[71]

Properly enacted, these measures would transform the international tax environment in a way that hasn't been seen for generations. None of the major Irish BEPS tools would survive if these measures were implemented fully, for example, but the OECD has never been interested in a genuinely transformative agenda in the international arena. Instead, it wants to create an even playing field for corporations to invest and compete in. To realise this, consider a paper on tax competition by the Chair of the OECD Committee on Taxation, Richard M. Hammer, and its Head of Fiscal Affairs, Jeffrey Owens.[72] In it, the authors address the need for a BEPS process by making a crucial distinction between 'harmful tax competition' that undermines the wider business environment and 'transparent and fair' competition which allocates capital effectively and ought to be encouraged.[73] The goal of the OECD, according to the authors, should be 'to create a fiscal climate which is more conducive to cross border business while promoting a fair sharing of the tax base between countries'.[74] What the OECD should have no interest in, however, is 'harmonising tax rates; adversely impacting cross border investment flows; eliminating commercially useful structures, such as holding companies; curtailing legitimate tax planning or denying governments the right to determine their own taxation policies'.[75] In other words, the OECD is a deeply neoliberal organisation, committed to the rights of global corporations so long as they compete within tolerable bounds. Harmonising tax structures would go a long way to undermining the offshore network, but this is ruled out by the OECD as going against 'fair competition'. Holding companies are also essential to profit shifting and base erosion, but these too would escape OECD regulations so long as they are not used too aggressively. Despite claiming global authority on international taxation, moreover, the OECD is an elitist organisation whose proposals disproportionately suit its own members. Fung makes the latter point in the following way:

Nicknamed the rich man's club, the OECD is neither inclusive with regard to its membership nor operates in a political vacuum; its policies serve, first and foremost, the interests of the member countries. As the self-proclaimed leader in setting standards and guidelines in respect of international tax matters…the OECD actively seeks out and engages with non-OECD countries in order to secure their commitment in the implementation of OECD instruments, standards and guidelines…. However, the decision-making power is vested in the OECD council alone.[76]

This combination of neoliberal policy making and elitist exclusivity biases the OECD BEPS process in five crucial ways. Firstly, as Richard Murphy points out, it is virtually impossible to distinguish between 'benign tax competition' and 'harmful tax competition' in the way the OECD proposes.[77] Over the last 35 years, for example, national states have eroded their own tax bases in a bid to win mobile capital flows as foreign direct investment. According to a recent IMF report, this form of base erosion has reduced corporate tax rates by an average of 50 per cent, but this is deemed completely benign by the neoliberals running the OECD.[78] Secondly, the OECD is committed to arm's length principles in internal transactions that effectively allow the parent company to shift profits from high to low tax places. Everyone knows that abuse of transfer pricing is the key mechanism for shifting profits out of higher tax countries, but until very recently the OECD remained committed to an international regulatory system based on these flawed principles. Thirdly, the OECD's favoured model convention – the set of rules it advocates for countries to sign – is decisively biased against poorer countries. This is because it allocates primary taxing rights to the country from which investment originates, rather than the country receiving the investment. In other words, the states that house the world's most powerful corporations should receive the lion's share of any international taxation, even if the bulk of the activity happens outside their jurisdiction. Fourthly, the BEPS process is neither legally binding nor universal in its application. This means countries can pick and choose which parts of the process they put into law – effectively allowing the semblance of compliance without the accompanying legal requirements. Fifth, and finally, the BEPS process is committed to the privacy of corporations in a way that undermines their formal commitment to openness and transparency. Publicly available country-by-country reporting is one of the most important mechanisms for increasing transparency in the international economy. The OECD support the idea of country-specific reporting on profits and activity, but only if all of the information is kept hidden from the public.

Collectively, these features of the BEPS project make it attractive to an Irish state that wants to promote adherence to the latest regulations without disrupting its offshore operations. By drawing a distinction between 'fair competition' and its 'harmful' counterpart, for example, the OECD helps to create the impression that Ireland's unusually low headline rate for corporation taxation is part of a legitimate strategy to attract inward investment and high paid employment. Earlier we outlined the nature of the pact between the Irish state and global corporations, which does rely on real investment and employment, but also on some of the world's most powerful BEPS tools. The upfront tax competition is also an essential prerequisite for the avoidance mechanisms, but this gets completely glossed over by the OECD's defence of the first and condemnation of the second. This is then used for political cover by the Irish state, as illustrated recently by Paschal Donohoe at a conference in Dublin Castle:

> Artificial profit shifting for tax purposes poses a real challenge and must continue to be addressed. However, I do not support measures which have as their core objective the end of legitimate and fair tax competition. The benefits of tax competition have long been recognised by the OECD and others, as long as this competition is fair.[79]

The second attractive aspect of the OECD initiative is its insistence on maintaining arm's length principles for transfer pricing (TP). Recall that Ireland's major BEPS tools rely on the opacity of internal group trading to funnel profits into the state using TP and intellectual property. It is virtually impossible to end this process if companies are granted arm's length principles, no matter how strictly they are supposedly being monitored. The OECD have three separate actions to tackle abuses of transfer pricing, for example, but assuming companies will apply internal prices as if they were trading with external companies is akin to allowing bank robbers to have access to their getaway car on condition that they promise not to speed. To see just how easy it is to manipulate TP rules, recall that Ireland's transaction net margin method (TNMM) is meant to compare internal profits with profits made from similar transactions on the open market when companies go to such long lengths to hide the real nature of their activities. Recall further that Ireland's TP rules only pick up companies under-declaring their Irish profits when the whole point of the offshore system is to over-declare foreign profits in the Irish state. Little wonder Paschal Donohoe has insisted that any new arrangements in international regulation 'must be based, to the greatest extent possible, on existing transfer pricing rules which are deeply embedded in the international tax framework'.[80]

Being part of the OECD confers a further important advantage on Ireland, in-so-far as the organisation has never placed any of its own members on tax haven blacklists. This allows Ireland to invoke the authority of the OECD as an independent arbiter, safe in the knowledge that no amount of evidence has ever been enough to blacklist one of its own.[81] Finally, the lack of any effective legal sanction means that Ireland can pick and choose the parts of the BEPS process that it enacts into law, and more importantly, supply its own interpretation of what these laws will actually mean. This explains how Ireland could recently pass a raft of laws around different BEPS Actions while increasing the profits moving artificially into the country since 2015 and how it could transpose the OECD Multilateral Instrument without ending newer versions of the Double Irish.[82]

3.2 European Union Initiatives

In 2011, The European Union launched its Directive on Administrative Co-operation (DAC) to 'strengthen the fight against cross border tax fraud and ensure that profits are taxed where they are made'.[83] To date there have been six areas brought under these proposals. DAC1 provided mandatory exchange of information in key areas, including directors' fees and income from immoveable property assets. This has since been expanded to include financial accounts information (DAC2); advance cross-border tax rulings (DAC3); Country-by-Country corporate accounts (DAC4); registers of beneficial ownership (DAC5); and automatic exchange of tax-planning schemes (DAC6).[84] The last three Directives specifically target the offshore system, with automatic exchange of information expected on the owners of corporate assets, the location and quantity of profits being made from these assets and any attempts to manipulate this information by tax specialists or accountants. Unlike the BEPS process, moreover, these Directives are mandatory for countries operating within the EU, creating a dilemma for the Irish government. Being part of the Single Market is essential for companies funnelling profits out of European countries, but this also means implementing Directives that potentially disrupt Ireland's offshore operations. To cope with this challenge the Irish state has deployed three basic tactics – delay implementation, dilute the impact and make a virtue of necessity when the Directives are eventually signed into law. The implementation of DAC5 is a case in point.

In September 2018, the Department of Finance claimed that Ireland was at the forefront of international tax transparency, partly on the basis of agreeing the EU's Fourth Anti-Money Laundering Initiative, which included a register of public ownership. What they didn't reveal, however, was that the Directive was meant to be signed in July 2017 but was twice delayed by the Irish state. When the initial deadline passed, Ireland was one of 17 European countries faced with infringement proceedings by the European Commission for failing to pass a law specifically designed to tackle cross-border criminality.[85] Then, in August 2018, Ireland was one of just three countries referred to the Court of Justice of the EU (CJEU) for continuing to hold out on implementation. Referring the case, the EU Commissioner for Justice, Vera Jourová, recommended that the CJEU impose a lump sum penalty and daily fines to prevent Ireland becoming a weak link in the fight against cross-border money laundering.[86] This external pressure eventually did the trick, as DAC5 was transposed into Irish law in November 2018.

A similar pattern emerged around the implementation of DAC4, moreover. Although Ireland signed the Directive requiring companies to report relevant tax information on a country-by-country reporting basis in 2015, they also made sure that this information was kept confidential and outside public scrutiny.[87] CBCR is one of the key methods for holding multinational companies to account, but the information needs to be public for it to work effectively. Despite this, the Irish state was one of twelve European countries to block an EU Commission proposal for public CBCR in November 2019 on the basis that it would disadvantage companies operating within the EU versus their counterparts in China and the US.[88] In other words, transparency for European citizens was put second to multinational competitiveness in a move that revealed the true priorities of the Irish establishment. The Department of Finance also claims to be a global leader around the mandatory disclosure of potential tax scams, but here again, their claims are misleading. Unlike the previous two Directives, which rely on increasing the transparency of corporate activities, DAC6 relies on the Irish government – a known tax haven – asking companies in the IFSC to let it know if they are planning tax schemes that might result in profit shifting or base erosion. Ireland was one of only three EU countries to have rules for mandatory disclosure even before DAC6 came into effect – but, hardly surprisingly, these rules were so toothless that only eleven disclosures were made in eight years, none of which related to widely used tax avoidance mechanisms.[89] Far from leading the charge on tax transparency and information sharing, this pattern of responses reveals a state that enthusiastically implements Directives when it is sure they won't be effective, uses its sovereignty to make others less effective and delays for as long as possible when they will definitely be effective.

Much the same applies when we turn to the EU's other major tax reforms – the Anti-Tax Avoidance Directives (ATADs). These were signed in July 2016 with the aim of transposing the BEPS proposals into European law and resulted in the following five initiatives:

1. *Anti-hybrid rules* to stop multinationals claiming tax deductions for the same costs in two different states or claiming a deduction in one country for a cost that never arose in another.
2. An *exit tax* to stop multinationals moving assets across borders without paying capital gains taxes.
3. *General Anti-Avoidance Rules (GAAR)* to stop activity undertaken purely for the purpose of avoiding taxes.

4. *Controlled foreign company (CFC) rules* to stop companies diverting profits into offshore entities in low tax countries.
5. *Interest limitation rules* to limit the deduction against borrowing costs to 30 per cent of a company's earnings before interest, tax depreciation and amortisation.[90]

As before, the Department of Finance created fanfare around signing ATADs, when in fact implementation has been delayed or diluted in every case.[91] The interest limitation rules are particularly important in this respect. Ireland's CAIA BEPS tool create significant opportunities for interest rate deductions by warehousing IP in Ireland which is paid for through intra-group loans. This currently allows multinationals to claim interest rate deductions at 80 per cent of the claimed cost of bought-in IP, instead of the 30 per cent that will be allowed if the new rules are adopted. In an explanatory note on the ATADs, Matheson flags the interest limitation rules as potentially the most significant ones, but assure their investors that 'Ireland will exercise the discretion afforded by the optionality under Article 4 to limit any adverse impact, particularly on the financial services industry'.[92] The optionality they refer to is a clause in the ATAD that allows countries to delay implementing the interest limitation rules until 2024, if they can prove their own laws in this area are equally effective. In their 'Ireland's Corporation Tax Roadmap', the Department of Finance state that they have not implemented the interest limitation rule for just this reason.[93] However, this has prompted the European Commission to once again threaten legal action as they disagree with the way that Ireland has chosen to avoid this Directive.[94] Ireland has also refused to implement the GAAR rules on the basis that the state has an equally robust one that goes back to 1989, and they have been able to put off the most important anti-hybrid laws until 2022. The state has implemented an Exit Tax, but instead of setting it at the normal capital gains rate of 33 per cent it has set the rate at just 12.5 per cent. It has also implemented controlled foreign company rules that will have little impact on Tax Haven Ireland. The objective of CFC rules is to stop multinationals diverting passive income – such as interest payments and royalties – into artificial structures in low tax economies. To achieve this aim, states have two different options:

- Option A imposes CFC charges on all undistributed passive income sent into low tax jurisdictions on the assumption that this is being done to avoid taxes.
- Option B imposes CFC charges on undisturbed income *when the activity is proven to be associated with BEPS activity* [our emphasis].[95]

In response to a state consultation on this matter, Oxfam gave three good reasons why Option B should be avoided: (1) It is costly and extremely difficult to prove non-genuine activity; (2) It is very easy to get around the measures, with just one employee often enough to escape the tag of non-genuine activity; and (3) Option B does nothing to stop CFC operations between known tax havens and developing countries.[96] Given these difficulties, Oxfam strongly advocated Option A as by far the most effective anti-avoidance measure. On the other hand, submissions from Arthur Cox, EY, Deloitte, Grant Thornton, KPMG and PwC all favoured at least including Option B – the one the government duly went for.[97] Responding to this, and the rest of the government's record on the ATADs, Oxfam made the following assessment:

It should be noted that Ireland had to implement most of the measures it is proposing in this report under EU Law (ATAD). Ireland has [therefore] chosen to implement the weakest options at the latest available date.... Ireland's reforms to address corporate tax avoidance to date have had little or no demonstrable impact on corporate tax avoidance. There is significant evidence that Ireland is still acting as one of the world's biggest conduits for tax avoidance.[98]

These are sentiments we share wholeheartedly. The Irish state claims it has done everything in its power to tackle corporate tax avoidance when all of the available evidence suggests otherwise.

10
The Social Costs

Ireland is often held up as a neoliberal success story. A former impoverished colony, it now ranks among the world's 20 richest countries on a Gross Domestic Product (GDP) per capita basis. Its economic growth rate regularly exceeds the EU average, and prior to the disaster associated with Covid-19, Ireland was the fastest-growing economy in the EU from 2014 to 2018.[1] Little wonder its former politicians are invited to advise poorer countries on how to develop.[2] Yet behind the spin and statistics, there is a dark secret at the heart of this official narrative. Ireland's headline economic success is based on corporate tax dodging on an industrial scale. To make this case, we noted that the Republic's development has gone through four distinct phases – each one rooted in an economy serving the interests of the elites. An initial decade of laissez-faire policy making was followed by a quarter of a century of economic nationalism. Up to the mid-1950s, however, the most important factor in the country's development was the failure of the Irish Revolution during 1916–23. This not only fractured the island into two reactionary states, it also cemented the class dynamics that eventually led to the small economy, open for – tax-dodging – business. In 1956, the state first showed its willingness to use the tax system to attract foreign direct investment (FDI) through its Exports Profits Reliefs Tax scheme. This, in turn, set up a wider dynamic between the state, foreign capital and domestic capital which had three important effects on the subsequent development of the offshore network. Firstly, it brought a significant amount of FDI into the country with an interest in minimising costs and regulations. Secondly, it created a subservient state that was anxious to please its new 'partners' at the same time as it protected key sectors for domestic capital. Thirdly, it created a culture of cronyism and corruption that was essential when the big opportunities for tax dodging came in the 1980s. Tax Haven Ireland can officially be dated to two events in that decade.

The first was the decision by Margaret Thatcher to deregulate the City of London in 1986. This created pressure throughout the global system for liberalised capital markets in general and for the Single European Market in particular. The second was the establishment of the International Financial Services Centre (IFSC) in 1987, by two men with stellar records for giving and receiving gifts – former Taoiseach Charles Haughey and City insider Dermot Desmond. This created the institutional capacity to move Ireland into the tax-dodging major leagues, just as international capital flows were becoming more prevalent. The subsequent development of the digital revolution – particularly in the context of neoliberal globalisation – is also an important maker in this process, as multinationals began to use complex legal structures to play different tax systems against each other, often using transfer pricing and intangible assets. During the 1980s and 1990s, Ireland attracted jobs and investment from American multinationals which both legitimised FDI in the eyes of the public and created a powerful feedback mechanism for Tax Haven Ireland. As the neoliberal period developed, the Irish elite were expected to offer the latest base erosion and profit shifting (BEPS) devices to their corporate clients, and they were more than happy to oblige. Today, Tax Haven Ireland is a complex network of state agencies, IFSC fixers and tax planners in the major corporations. But it is also deeply embedded in the real economy via the global companies that use Ireland as their base for real activity alongside profit shifting. All of this has made Ireland into one of the world's most important tax havens and in this final chapter we look at the social and human costs associated with this reality.

THE COST TO THE POOR

Tax dodging hits the poorest hardest. Research by Oxfam estimates that developing countries lose between $100 to $160 billion annually as a direct result of tax avoidance.[3] The OECD suggest the figure could be hundreds of billions, but even this underestimates the human damage being done.[4] For one thing, poorer countries rely more heavily on corporation taxes than their OECD counterparts, amplifying the damage when tax is avoided.[5] For another, poorer countries are disproportionately disadvantaged by transfer pricing that assigns value to developed economies rather than production or sales in Africa, Asia and Latin America. Thirdly, the human costs are much greater in countries that already face mass poverty without strong welfare systems to protect their citizens. In these senses, the bald statistics hide a far more horrific reality. Oxfam predict that if poorer countries could get hold of the money they lose in taxes, it would provide education for 124 million children and prevent the deaths of more than eight million mothers and children annually.[6] Few would blame the Irish government for directly causing these deaths, but it is certainly a consequence of their policies – and they know it. In 2015, the Department of Finance published an analysis of the Irish tax system's impacts on the developing world.[7] The context was the controversy surrounding the 'Double Irish' and the objective, at least on paper, was to ascertain whether Ireland was undermining poorer countries through its tax regime. True to form, the report presented a sanguine view of Ireland's impact, based on the supposedly low level of interaction between the respective taxation systems. This allowed government spin doctors to give the tax code a clean bill of health. However, Christian Aid soon demolished this rosy assessment when they demonstrated that multinationals regularly establish their 'regional headquarters' in Ireland before sucking profits out of developing economies.[8] Microsoft created a range of phones specifically for sale in Africa and Asia, for example, but then booked the resulting profits through Irish holding companies to avoid their taxes. The charity also found evidence that, thanks to the Capital Allowances for Intangible Assets scheme, global companies are sending 'non-negligible royalty payments from poorer countries into Ireland' although 'the impact on individual developing economies remained unknown…due to confidentiality provisions in the statistics act'.[9] In the same vein, Professor Sheila Killian challenged the assumption that seemingly low capital flows meant that there was no impact on developing countries. Instead, she insisted, this often pointed to a lack of reliable information as companies use 'sophisticated tax planning strategies to skip from country to country – and sometimes back again'.[10] The best way to guard against this behaviour is to write strong anti-avoidance measures into bilateral tax treaties with poorer countries, but this is the very opposite of what the Irish government have been doing. Professor Killian takes up the story:

> The [Department of Finance] spillover analysis was conducted while negotiations for a new Zambian tax treaty were ongoing, and the report mentions the Zambian tax treaty should be negotiated 'without delay', since [the law] does not [currently] allow the source state to levy any withholding taxes on dividends, interest and royalties….
>
> [So] it is astounding that, given this analysis, and the concrete harm demonstrated by ActionAid's work, *the new double tax treaty still lacks anti-abuse provisions, and does not allow any withholding tax on management fees* [our emphasis].[11]

A similar picture emerges in the tax deal done with Ghana in 2018. As far back as 2012, the Department of Foreign Affairs and Trade (DFAT) warned that the tax treaty being constructed risked undermining state revenues in Ghana through BEPS.[12] Despite this, however, the Irish state signed an agreement that explicitly cut royalties from Ghana to Ireland from 15 per cent to 8 per cent and cut the rate on technical services fees from 20 per cent to 10 per cent.[13] The agreement was also designed to deny Ghana the right to tax capital gains from the sale of assets in its territory, if the sale is executed through the offshore sale of shares in an Irish holding company.[14] The results of this were important, moreover, as at the end of the negotiations, investment from Ireland into Ghana went from a negligible amount in 2011 to $4.5 billion just two years later.[15] Indeed, Ireland became the single largest source for direct investment into Ghana with Mike Lewis from Christian Aid arguing that limiting Ghana's taxing rights over income, profits and economic activity…may thus have a significant impact on Ghanaian tax revenues.[16] Ghana's spending on social protection was already low when judged by African standards, and this tax treaty will ensure it gets worse. Northern Ghana is particularly impoverished for example, with a mortality rate for children under five years' old at a shocking 111 per 1000.[17] To put this in perspective, the equivalent rate in Ireland is just 4 per 1000, yet the Irish government is helping to rob money that could be used to save lives, simply to line the pockets of wealthy shareholders. The Department of Foreign Affairs more or less accepted this judgement in their own assessment:

> Countries with these treaties can...be used to channel money between jurisdictions to minimise tax payable, particularly if withholding taxes are minimised to encourage investment – a practice which would clearly not be encouraged in relation to developing nations.[18]

Officials may defend these deals as the exception, but we know from Christian Aid – among others – that Ireland has undermined tax systems right across the developing world.[19] Recent tax treaties have only reinforced this position, moreover, while the poor in the developed world are also being affected.[20] In Chapter 4, we noted that US companies were hoarding more than $1 trillion abroad to avoid paying 35 per cent taxes on their global earnings.[21] In effect, these companies were engaging in an investment strike, aimed at forcing the US authorities to adjust their tax laws in a pro-business direction. Donald Trump duly became their champion in 2017, when he introduced the Tax Cuts and Jobs Act with the aim of bringing that cash back into the states. Within a year, a staggering $777 billion flowed back to the US, with companies in Ireland sending the third largest amount.[22] Trump also shifted from a global to a territorial tax system and cut the domestic corporation profit tax rate from 35 to 21 per cent.[23] The silent investment strike – facilitated by Ireland – had worked. The immediate impact was a surge in US stock market value, as multinationals engaged in share buy-back schemes that created a windfall for the US 1 per cent. By contrast, the 40 million Americans who live below the poverty line saw little benefit because they don't own stocks in corporations. US welfare provision barely exists, and, as a result, 1.5 million children are currently homeless. A few blocks from the cultural symbol of America – Hollywood – the streets of Los Angeles are lined with make-shift tents where some of these children undoubtedly live. A lack of a proper public healthcare system also means the poorest people sometimes choose between food and meeting their medical requirements. Indeed, so shocking is the inequality, that hundreds line up for healthcare in field-camps provided by volunteers.

By offering itself as a location for US corporate tax dodgers, Ireland makes its own contribution to this obscene state of global affairs. But why should anyone care about the poor in Zambia, Ghana or America? Don't the Irish need to look after our own and forget about the plight of other people? This is certainly the way the corporate elites would like us to think. From their boardrooms and penthouse suites, global capitalists see the world as one big market place. Their cosmopolitanism consists of seeking tax-free profits across the planet while hoping local populations remain imprisoned by their national perspectives. The more each country competes to 'attract' them, the quicker the 'race to the bottom' takes place, making them rich. Decades ago, the case for an internationalist outlook was outlined by one of the leaders of the 1916 Irish rebellion – James Connolly. He suggested that 'the internationality of Capital and Capitalism' needs to be matched by that of labour. Workers, he wrote, should be 'interested in every revolt of Labour all over the world, for the very individuals against whom that revolt may be directed may...be the parasites who are sucking their blood also'.[24] But while internationalism is clearly progressive and desirable, most people still think in national terms. And although a recent survey showed that '86 percent of Irish people believed that big companies were using tax loopholes to dodge their fair share of tax', many still assume that their presence in Ireland is beneficial.[25] Some may even claim that after hundreds of years of colonisation, Ireland is entitled to bend the rules to support its population. However, the wider population doesn't benefit from Tax Haven Ireland – a tiny elite, and their hangers-on, do. More specifically, it is the accountancy firms, the corporate lawyers and the hedge fund managers that have a vested interest in tax avoidance and who also support Ireland's right-wing parties – Fine Gael and Fianna Fáil. For the rest of society, tax dodging brings a host of problems.

THE COSTS IN IRELAND

One of the stranger effects of Tax Haven Ireland is how ingrained the narrative around corporate taxation has become. Most teenagers don't know the tax rates they will pay when they leave school, but they know that Ireland charges 12.5 per cent tax on corporate profits – and they are expected to internalise how important this is for jobs and prosperity. Similarly, when a left-wing politician recommends that corporations 'pay their fair share', they are met with howls of derision and warned that multinationals will move their jobs if they are asked to pay any more taxes. The Irish state lobbies Europe to maintain taxation as a national competency, but try increasing corporate taxes and it quickly becomes apparent who decides tax policy, and it isn't the elected representatives. Threatening to leave is a form of economic terrorism, but it never gets framed this way in national debates. Instead, any discussion of the harm tax dodging brings to Irish society is met with the same refrain – 'they give us jobs'. This is a peculiar way of framing the issue – no less strange for the countless times it is repeated.

'Giving us jobs' suggests that multinationals are benefactors heaping generosity on Irish workers, when it would be more accurate to suggest that 'Ireland gives global companies tax-free profits and they employ Irish workers to make even more money'. The whole issue is surrounded by so much propaganda that many imagine the country is entirely dependent on this notional generosity. Few are aware of the exact numbers employed by multinationals and most overestimate it. According to the Bureau of Economic Analysis, for example, there were 130,000 people working for US-majority-owned companies in 2017, making up 5.4 per cent of the workforce. The Industrial Development Authority (IDA) uses somewhat higher figures and, according to them, US companies employed 162,000 workers or 6.5 per cent of the workforce. If foreign investment from other countries is included, it amounts to 229,000 or 9.3 per cent of the workforce.[26] More than half of those employed are concentrated in one area – a category known as International and Financial. Overall, then, foreign companies employ less than one tenth of the Irish labour force and half of these jobs are in the category where tax dodging is most obviously prevalent.

Far from being grateful for these jobs, moreover, Irish workers actually subsidise them through the taxation system. Multinationals get highly educated workers, national infrastructure and transport networks, all without having to pay very much in return. In 2017, for example, Irish workers paid €22.5 billion out of €136 billion in wages versus €8.1 billion from corporations out of €167 billion in gross earnings.[27] Or to put this another way, workers paid an effective tax rate that was more than three times higher than the bosses who employ them. One reason for this is the low level at which Irish workers hit the highest rate of income tax compared to other OECD countries.

Have a look at the figures in Table 10.1.

Table 10.1   Taxation on Personal Income from Central Government – Thresholds and Tax Rates

Country	Threshold (€)	Tax Rate (%)
Ireland	34,550	40
Germany	54,949	42
France	73,779	41
Italy	55,000	41
Spain	60,000	22.5
Finland	74,000	32.5

Source: OECD Data set. www.stats.oecd.org/Index.aspx?DataSetCode=TABLE_I6.

A second reason is that Irish employers pay just 11 per cent for their social insurance versus an EU average of 21 per cent.[28] A third, is that, since the Great Recession, Irish workers have been forced to pay a bigger portion of the overall tax take – up from 21 per cent in 2007 to 32 per cent in 2018.[29] Taken collectively, these facts reveal a taxation system that has been deliberately stacked against workers to make up the shortfall from corporations. Meanwhile, working people get relatively poor services, even though they pay around the EU average in social insurance contributions.[30] At just 9 per cent in 2018, Ireland had the lowest level of social protection spending in the European Union when benchmarked against the country's GDP.[31] One reason for this is the artificial inflation of the GDP figures that comes from tax-dodging multinationals. Ireland posts a figure of €300 billion for GDP versus €200 billion for Gross National Income, but even when public services are benchmarked against this lower figure, Ireland is still a laggard. Before the costs associated with Covid-19, Ireland had earmarked €70 billion for current and capital spending for 2020, when the average for a European economy of equivalent size would have been €85 billion.[32] This creates a number of knock-on effects that reduce living standards across the country. Here, we outline some of the most important:

- Hospital waiting lists are the worst in Europe. The Health Service Executive have set a target of 18 months for patients to be seen and this will only get worse due to Covid-19.[33]
- A lack of public housing means Irish people pay the second highest mortgage rates in the European Union and people in Dublin pay the second highest rents.[34]
- Childcare fees average €771 per month making them the third highest in the EU.[35]
- Irish primary school classes are among the largest and worst funded in Europe. The average class size is 25 as against an EU average of 20.[36]
- Ireland has the highest level of university fees in the EU. Nine other countries provide free fees.[37]

When we compare the level of taxes an average worker pays against their public services, it becomes abundantly clear that tax dodging carries a significant social cost.

However, it is not just a mechanical relationship between low corporate taxes, high employee taxes and poor public services. Tax dodging also creates a political culture that promotes business interests over every other concern. 'Ireland is open for business' proclaims every diplomat from the Department of Foreign Affairs and behind this slogan lies an attitude which venerates the 'entrepreneur' as the historic agent of social progress. Each morning, the state's news programme starts with 'The Business News' to inform the public of corporate exploits and successes. Faculties of Business and Enterprise mushroom in Irish universities, where even laid-back arts students are subjected to courses on 'entrepreneurship'. Business speak, with its banal language of 'excellence', 'benchmarking' and 'innovation', has spread out from managerial textbooks to every corner of society. Ireland is by no means unique in this pattern, as a culture of neoliberalism sweeps across the globe, but it embraces it to an unusual degree. The Irish state has forged a 'frictionless' relationship with business interests whereby these are served with unsurpassed enthusiasm and their insatiable demands for change are met regularly.

Take the scandal of Ireland's housing crisis as an example. The simple demand that the state provides social housing – as it did in previous decades – is rebuffed with the claim that the private sector must be 'incentivised to increase supply'. The state controls more than one quarter of all zoned residential development land, enough to build 114,000 dwellings. By using this land, it could build social housing for half the price that private developers charge and lower costs across the industry.[38] But instead, the political rhetoric is about encouraging the private sector, even though they created the problem in the first place. Tokenistic measures, known as rent pressure zones, are deployed to curb rising rents, but enough loopholes are inserted to allow landlords to evict tenants and increase their rents. 'Incentivisation' also means that when property developers seek greater flexibility in planning laws, it is granted. Vast tracts of public land are sold on the cheap, to the same developers who crashed the economy a decade previously. With this political culture in place, moreover, it is easy to grasp how lax tax rules designed to attract securitisation into Ireland could be easily adjusted for the housing market. Thus, we have already seen how the provisions of Section 110 of the Taxes Consolidation Act 1997 were tweaked to allow vulture funds to hold vast tracts of Irish based property assets – and then to increase rents to incredible levels.[39] Most people know that tax dodging deprives society of much-needed resources, but few join the dots from their own lives in a housing crisis to tax dodging in the IFSC. Yet the fact remains that Ireland's offshore network helped to engineer a housing crisis of epic proportions and then sat back while foreign vultures and Irish developers made extraordinary profits from rents and higher prices.

A RISKY STRATEGY

In August 2019, the Irish Central Bank (ICB) released a report that assessed financial risks in the IFSC.[40] Their stand-out point was that the IFSC currently houses one of the world's major shadow banking networks with trillions in assets managed completely outside the normal banking sector. Most of the time this money flows in and out of Ireland without people even noticing it. However, this doesn't mean that a major financial crisis isn't possible or that the risks would be confined to high-paid asset managers if it were to occur. We know from bitter experience that Irish governments will not hesitate to protect their own privileges over public service. We also know that in 2008, a little-known German bank – Depfa – cost German taxpayers an incredible €124 billion when it collapsed during the Great Recession.[41] This proved to be Germany's single largest financial bailout, but Depfa was originally registered in the IFSC and was very nearly a problem for Irish taxpayers. This shows the dangers that could still be lurking in the under-regulated offshore system. One potential channel of disruption identified by the ICB report was the growing links between IFSC Special Purpose Vehicles and the domestic real estate sector. A second, was a shifting risk profile as funds currently housed in London reassess their options after Brexit. A third, was the sheer scale of the increase in shadow banking assets in the IFSC, which potentially risked destabilising the wider Irish economy. The authors' summary is outlined here:

> The rapidly growing and changing nature of the Dublin financial centre, coupled with the visible fragmentation of finance in Europe... raises questions about the evolution of financial stability risks. First, a large share of intermediation could be provided by third-country firms, raising questions on how to organise regulatory relations going forward to balance efficiency and stability. Second, the fragmentation of finance inside the EU27 across different sectors can on the one hand imply new risks in terms of greater financial complexity in firms, but on the other hand it may also be mitigating concentration risk. Third, the growth of the IFSC – similar to non-financial multinational firms – may be changing Ireland's risk profile.[42]

The aftermath of Covid-19 is likely to amplify these risks as governments fight to attract mobile capital looking for safe havens from the coming disaster. And these are not the only challenges currently facing the country. In the past, Ireland's size meant that it was able to avoid inspection by EU authorities by flying under the radar. However, the sheer scale of avoidance that has now been identified, means that bigger states are no longer happy to allow companies to sell most of their products in France or Germany while paying most of their taxes in Ireland, Luxembourg and the Netherlands. The EU Commission's proposal for a 3 per cent tax on the revenues of major technology companies may well be a sign of things to come, and if this fails, they may still try to impose a Common Consolidated Corporation Tax Base (CCCTB).[43] Relaunched in 2016, the CCCTB is a proposal to reduce the ability of multinationals to play tax codes against each other by creating one consolidated set of tax rules across the EU. It is also an attempt to end profit shifting, as multinationals would have to submit accounts for the entire EU and pay taxes on a formulary basis that reflected their sales, employment and investment.[44] Although these proposals have been blocked by Ireland and Denmark, powerful EU countries are becoming more determined to implement them unilaterally.

The UK could previously be relied upon to stand against this reform agenda, but Brexit not only takes Ireland's most important political ally off the pitch, it creates the potential for an even less regulated financial centre on Ireland's doorstep. Reflecting on these pressures, the University College Dublin academic Dr Aidan Regan suggested that

> Ireland will find it much harder to block the Common Consolidated Corporate Tax Base (CCCTB) reforms this time due to Brexit. Ireland, the Netherlands, Luxembourg and other small economies always aligned in behind Britain as the big brother. Now that the big brother is not around, these countries are more exposed.[45]

Recent changes to the US tax code could also be disruptive, particularly the introduction of a charge on 'global intangible low tax income' – defined as excess income earned by a foreign subsidiary that is above a 10 per cent return on tangible business assets.[46] Trinity College Dublin Professor Frank Barry has estimated that some of Trump's tax changes will actually benefit Ireland – at least in the short term.[47] However, recent moves by Google indicate that it might not be as plain sailing as Barry believes. Over the last two years, Google Irish Holdings Unlimited has paid out $50 billion in shareholder dividends, while it also paid nothing to the Irish exchequer for $15 billion profit declared in 2018.[48] Google enjoyed these extraordinary benefits from the extension of the Double Irish until 2020, but if the Irish government thought the company would be grateful, they were sadly mistaken. Instead of gratitude, Google has decided to move its intellectual property holdings back to the US to take advantage of recent changes in US tax laws.

Beyond these changes in Ireland's most important trading partners, there are growing signs that the entire system of transfer pricing using intangible assets could be coming to an end. Having championed arm's length principles and international tax competition throughout the initial phase of the BEPS process, the OECD is now moving into line with the EU and the IMF by accepting a more co-ordinated approach to taxing the profits of global corporations. For the first time in January 2019, the OECD publicly conceded that the challenges of the digital economy meant that 'solutions' would have to 'go beyond the arm's length principle'.[49] This was followed up in March 2019, when Christine Lagarde, then Managing Director of the IMF, called the current system 'outdated' and urged a move towards formula-based approaches such as the CCCTB.[50] Finally, in May 2019, the OECD published a roadmap of reforms based on two key pillars. The first is a set of *Revised Nexus and Profit Allocation* rules that seek to make sure profits are apportioned where real activity is taking place. The second is a *Global Anti-Base Erosion Proposal* that would impose a minimum effective tax rate on global corporations.[51] These proposals are not yet agreed by the various countries signed up to the wider BEPS process, but the new roadmap is still a significant development as Grant Thornton outlines:

While there are a lot of twists, turns and boulders in the road ahead… [t]he OECD's programme of work represents the direction of travel. Even if some of the controversial and hard to implement elements are reined in or dropped altogether, many and possibly even most countries will adopt some form of the proposals, even if others don't. *The most important ramification is the death knell for the arm's length principle as we know it* – some of the threads will survive, but its universal application and the reasonable certainty that come with it will be gone [our emphasis].[52]

If this is even vaguely accurate, the effects on Tax Haven Ireland will be enormous.

THE IMPACT OF COVID-19

The crisis associated with Covid-19 could also have major implications for Tax Haven Ireland, as states everywhere look to protect their revenues from the oncoming disaster. This was certainly the case after the Great Recession and this time the stakes will be even higher. A recent report by the World Bank highlighted how widespread the crisis is likely to be, with more economies expected to face recession than in any crisis since 1870.[53] The same report emphasised how deep the crisis is likely to be, with developed states expected to contract by 8 per cent and those in the periphery by around 3 per cent.[54] One way to underline the severity of these numbers is to compare them to the worst year of the Great Recession. In 2009, global GDP fell by 0.1 per cent, while many of the emerging economies continued to grow strongly.[55] Reflecting on the scale of the current crisis, IMF chief economist Gita Gopinath stated that 'the magnitude and speed of collapse in activity is unlike anything experienced in our lifetimes and [is] likely to dwarf the losses associated with the Great Recession.'[56] When she wrote these lines, the IMF expected total losses of $9 trillion for 2020 and 2021. Just three months later, they had revised their forecast to $12.5 trillion, due to a 'larger than anticipated hit to activity during lockdown, economic scarring caused by disruption to supply chains and a loss in productivity from social distancing measures'.[57] In Ireland, the government expects a decline of roughly 10 per cent of GDP and a cost to the country of roughly €40 billion, but these figures come with a severe health warning.[58] No one really knows how damaging the crisis in the global system will be or how much disruption to business as normal will occur. Never before has the economy been shut down with such speed and severity in so many countries simultaneously. The IMF give a sense of the impending challenge:

This is a truly global crisis as no country is spared. Countries reliant on tourism, travel, hospitality, and entertainment for their growth are experiencing particularly large disruptions. Emerging market and developing economies face additional challenges with unprecedented reversals in capital flows as global risk appetite wanes and currency pressures, while coping with weaker health systems, and more limited fiscal space to provide support. Moreover, several economies entered this crisis in a vulnerable state with sluggish growth and high debt levels.[59]

The last point is particularly important. In the aftermath of the Great Recession, governments staved off a 1930s-style depression with aggressive use of monetary policy alongside brutal austerity. This eventually succeeded in stabilising the global economy, but despite having historically low labour costs, free money and an entire tax-dodging network at their disposal, multinationals have not engaged in high levels of investment and employment. Instead they have pumped extra money into share buy-back schemes and other forms of financial speculation. To give just one example, the Boeing Company, put in a claim to the US government for $60 billion to help them cope with the downturn in the airline industry. Yet over the last ten years the company has already received $60 billion in virtually free money, all of which was used either to buy back its own shares ($43 billion) or to give shareholder returns ($17 billion).[60] The key reason for this anomaly has been a tendency for profit rates to decline over many decades.

After the Second World War, profit rates were high enough to drive a cycle of investment and accumulation, even as interest rates increased to their normal levels.[61] Yet, this time around, anaemic profit rates have meant that most of the money sloshing around the system has been used to inflate asset prices, something Karl Marx defined as 'fictious capital'. It has also been used to keep an increasing number of zombie companies in operation. Using data for 32,000 enterprises across 14 developed economies, the Bank of International Settlements (BIS) tracked firms that are more than ten years old and unable to cover their 'debt servicing costs from current profits over an extended period'.[62] Their analysis demonstrated a sixfold increase in these so-called Zombie corporations, which have increased from just 2 per cent in the late 1980s to 12 per cent in 2018. In the US, the number rises to 18 per cent, as nearly one in five companies now survives on low interest rates in short-term money markets. No less telling, is the fact that each crisis in the neoliberal era has witnessed a proliferation of unprofitable firms that are never dealt with fully in the subsequent upswing.[63] The overall result has been a 'crowding out of real investment' with the BIS noting that past weakness in profitability is the strongest indicator of future profit difficulties.[64] In other words, unprofitable firms are increasingly clogging up the system, with global leaders caught between their fear of further contagion and their realisation that lower-than-normal interest rates are causing all manner of secondary complications – including a massive rise in corporate debt. The level of debt in America's corporate sector is currently at a record-breaking 75 per cent of GDP and among large American companies, debt burdens are precariously high in the automotive, hospitality and transportation sectors – industries taking a direct hit from Covid-19. The Chinese figures are similarly alarming, with corporate debt up 400 per cent to $21 trillion since the Great Recession, one tenth of which is in zombie firms which rely on government-directed lending to stay afloat.[65] An economy firing on all cylinders would find it difficult to cope with a shock like Covid-19, but with debt piling up and zombie companies already proliferating, this could cause the entire system to go into lockdown.

And if this were to happen, Tax Haven Ireland could well become a very weak link in an already weak chain. Despite half a decade of consistently strong headline growth, Ireland's gross national debt was four times higher in 2020 than it had been back in 2008. The combined effect of recapitalising banks and allowing corporations to dodge taxes on a grand scale – most infamously in refusing to take Apple's €13 billion in back taxes – meant that national debt remained stubbornly high throughout the recovery and is now set to increase significantly. Budget 2021 earmarked €18 billion in extra spending for example, with the government expecting that Covid-19-related measures will add €40 billion to the national debt over the coming period.[66] Household debt has declined with the growth of employment, but with debt levels of €29,000 per capita, they were still the sixth highest in the EU before the latest drop in employment.[67] This makes the country more vulnerable than it would otherwise be, thanks to the corporate friendly policies pursued after the Great Recession.[68]

The other major risk facing Tax Haven Ireland is its dependence on financial flows based on intangibles. As one of the world's most open economies, Ireland is likely to be disproportionately affected by the Covid-19 crisis and faces the possibility of hot money fleeing the IFSC in search of safe havens. Assessing these risk factors in 2019, the ICB noted that 'Ireland is exposed to disruptions to the international trading environment through its participation in global value chains... and is particularly exposed to abrupt shifts in international trading and tax arrangements.'[69] One of the most noticeable features of neoliberal globalisation has been the speed with which capital moves out of less-established financial centres at the first sign of distress. This was the pattern during the South-East Asian crisis in the late 1990s, for example, and, on a more modest scale recently, as funds flowed out of Mexico and Turkey back into the dollar. Ireland might legitimately regard itself as a more developed economy than either of the latter two, but the economy is heavily dependent on decisions by US executives with no loyalty to Ireland or its population.

Ireland's development strategy is therefore under increasing pressure at the same time as Brexit, a global health pandemic, a global economic crisis and a climate emergency pose historic challenges to the island and its people. We know the elites have no interest in change that challenges their power, but we also know that the current crises point towards the dire need for a different kind of society. Having insisted for decades on the sanctity of the market, our rulers have suddenly had to admit that private solutions are a barrier to the universal healthcare needed to tackle Covid-19; having insisted repeatedly that there is no money for housing and healthcare, they have suddenly found trillions to hand to their friends in big business; having insisted for decades that there is no such thing as society, they are now extolling the virtues of supporting the vulnerable; having glorified the wealthy as the heroes of society, they have suddenly had to rely on healthcare workers, warehouse operatives, retail workers and other members of the working classes to solve this crisis when the rich have become impotent.

In this environment of heightened risks and opportunities, it is time for working people to be bold and decisive. For a hundred years now, the Irish elites have controlled economic and political decisions to further their own agenda. Each time the pattern has been the same, moreover, as a model for development initially brings some minimal success before collapsing in unemployment and emigration. With Brexit happening and the world in turmoil, now is the time to move beyond the failed policies of Tax Haven Ireland in two decisive directions. On the one hand, we must move away from the economic terrorism of tax haven capitalism to a society that puts people before profit and the planet before the ruling classes. On the other hand, we must move away from the two reactionary states ushered in by British imperialism and upheld by the Irish border. In the years after the Great Recession, the Irish elites imposed their own agenda by bailing out banks, holding down wages and forcing austerity onto the general public.[70] This created a disastrous rise in child poverty and deprivation, but it also created a substantial recovery in wealth and higher incomes. Official statistics reveal that corporate profits and higher incomes more than doubled from 2013 to 2020 – at the same time as household wealth increased by nearly 80 per cent.[71] Much of this wealth remains in the hands of the very richest and with Brexit and Covid-19 interacting with economic and environmental catastrophe, now is the time to challenge the logic of tax haven capitalism through investment in public infrastructure and the establishment of national companies in banking, construction and environmental protection.

In a number of pre-budget submissions written for People Before Profit over the last few years, the current authors demonstrated the possibility of imposing targeted taxes on the richest 10 per cent of the population in order to renew our public services, repair the damage caused by the Great Recession and begin the move away from a high carbon, low justice, tax-dodging economy to one that respects the needs of people and the planet. Much of this analysis remains valid today, but as the scale of the crises become ever more daunting, so the policies needed to tackle them must become ever more radical.

Tax haven Ireland has been at the centre of everything wrong with global capitalism in the early part of the twenty-first century. It has enriched the few at the expense of the many, while tearing down democratic structures and fuelling a climate disaster that risks the lives of people, animals and future generations.[72] One hundred years ago, James Connolly invoked the downtrodden to take back the earth. In modern Ireland, this means nothing less than putting a stop to the capitalist theft represented by Tax Haven Ireland and building an eco-socialist movement to create a fairer society for all. It can, and must, be done.

Postscript

BEPS Agreement – The End of the Road?

On 1 July 2021, the OECD announced that 130 countries had reached an agreement to impose a 15 per cent minimum tax rate on corporations with turnover above €750 million per annum.[1] Coming after nearly a decade of negotiations, the agreement is the culmination of Pillar Two of the Inclusive Framework on Base Erosion and Profit Shifting (BEPS) and has the backing of the world's most powerful countries – the Group of Seven (G7) and the Group of Twenty (G20). It also represents more than 90 per cent of global GDP and is strongly supported by the Biden administration in the US. Heralding the significance of the deal, OECD Secretary General Mathias Cormann stated that, 'After years of intense work and negotiations, this historic package will ensure that large multinational companies pay their fair share of tax everywhere'.[2]

Worth an estimated €150 billion annually, the deal will tinker at the edges of the global evasion network rather than dismantling it – but it has put Ireland into a difficult situation, nevertheless. As noted in Chapter 9, Ireland has strategically deployed support for the BEPS initiative to cover its role in the tax evasion system. Government ministers refer to the Inclusive Framework as the only basis for a global agreement on taxation, but when it came to actually signing up, Ireland was among a handful of states that refused. The others were Barbados, Saint Vincent and The Grenadines – three Caribbean tax havens; two African states, Nigeria and Kenya; and two aspiring low tax destinations in Europe – Hungary and Estonia.[3] As usual, the Minister for Finance, Pascal Donohoe, made all the right noises about being committed to BEPS and acting constructively to meet any outstanding challenges, but Ireland has been weakened by such a public refusal to cooperate in the fight against tax avoidance.[4]

Why have the elites decided on this course when most offshore jurisdictions have signed up and headline rates can so easily be manipulated
to ensure companies pay a fraction of these amounts? Responding to the
reputational damage, Donohoe gave three reasons for Ireland's failure
to agree the deal: fears that the 15 per cent rate may be forced up over
time; worries about the reputational damage caused by moving away
from Ireland's current 12.5 per cent rate; defence of the rights of smaller
nations to engage in 'legitimate tax competition'.[5] These responses deliberately miss the *real politick* in Ireland's position, however.

As the world's major conduit for US profits from intellectual
property (IP), Ireland has made its stand with the imprimatur of the
US Chamber of Commerce to support business lobbyists in the United
States.[6] Although it is strongly supported by the Biden administration,
the OECD Agreement has not yet been ratified by Congress and with
strong opposition among Republicans, Ireland's stance is designed to aid
lobbyists meeting legislators on Capitol Hill. The idea is to signal how
damaging the proposals will be for US companies operating out of Ireland,
in the hope that this will convince some wavering representatives. The
deal will be fatally undermined without American support, so Ireland is
adding its weight to the efforts of corporate lobbyists, while hedging its
bets until the US position becomes clearer. Running alongside the BEPS
process, corporate America is also involved in a separate tug-of-war with
Biden over proposed reforms that would reverse decades of favourable
tax treatment for the corporate sector. These include increasing the
minimum corporation tax rate from 21 to 28 per cent, repeal of laws
that reduce US corporation taxes on foreign intangible profits, and a
doubling of the Global Intangible Low Tax Income (GILTI) rate from
10.5 per cent to 21 per cent.[7] Success in one part of Biden's strategy will
create momentum in the other, defeat in one will make the other more
challenging, so the Irish establishment are willing to take some reputational damage in the hope that they can support their offshore partners
in the US multinationals.

Complementing the strategy to tackle base erosion outlined above,
Pillar One of the Agreement is focused on profit shifting by corporations
with a global turnover above €20 billion and before-tax-profits above

10 per cent.[8] Under the current rules, multinationals increasingly locate the bulk of their IP in low tax jurisdictions before allocating the bulk of their profits to these same destinations. This creates an anomaly in the system, however, as high tax countries get relatively little revenue, despite the fact that the majority of profits are derived within their borders. To address this anomaly, Pillar One allows between 20–30 per cent of residual profits (above the base line of 10 per cent), to be reallocated to countries where multinational users and customers are located, provided the company derives at least €1 million within that jurisdiction.[9] This means companies can no longer avoid taxes where they have no IP or physical infrastructure, forcing some realignment of the system overall. Explaining Ireland's decision to accept Pillar One, Minister Donohoe said that despite the fact that it will cost Ireland €2 billion annually in lost revenue, this is a price worth paying for the fairness, transparency and global stability that the deal will deliver.[10]

If the state loses 20 per cent of its corporation tax revenue through explicitly anti-avoidance measures, this surely vindicates our claim that Ireland has been, and remains, a central location for profit shifting by US multinationals. Yet before this part of the Agreement can actually come into force, it requires a complex legal instrument which leaves plenty of time to water it down as the deadline draws closer.[11] The Agreement is also viewed by corporate America as the lesser of two evils, as it is expected to replace the European Commission's Digital Tax Initiative, which itself is designed to take 3 per cent of all corporate earnings and is therefore considerably more difficult to avoid.[12] The Irish state wants neither an anti-shifting rule nor a tax on digital revenues, but it is far more comfortable with the OECD proposal than with unilateral moves by the European Commission.

So, have we finally entered a brave new world, where, as Mathias Cormann claims, 'large multinational companies pay their fair share of tax everywhere'? When even the OECD predict that their anti-profit-shifting measure will reallocate just €100 billion annually, we remain to be convinced.[13] Despite the fanfare and the increased challenges to its practices, Tax Haven Ireland will likely survive the latest OECD initiative with intense backroom lobbying, slick media performances and the backing of Corporate America. What it will find harder to survive, however, is an increasingly angry population forced to live with the fall out in housing, healthcare and education. These are the people we put our faith in. These are the people we fight alongside to change Ireland for the better.

Notes

INTRODUCTION

1. T. R. Tørsløv, L. S. Wier and G. Zucman. 'The Missing Profits of Nations. National Bureau of Economic Research'. Working Paper 24701 http://www.nber.org/papers/w24701.
2. Central Statistics Office. 'Statistical Year Book of Ireland 2019'. www.cso.ie/en/releasesandpublications/ep/p-syi/statisticalyearbookofireland2019/bus/businessinireland/.

1 PORN, TAX DODGING AND EXPLOITATION

1. 'An Irishman's Diary on Arthur Cox – Solicitor, Senator and Priest'. *Irish Times*. 10 March 2015.
2. *Ibid.*
3. T. Basu. 'Porn Site Offers $25,000 Scholarship for Answering "How do you strive to make others happy?"'. *Time.* 2 September 2015.
4. 'Inside Pornhub's Crusade to Tear Down the Barriers on Watching Sex Online'. *Adweek.* 18 December 2014. www.adweek.com/brand-marketing/inside-pornhubs-crusade-tear-down-taboos-watching-sex-online-161910/.
5. G. Dines. *Pornland: How Porn Hijacked Our Sexuality*. Boston. Beacon Press. 2011.
6. A.J. Bridges et al. 'Aggression and Sexual Behaviour in Best-Selling Porn Videos: A Content Analysis Update'. *Violence Against Women*. Vol. 16, No. 1, 2010, pp. 1065–85.
7. K. Forrester. 'Making Sense of Modern Pornography'. *New Yorker.* 26 September 2016.
8. 'Interview with Fabian Thylmann'. www.eu-startups.com/2016/09/interview-with-fabian-thylmann-the-german-entrepreneur-who-once-built-the-biggest-adult-entertainment-company-in-the-world/.
9. M. Bergeron, 'The MindGeek Enigma: From Luxembourg to Montreal'. *La Presse.* 10 October 2016.
10. D. Gusovsky. 'Taxes, Multinational Firms and Luxembourg Revealed'. *CNBC.* 6 November 2014. www.cnbc.com/2014/11/06/taxes-multinational-firms-luxembourgrevealed.html.
11. P. Hamilton. 'Pornography Company Records €19 Million Profit at Irish Arm'. *Irish Times.* 3 January 2018.

12. 'Dublin-based Firm Collected €356 Million in Revenue from Porn Subscriptions'. *The Journal*. 28 August 2017.

13. R. Wood. 'Ten Notorious Tax Cheats: Queen of Medan Leona Helmsley Proves Little People Can Put You in Jail'. *Forbes*. 17 April 2017.

14. Leahy O'Riordan Taxation Service. www.leahy.ie/taxation-service (accessed 30 June 2018).

15. *Ibid.*

16. 'JP McManus Charitable Foundation Donated €1.7m'. *Irish Times*. 3 August 2017.

17. 'McManus Paid No Irish Tax for 20 Years'. *Sunday Times*. 5 June 2016.

18. F. Reddan. 'Ireland's Tax Exiles Now Number over 3,000'. *Irish Times*. 10 April 2015.

19. 'JP McManus Versus United States: Tax Refund Suit RCFC 56 Summary Judgement No 15-946T. 3 March 2017.

20. S. Carroll. '10 Wealthy Non-resident Irish Citizens Paid €200,000 Domicile Levy in 2011'. *Irish Times*. 23 November 2012.

21. Dail Debates, Parliamentary Question. 13 July 2017.

22. 'New Report Shows That 83 of Ireland's Wealthiest People Pay Lower Rate of Income Tax Than the Average Worker'. *The Journal*. 29 September 2018. www.thejournal.ie/ireland-rich-taxpayers-hwi-2015-4260493-Sep2018/.

23. Companies Registration Office Annual Report 2017.

24. Statistic and Research Branch, Revenue Commissioners, *Corporation Tax 2017 Payments and 2016 Returns*. Dublin. Revenue Commissioners. 2018.

25. 'Ireland's Reliance on Just 5 Multinationals Is a Threat to the Economy'. *Irish Times*. 1 August 2018. www.irishtimes.com/business/economy/ireland-s-reliance-on-five-huge-multinationals-is-a-threat-to-the-economy-1.3582410.

26. EU Commission. *2020 European Semester Ireland: Country Report*. Brussels. EU Commission. 2020, p. 29.

27. Statistical Yearbook of Ireland 2019. www.cso.ie/en/releasesandpublications/ep/p-syi/statisticalyearbookofireland2019/bus/businessinireland/.

28. Corporation Tax 2019 Payments and 2018 Returns. www.revenue.ie/en/corporate/documents/research/ct-analysis-2020.pdf.

29. International Consortium of Investigative Journalists Lux Leaks Data Base. www.icij.org/investigations/luxembourg-leaks/explore-documents-luxembourg-leaks-database/.

30. C. Keena. 'Sisk Family Routed Money through Luxembourg'. *Irish Times*. 6 November 2014.

2 GLOBAL PLUNDER

1. N. Shaxson. *Treasure Islands: Tax Havens and the Men Who Stole the World*. London. Vintage. 2012, p. 17.

2. *Ibid.*, p. 17.

3. R. Peet. *Unholy Trinity: The IMF, World Bank and WTO*. London. Zed Books. 2009, p. 105.

4. A. Shah. 'Structural Adjustment: A Major Cause of Poverty'. www.globalissues. org/article/3/structural-adjustment-a-major-cause-of-poverty; www.oxfam ireland.org/blog/tax-dodging.

5. S. Killian. 'Mantras and Myths: A True Picture of the Corporation Tax System in Ireland'. 2017, p. 3. www.oxfamireland.org/sites/default/files/upload/pdfs/ mantras-myths-final.pdf.

6. L. Trotsky. *The Permanent Revolution and Results and Prospects*. London. Well Red Books. 2004, p. 169.

7. R. Palan, R. Murphy and C. Chavagneux. *Tax Havens: How Globalization Really Works*. Ithaca. Cornell University Press. 2010, p. 118.

8. G. Zucman. *The Hidden Wealth of Nations: The Scourge of Tax Havens*. Chicago. The University of Chicago Press. 2015, p. 9.

9. *Ibid.*, p. 13.

10. Shaxson. *Treasure Islands*, pp. 184, 192.

11. Palan et al. *Tax Havens*, p. 111; Shaxson. *Treasure Islands*, p. 53.

12. J. Garcia-Bernardo et al. 'Uncovering Offshore Financial Centres: Conduits and Sinks in the Global Corporate Ownership Network'. *Nature*. Vol. 7, Article No. 6246, 2017. www.nature.com/articles/s41598-017-06322-9.

13. T. Norfield. *The City: London and the Global Power of Finance*. Verso. London. 2016, p. 108.

14. P. Savona and G. Sutija. *Euro Dollars and International Banking*. London. Macmillan Publishers. 1985.

15. Norfield. *The City*, p. 49.

16. Palan et al. *Tax Havens*, p. 139.

17. Shaxson. *Treasure Islands*, p. 252.

18. Palan et al. *Tax Havens*, p. 135.

19. 'Addicted to Tax Havens: The Secret Life of the FTSE 100'. www.actionaid.org. uk/sites/default/files/doc_lib/addicted_to_tax_havens.pdf.

20. D. Harvey. *A Brief History of Neoliberalism*. Oxford. Oxford University Press. 2005, p. 19.

21. *Ibid.*, pp. 41–4.

22. Shaxson. *Treasure Islands*, p. 83.

23. *Ibid.*

24. B. O'Boyle. 'Reproducing the Social Structure: A Marxist Critique of Anthony Giddens's Structuration Methodology'. *Cambridge Journal of Economics*. Vol. 37, No. 5, 2013, pp. 1019–33.

25. K. Pomerleau. 'Corporate Income Tax Rates Around the World 2014'. www. taxfoundation.org/corporate-income-tax-rates-around-world-2014.

26. Palan et al. *Tax Havens*, p. 154.

27. Harvey. *Brief History of Neoliberalism*, p. 26; Margaret Thatcher Foundation. www.margaretthatcher.org/document/109497.

28. D. Dorling. *Inequality and the 1%*. London. Verso. 2015, p. 18.

29. Shaxson. *Treasure Islands*, p. 77.

30. D. Hardoon. 'An Economy for the 99%'. Oxfam. 2017. www.oxfam.org/sites/ www.oxfam.org/files/file_attachments/bp-economy-for-99-percent-160117-summ-en.pdf.

31. *Ibid.*, p. 9.

32. C.E Altamura. 'Recycling Oil Wealth: European Banks, the Eurodollar Market and the Latin American Debt Boom of the 1970s'. Unpublished PhD thesis. www.worldbhc.org/files/full%20program/A4_B4_RecyclingOilWealthWBHC. pdf, p. 12.

33. Peet. *Unholy Trinity*, p. 66.

34. D. Budhoo. 'IMF/World Bank Wreak Havoc on the Third World'. In K. Danahar, *50 Years Is Enough*. Boston. South End Press. 1999, pp. 20–1; Peet. *Unholy Trinity*, p. 105.

35. Harvey. *Brief History of Neoliberalism*, p. 89.

36. Altamura. 'Recycling Oil Wealth', pp. 1, 9.

37. *Ibid.*

38. Palan et al. *Tax Havens*, p. 62.

39. *Ibid.* p. 63.

40. Zucman. *Hidden Wealth of Nations*, p. 35.

41. Palan et al. *Tax Havens*, p. 63.

42. UNESCO Report, *Eliminating Unhealthy Water/Providing Clean Water for All*. www.unesco.org/education/tlsf/mods/theme_a/interact/www.worldgame.org/ wwwproject/what04.shtml.

43. *Ibid.*

44. R. Murphy. *Dirty Secrets: How Tax Havens Destroy the Economy*. London. Verso. 2017, p. 111.

45. *Ibid.*, p. 107.

46. Palan et al. *Tax Havens*, p. 66.

47. *Ibid.*

48. *Ibid.*

49. Murphy. *Dirty Secrets*, p. 109.

50. *Ibid.*, pp. 116–18.

51. 'Panama Paper: Europol Links 3,500 Names to Suspected Criminals'. www. theguardian.com/news/2016/dec/01/panama-papers-europol-links-3500-names-to-suspected-criminals.

52. 'Fund Run by David Cameron's Father Avoided Paying Tax in Britain'. www. theguardian.com/news/2016/apr/04/panama-papers-david-cameron-father-tax-bahamas.

53. B. Obermayer and F. Obermaier. *The Panama Paper: Breaking the Story of How the Rich and Powerful Hide Their Money*. London. One World Books. 2016, p. 332.

54. 'Cameron Stepped in to Protect Offshore Trusts from EU Crackdown in 2013'. www.theguardian.com/politics/2016/apr/07/david-cameron-offshore-trusts-eu-tax-crackdown-2013.

55. Shaxson. *Treasure Islands*, p. 129.

56. A. Maingot. 'Offshore Secrecy Centres and the Necessary Role of States: Bucking the Trend'. *Journal of Interamerican Studies and World Affairs*. Vol. 37, No. 4, 1995, pp. 1–24.

57. *Ibid.*

58. 'HSBC to Pay $1.9 billion Fine in U.S Money Laundering Case'. www.reuters.com/article/us-hsbc-probe-idUSBRE8BA05M20121211.

59. 'Who Is Behind Mexico's Drug Related Violence'. www.bbc.com/news/world-latin-america-10681249.

60. 'HSBC to Pay $1.9 Billion Fine'.

61. Shaxson. *Treasure Islands*, p. 19.

62. 'Western Banks, Terrorism and IS: The Nihilism of Dark Finance Fuelling Global Insecurity'. www.ibtimes.co.uk/western-banks-terrorism-isis-nihilism-dark-finance-fuelling-global-insecurity-1474508.

63. *Ibid.*

64. Shaxson. *Treasure Islands*, p. 27.

65. J. Stewart. 'Low Tax Financial Centres and the Financial Crisis: The Case of the Irish Financial Services Centre'. *Institute for International Integration Studies (IIIS) Discussion Paper Series*. No. 420, January 2013, pp. 1–22.

66. *Ibid.*, p. 2.

67. *Ibid.*, p. 3.

68. 'Madoff Probe Focuses on Tax Havens'. www.theguardian.com/business/2008/dec/28/bernard-madoff-fraud-investigation-offshore.

69. Stewart. 'Low Tax Financial Centres', p. 5.

70. 'Madoff Probe Focuses on Tax Havens'.

71. 'Banking Bailout: The Rise and Fall of RBS'. www.telegraph.co.uk/finance/newsbysector/banksandfinance/4291807/Banking-bailout-The-rise-and-fall-of-RBS.html.

72. 'RBS Avoided £500 million in Tax in Global Deals'. www.theguardian.com/business/2009/mar/13/rbs-tax-avoidance.

73. 'Depfa Saga Ends but at What Cost to Germany'. www.irishtimes.com/business/financial-services/depfa-saga-ends-but-at-what-cost-to-germany-1.2042911.

74. Stewart. 'Low Tax Financial Centres and the Financial Crisis', p. 15.

75. *Ibid.*, p. 4.

3 MAKING TREASURE IRELAND

1. See, for example, S. Dorgan. 'How Ireland Became a Celtic Tiger'. The Heritage Foundation. 2006. www.heritage.org/europe/report/how-ireland-became-the-celtic-tiger; S. Grimes and P. Collins. 'Building a Knowledge Economy in Ireland through European Research Networks'. 2002. www.doi.org/10.1080/09654310303641.

2. J. Knirck. *Afterimage of the Revolution: Cumann na nGaedheal and Irish Politics, 1922–1932*. Madison. University of Wisconsin Press. 2014, p. 43.

3. 'British Parliamentary Report: Enclosing the Land'. www.parliament.uk/about/living-heritage/transformingsociety/towncountry/landscape/overview/enclosingland/.

4. K. Marx. 'Letter to Sigfrid and August Meyer, 9 April 1870'. In K. Marx and F. Engels, *Selected Correspondence*. Moscow. Progress Publishers. 1975, pp. 220–4.

5. C. Van Egeraat and P. Breathnach. 'The Manufacturing Sector'. In B. Bartley and R. Kitchin, *Understanding Contemporary Ireland*. London. Pluto Press. 2007, p. 128.

6. History Ireland. 'Food Exports from Ireland 1846–47'. www.historyireland.com/18th-19th-century-history/food-exports-from-ireland-1846-47/.

7. K.A. Kennedy, T. Giblin and D. McHugh. *The Economic Development of Ireland in the Twentieth Century*. London. Routledge. 1988, p. 36.

8. P. Kirby. *Celtic Tiger in Collapse: Explaining the Weaknesses of the Irish Model*. New York. Palgrave Macmillan. 2010, p. 16.

9. J. Haughton. 'Historical Background'. In J. O'Hagan and C. Neman, *The Economy of Ireland: National and Sectoral Policy Issues*. Dublin. Gill and Macmillan. 2008, p. 14.

10. Kennedy et al. *Economic Development of Ireland in the Twentieth Century*, p. 36.

11. C. McCabe. *Sins of the Father: The Decisions That Shaped the Irish Economy*. Dublin. The History Press Ireland. 2014, p. 141.

12. *Ibid.*, p. 142.

13. Kennedy et al. *Economic Development of Ireland in the Twentieth Century*, p. 37.

14. K. Allen. 'Into the Lime Light: Tax Haven Ireland'. *Irish Marxist Review*, Vol. 5, No. 16, 2016, p. 15.

15. Kennedy et al. *Economic Development of Ireland in the Twentieth Century*, p. 48.

16. Allen. 'Into the Lime Light', p. 15.

17. M. Daly. 'The Fianna Fáil Economic Revolution'. In M. Daly, *Industrial Development and Irish National Identity, 1922–1939*. Syracuse. Syracuse University Press. 1992, pp. 59–74. www.jstor.org/stable/pdf/j.ctv64h6t9.9.pdf?refreqid=excelsior%3A9cad8e8789198443e4096c0e601f72c4.

18. Kennedy et al. *Economic Development of Ireland in the Twentieth Century*, p. 44.

19. Allen. 'Into the Limelight', p. 15.

20. Van Egeraat and Breathnach. 'The Manufacturing Sector', p. 129.

21. Daly. 'The Fianna Fáil Economic Revolution', p. 70.

22. Sean McEntee papers, P 67/350/10 UCD Archives.

23. McCabe. *Sins of the Father*, p. 150.

24. E.O. Malley. *Industry and Economic Development*. Dublin. Gill and Macmillan. 1989, p. 68; Haughton. 'Historical Background', p. 20.

25. C. Keena. *The Ansbacher Conspiracy*. Dublin. Gill and Macmillan. 2003, p. 10.

26. *Ibid.*, p. 65.

27. *Ibid.*, p. 63.

28. Clancy Emma. 'Irish State Marketed for Tax Avoidance since the 1950s'. 2016. www.emmaclancy.com/2016/07/30/irish-state-marketed-for-tax-avoidance-since-1950s/.

29. S. Coffey. 'Review of Ireland's Corporation Tax Code: Presented to the Minister for Finance and Public Expenditure and Reform'. 2017, p. 14. www.finance.gov. ie/wp-content/uploads/2017/09/170912-Review-of-Irelands-Corporation-Tax-Code.pdf.

30. *Ibid.*

31. 'How Foreign Firms Transformed the Irish Economy'. www.irishtimes.com/ business/how-foreign-firms-transformed-ireland-s-domestic-economy-1.1593462.

32. Kirby. *Celtic Tiger in Collapse*, p. 20.

33. F. Barry. 'Industrialisation Strategies for Developing Countries: Lessons from the Irish Experience'. *Development Policy Review*, Vol. 9, No. 1, 1991, p. 85.

34. P.J. Drudy. 'Housing: The Case for a New Philosophy'. 2005, p. 42. www. socialjustice.ie/sites/default/files/attach/publication/3296/4pjdrudy.pdf.

35. *Ibid.*, p. 109.

36. *Ibid.*, p. 107.

37. P.J. Drudy and M. Punch. *Out of Reach: Inequalities in the Irish Housing System*. Dublin. New Island Press. 2005, p. 15.

38. *Ibid.*, p. 25.

39. Keena. *Ansbacher Conspiracy*, p. 42.

40. F. McDonald and K. Sheridan. *The Builders*. London. Penguin Books. 2009, p. 25.

41. *Ibid.*, p. 25.

42. McCabe. *Sins of the Father*, p. 31.

43. M. Norris and T Fahey. 'From Asset Based Welfare to Welfare Housing? The Changing Function of Social Housing in Ireland', *Housing Studies*. Vol. 26, No. 3, pp. 459–69.

44. McDonald and Sheridan. *Builders*, p. 26.

45. *Ibid.*, p. 78.

46. For some useful details on this period, see F. Barry. 'Politics, Institutions and Post War Growth in Ireland'. 2006. www.helsinki.fi/iehc2006/papers1/Barry. pdf.

47. *Ibid.*, p. 76.

48. *Ibid.*, p. 82.

49. F. O'Toole. *Ship of Fools: How Stupidity and Corruption Sank the Celtic Tiger*. London. Faber and Faber. 2009, p. 27.

50. *Ibid.*, p. 44.

51. *Ibid.*

52. '£7,000 TD's Salary Stand-First Proved Small Beer to Haughey'. www. irishtimes.com/news/7-000-td-s-salary-stand-first-proved-small-beer-to-haughey-1.296167.

53. Keena. *Ansbacher Conspiracy*, p. 46.

54. *Ibid.*, p. 35.

55. O'Toole. *Ship of Fools*, p. 62.

56. 'Dermot Desmond on the IFSC Past and Future'. Finance-Magazine.com. www. finance-magazine.com/display_article.php?i=2300&pi=142.

57. L. Murphy. 'Financial Engine or Glorified Back Office? Dublin's International Financial Services Centre Going Global'. *Area*. Vol. 30, No. 2, 1998, p. 160.

58. J. Stewart. Low Tax Financial Centres and the Financial Crisis: The Case of the Irish Financial Services Centre IIIS Discussion Paper No 420/Jan 2013 p. 7.

59. Murphy. 'Financial Engine or Glorified Back Office?', p. 161.

60. *Ibid.*, p. 161.

61. *Ibid.*, p. 161.

62. Kirby. *Celtic Tiger in Collapse*, p. 34.

63. Dorgan. 'How Ireland Became a Celtic Tiger'.

64. S. O'Riain. 'Falling Over the Competitive Edge'. In M. Peillon and M.P. Corcoran (eds), *Place and Non-Place: The Reconfiguration of Ireland*. Dublin. Institute of Public Administration. 2004, p. 36.

65. *Ibid.*, p. 35.

66. Kirby. *Celtic Tiger in Collapse*, p. 35.

67. J. Stewart. 'Low Tax Financial Centres and the Financial Crisis: The Case of the Irish Financial Services Centre', *Institute for International Integration Studies (IIIS) Discussion Paper Series*, No. 420, January 2013, p. 6.

68. R. Palan, R. Murphy and C. Chavagneux. *Tax Havens: How Globalization Really Works*. Ithaca. Cornell University Press. 2010, p. 67.

69. Stewart. 'Low Tax Financial Centres and the Financial Crisis', p. 6.

70. *Ibid.*

71. *Ibid.*, p. 55.

72. K. Allen with B. O'Boyle. *Austerity Ireland: The Failure of Irish Capitalism*. London. Pluto Press. 2013, p. 74.

73. O'Toole. *Ship of Fools*, p. 102.

74. O'Toole. *Ship of Fools*, p. 87.

75. S. Ross. *The Bankers: How the Banks Brought Ireland to Its Knees*. Dublin. Penguin Ireland. 2009, p. 123.

76. M. Coakley. *Ireland in the World Order: A History of Uneven Development*. London. Pluto Press. 2012, p. 170.

77. P. Honohon. 'Resolving Ireland's Banking Crisis'. *The Economic and Social Review*. Vol. 40, No. 2, 2009, p. 218.

78. *Ibid.*, p. 263.

79. *Ibid.*

80. See the following article for more details: www.researchrepository.ucd.ie/ bitstream/10197/1447/1/Commission_on_Taxation_Report_2009.pdf.

4   DIRTY SECRETS

1. T. R. Tørsløv, L. S. Wier and G. Zucman. 'The Missing Profits of Nations. National Bureau of Economic Research'. Working Paper 24701 http://www.nber. org/papers/w24701.

2. *Ibid.*
3. *Ibid.*, p. 2.
4. This information was estimated using the average wages in both the multinational and domestic sectors and assuming that profits in both should be 35 per cent of this total. The relevant information can be found in the following reports: www.revenue.ie/en/corporate/documents/research/ct-analysis-2019.pdf, p. 1, and www.idaireland.com/getmedia/a4a188d7-e067-4c6d-8d00-ab771bd7122d/IDA_Annual_Report_2018.pdf.aspx, p. 2.
5. Central Statistics Office. 'Statistical Year Book of Ireland 2019'. www.cso.ie/en/releasesandpublications/ep/p-syi/statisticalyearbookofireland2019/bus/businessinireland/.
6. L. McCarthy. 'Corporation Tax Returns 2018 Payments and 2017 Returns'. www.revenue.ie/en/corporate/documents/research/ct-analysis-2019.pdf.
7. *Ibid.*, p. 7.
8. J. Garcia-Bernardo et al. 'Uncovering Offshore Financial Centres: Conduits and Sinks in the Global Corporate Ownership Network'. *Nature.* Vol. 7, Article No. 6246, 2017. www.nature.com/articles/s41598-017-06322-9.
9. *Ibid.*, pp. 6–9.
10. D. Mackenzie and A. Coghlan. 'Revealed – the Capitalist Network That Runs the World'. *New Scientist.* 2011. www.newscientist.com/article/mg21228354-500-revealed-the-capitalist-network-that-runs-the-world/.
11. Garcia-Bernardo et al. 'Uncovering Offshore Financial Centres', p. 1.
12. United Nations Conference on Trade and Development. '80% of Trade Takes Place in "Value Chains" Linked to Transnational Corporations, UNCTAD Report Says'. 2013. www.unctad.org/en/pages/PressRelease.aspx?OriginalVersionID=113.
13. L. Voytko. 'Shell Companies Hide $15 Trillion from Taxes, Study Reports'. *Forbes Magazine.* 2019. www.forbes.com/sites/lisettevoytko/2019/09/09/shell-companies-hide-15-trillion-from-taxes-study-reports/#368c7be67269.
14. Tørsløv et al. 'The Missing Profits of Nations', pp. 3, 20.
15. Garcia-Bernardo et al. 'Uncovering Offshore Financial Centres', p. 6.
16. *Ibid.*, p. 5.
17. *Ibid.*, p. 6.
18. R. Avi-Yonah. 'International Tax Evasion: What Can be Done?' *The American Prospect.* 2016. www.prospect.org/power/international-tax-evasion-can-done/.
19. A. Mitchell. 'What Is a "Check-the-Box" Election'. 2010. www.intltax.typepad.com/intltax_blog/2010/06/what-is-a-checkthebox-election.html.
20. See the Taxes Consolidation Act 1997 for more details: www.oireachtas.ie/en/bills/bill/1997/42/. We look at the implications of the changes to the securitisation industry in Chapter 6 and Chapter 8.
21. Taxes Consolidation Act. 1997, p. 94. www.data.oireachtas.ie/ie/oireachtas/act/1997/39/eng/enacted/a3997a.pdf.
22. Industrial Development Authority. 'Taxation in Ireland 2016'. 2016, p. 3. www.idaireland.com/newsroom/publications/taxation_ireland.

23. 'Double Tax Treaties: Irish Revenue Commissioners'. www.revenue.ie/en/tax-professionals/documents/commentary-irishtaxtreaties.pdf.
24. J. Duffy, J. Ryan and K. Stapleton. 'Transfer Pricing Overview'. Matheson. 2010, p. 180. www.matheson.com/images/uploads/documents/Transfer_Pricing_Ireland.pdf; A&L Goodbody. 'Guide to Investing in Ireland: Taxation'. p. 1. www.algoodbody.com/media/Taxationv21.pdf.
25. 'Ireland's Double Tax Treaty Network: An Update in 2 Minutes'. www.pearse-trust.ie/blog/irelands-double-taxation-treaty-network-update.
26. Revenue Commissioners. 'Summary of Corporation Tax Returns'. 2019. www.revenue.ie/en/corporate/documents/statistics/income-distributors/corporation-tax-calculation.pdf.
27. IDA Ireland. 'IDA Ireland 2018 Results: Highest number Ever Employed in the Multinational Sector – 229,057'. www.idaireland.com/newsroom/ida-ireland-2018-results-highest-number-ever-emp.
28. *Ibid.*
29. Tørsløv et al. 'The Missing Profits of Nations'.
30. Revenue Commissioners. 'Summary of Corporation Tax Returns', p. 3.
31. R. Palan, R. Murphy and C. Chavagneux. *Tax Havens: How Globalization Really Works*. Ithaca. Cornell University Press. 2010, p. 63.
32. M. Brehm Christensen and E. Clancy. 'Exposed: Apple's Golden Delicious Tax Deals'. 2018, p. 44. www.sinnfein.ie/files/2018/Apple_Tax_Deals_report_final_21.06_.18_.pdf.
33. *Ibid.*
34. S. Killian. 'Mantras and Myths: A True Picture of the Corporate Tax System in Ireland'. 2017, p. 6. www.oxfamireland.org/sites/default/files/upload/pdfs/mantras-myths-final.pdf.
35. A&L Goodbody. 'Guide to Investing in Ireland: Taxation', p. 1.
36. J. Duffy and T. Bailey. 'The Anti-Tax Avoidance Directive: Winds of Change or an Easterly Breeze'. Matheson. 2016, p. 107. www.matheson.com/images/uploads/documents/The_Anti-Tax_Avoidance_Directive_in_Ireland_-_Winds_of_Change_or_an_Easterly_Breeze.pdf.
37. *Ibid.*
38. *Ibid.*
39. Dillon Eustace. 'Holding Companies in Ireland'. www.dilloneustace.com/download/1/Publications/Tax/Holding%20Companies%20in%20Ireland.pdf.
40. P.K. Schmidt. 'Taxation of Controlled Foreign Companies in the Context of the OECD/G20 Project on Base Erosion and Profit Shifting'. *Nordic Tax Journal*. No. 2, 2016, p. 89.
41. Oxfam. 'Analysis of Ireland's Corporation Tax Roadmap'. p. 7. www.oxfamireland.org/sites/default/files/ireland_s_corporate_tax_roadmap_final.pdf.
42. Dillon Eustace. 'Holding Companies in Ireland', p. 2.
43. PricewaterhouseCoopers. 'World Wide Taxes Summary: Corporate Withholding Taxes'. https://www.taxsummaries.pwc.com/ID/Ireland-Corporate-Withholding-taxes.

44. Industrial Development Authority. 'Taxation in Ireland 2016', p. 9.

45. *Ibid.*, p. 9.

46. PricewaterhouseCoopers. 'World Wide Taxes Summary'.

47. *Ibid.*

48. R. Duffy. 'Fine Gael Ministers Discussed US Corporations "Paying Little or No Tax Here" in the 1980s'. 2018. www.thejournal.ie/tax-arrangements-state-papers-4405807-Dec2018/.

49. IFSC. 'John Bruton to Become Chairman of IFSC Ireland Commencing September 1 2010'. *IFSC Newsletter*. www.ifsc.ie/article.aspx?idnews=45721.

50. Tørsløv et al. 'The Missing Profits of Nations', p. 31.

51. Wikipedia is an excellent resource on the Irish tax Haven. Much of the following comes from information gleaned from the following website: www.en.wikipedia.org/wiki/Double_Irish_arrangement.

52. J. Drucker. 'Controversial Tax Strategies Brain Child of O'Rourke's Son'. *Irish Independent*. 2013. www.independent.ie/business/irish/controversial-tax-strat-egies-brainchild-of-orourkes-son-29721835.html.

53. C. Humphries. 'Government Says "Not to Blame for Apple's Low Tax Rate"'. *Irish Independent*. 2013. www.independent.ie/business/irish/government-says-not-to-blame-for-apples-low-tax-rate-29284001.html.

54. P. Bodkin. 'The Double Irish Is Dead, Long Live the "Knowledge Development Box"'. 2014. www.thejournal.ie/double-irish-dead-1723096-Oct2014/.

55. M. Lewis. 'Impossible Structure: Tax Outcomes Overlooked by 2015 Tax Spillover Analysis'. 2017, pp. 5, 6. www.christianaid.ie/sites/default/files/2018-02/impossible-structures-tax-report.pdf.

56. Bodkin. 'The Double Irish Is Dead'.

57. *Ibid.*

58. J.L. Rubinger and S. Ayers Le Pree. 'Death of the Double Irish Dutch Sandwich: Not So Fast'. www.taxeswithoutbordersblog.com/2014/10/death-of-the-double-irish-dutch-sandwich-not-so-fast/.

59. Lewis. 'Impossible Structure'.

60. M. Carty. 'Ireland's Tax Deals with Apple Under the Spotlight in European Parliament'. www.sinnfein.ie/contents/47370. 2017.

61. Lewis. 'Impossible Structure', pp. 5, 6.

62. *Ibid.*

63. F. Daly et al. 'Commission on Taxation Report 2009'. www.researchrepository.ucd.ie/bitstream/10197/1447/1/Commission_on_Taxation_Report_2009.pdf.

64. 'Capital Allowances for Intangible Assets Under Section 291A of the TCA 1997'. www.revenue.ie/en/tax-professionals/tdm/income-tax-capital-gains-tax-corporation-tax/part-09/09-02-05.pdf.

65. Daly et al. 'Commission on Taxation Report 2009'.

66. KPMG. 'Intellectual Property Tax'. Quoted in the following: www.en.wikipedia.org/wiki/Double_Irish_arrangement.

67. Brehm Christensen and Clancy. 'Exposed: Apple's Golden Delicious Tax Deals', p. 5.

68. *Ibid.*, p. 6

69. The Wikipedia entry on this issue is particularly impressive, as well as its analysis of Tax Haven Ireland more generally. See www.en.wikipedia.org/wiki/ Ireland_as_a_tax_haven#:~:text=Ireland%20has%20been%20labelled%20 a,via%20their%20tax%20treaty%20network and www.en.wikipedia.org/wiki/ Double_Irish_arrangement for more details.

70. www.en.wikipedia.org/wiki/Ireland_as_a_tax_haven#:~:text=Ireland%20 has%20been%20labelled%20a,via%20their%20tax%20treaty%20network.

71. The figures in this table differ slightly from the earlier one due to the approximate nature of the figures available and our need to simplify. However, the key line of argument does not rest on specific figures – which vary slightly in different official reports, but on the overall trends across these reports.

72. Industrial Development Authority. 'Taxation in Ireland 2016', p. 8

73. Revenue Commissioners. 'Summary of Corporation Tax Returns', pp. 1–3.

74. *Ibid.*

75. *Ibid.*

5 THE FIXERS

1. 'Dublin Moves to Block Controversial Tax Gambit'. *Wall Street Journal*. 15 October 2015.

2. C. Keena. 'Report Shines Harsh Light on Dunne's Link with Haughey'. *Irish Times*. 22 December 2006.

3. Irish Funds Industry Association. www.ifsc.ie/company.aspx?idcategory=96 &idcompany=235.

4. Quoted in TASC. *Tax Justice: Following the Tax Trail*. Dublin. TASC. 2012, p. 19.

5. Revenue Commissioners. *Tax and Duty Manual 37-00-00a*. The Revenue Technical Service. p. 12.

6. 'Section 110 of the New Finance Bill Will Help the Irish Securitisation Industry Play Catch Up'. *Finance Dublin.Com*, March 2003.

7. Matheson. *Irish Tax Firm of the Year*. Dublin, 2016.

8. Matheson. *The Knowledge Development Box: Public Consultation*. Dublin. Matheson. 8 April 2015.

9. *Ibid.*

10. Matheson. *Establishing an ICAV*. Dublin. Matheson. No date.

11. 'Loophole Lets Firms Earning Millions Pay €250 Tax, Dail Told'. 6 July 2017. www.irishtimes.com/news/politics/oireachtas/loophole-lets-firms-earning-millions-pay-250-tax-d%C3%A1il-told-1.3145769.

12. S. Donnelly. 'Why Letting Section 110 SPVs Open in Irish Domestic Economy Will Damage Our Tax Base and Our Reputation as a "Low-Tax" Economy'. September 2016. www.stephendonnelly.ie/wp-content/uploads/2016/10/ Closing-Down-Section-110-for-Vulture-Funds.pdf.

13. Revenue Commissioners. *Tax and Duty Manual 37-00-40 Large Cases Divisions: Opinions/Confirmations on Tax/Duty Consequences of a Proposed Course of Action*. Dublin. Revenue Commissioners. 2019, p. 2.

14. *Ibid.*

15. Maples and Calder. www.maplesandcalder.com/expertise/tax/tax-controversy-l itigation/.

16. Maples and Calder. *International and Irish Tax Update March 2016*. Dublin. Maples and Calder. 2016.

17. A. Finnerty and C. McLaughlin. 'Inversions to Ireland'. *Practical Law Journal*. 25 March 2014.

18. 'DAA Chairman Says It Is Time to Re-Assess Salary Cap on Semi State Bosses'. *Irish Independent*. 1 September 2018.

19. 'Cox's Conflicts'. *The Village Magazine*. 25 April 2012.

20. 'Investigation into IBRC Sale to O'Brien Firm Costs Almost €3.3 Million'. *Irish Times*. 7 April 2018.

21. D. Barrett, B. Godfrey and B. Golden. 'New Data Collection on Special Purpose Vehicles in Ireland: Initial Findings and Measuring Shadow Banking'. *Central Bank Quarterly Bulletin*. No. 4, October 2016. www.centralbank.ie/docs/default-source/publications/quarterly-bulletins/QB4-16/gns-5-1-15-new-data-collection-on-special-purpose-vehicles.pdf?sfvrsn=2.

22. Written Answer from Minister of Finance to Richard Boyd Barrett TD 24 July 2018.

23. *Ibid.*

24. *Ibid.*

25. 'SFM: The Vulture Funds' Enforcer That Calls in Irish Property Debts'. *Irish Times*. 26 March 2016.

26. J. Garcia-Bernardo et al. 'Uncovering Offshore Financial Centres: Conduits and Sinks in the Global Corporate Ownership Network'. *Nature*. Vol. 7, Article No. 6246, 2017. www.nature.com/articles/s41598-017-06322-9.

27. 'Dutch Inquiry Calls for Overhaul of Trust Office Industry'. *Reuters*. 5 July 2017.

28. 'Intertrust Ireland to Create 60 New Jobs in Dublin'. *Irish Times*. 2 July 2018.

29. Government Accountability Office. *Public Accounting Firms: Mandated Study on Consolidation and Competition*. Washington, DC. GAO. 2003.

30. 'PwC Promoted Tax Avoidance on an Industrial Scale, Say MPs'. *BBC News*. 6 February 2015.

31. House of Commons Committee of Public Accounts. *Tax Avoidance: The Role of Large Accountancy Firms*. London. House of Commons. 15 April 2013, p. 5.

32. Professor Prem Sikka sent us this information in a personal correspondence. He was a member of the UK Commission.

33. US Senate, Permanent Sub-Committee on Investigations. *The US Tax Shelter Industry: The Role of Accountants, Lawyers and Financial Professionals*. Washington, DC: US Government Printing Office. 2005, p. 9.

34. *Ibid.* See also A. Mitchell and P. Sikka. 'The Pinstripe Mafia: How Accountancy Firms Destroy Societies'. Basildon. Association for Accountancy and Business Affairs. 2011. www.visar.csustan.edu/aaba/PINSTRIPEMAFIA.pdf.

35. E. Doyle, J.F. Hughes and K.W. Glaister. 'Linking Ethics and Risk Management in Taxation: Evidence from an Exploratory Study in Ireland and the UK'. *Journal of Business Ethics.* Vol. 86, No. 2, 2009, pp. 177–98.

36. *Ibid.*

37. 'Ernest and Young Settle with N.Y. for $10 Million over Lehman Auditing'. *Reuters.* 15 April 2015.

38. 'A New Frontier'. *Accountancy Ireland.* 1 August 2015.

39. 'Man Making Ireland Tax Avoidance Hub Proves Local Hero'. *Bloomberg.* 28 October 2013.

40. 'PwC Letter to Marius Kohl'. 27 September 2007. Lux Leaks.

41. 'PwC Letter to Marius Kohl'. 14 January 2009. Lux Leaks.

42. 'Italy Was Key Destination for Spouses on Road to Avoiding Tax'. *Irish Times.* 25 March 2009.

43. *Ibid.*

44. P. Bourdieu. *Acts of Resistance.* New York. New Press. 1999, p. 25.

45. PricewaterhouseCoopers. *Irish Water Report Phase 1.* Dublin. PwC. 2011, p. 18.

46. PricewaterhouseCoopers. *Report on Pension Charges in Ireland.* Dublin. PwC. 2012, p. 228.

47. 'Written Answer from Minister of Finance to Richard Boyd Barrett TD'. 24 July 2018.

6 THE IRISH FINANCIAL SERVICES CENTRE

1. S. Andrews. 'Larry Fink's $12 Trillion Shadow'. *Vanity Fair.* April 2010. www.vanityfair.com/news/2010/04/fink-201004.

2. 'Blackstone's $9.6 Billion Bet on the U.S. Housing Recovery Files to Go Public'. *Forbes.* 6 January 2017.

3. W. Lazonick. 'Profits without Prosperity'. *Harvard Business Review.* September 2014.

4. B. Golden and P. Hughes. 'Shining a Light on Special Purpose Entities in Ireland'. *Economic Letters.* 11/EL/18, 2018, p. 3. www.pdfs.semanticscholar.org/b3ec/47a3e3496d99655402563781e4b91b5c2c16.pdf.

5. L. Murphy. 'Financial Engine of Glorified Back Office: Dublin's International Financial Services Centres Going Global'. *Area.* Vol. 30, No. 2, 1998, p. 160.

6. Tax Justice Network. 'How Ireland Became an Offshore Tax Haven'. www.taxjustice.net/2015/11/11/how-ireland-became-an-offshore-financial-centre/.

7. *Ibid.*

8. 'Dermot Desmond on the IFSC Past and Future'. www.finance-magazine.com/display_article.php?i=2300&pi=142.

9. N. Shaxson. *Treasure Islands: Tax Havens and the Men Who Stole the World.* London. Vintage. 2012, p. 17.

10. Murphy. 'Financial Engine or Glorified Back Office', p. 163.
11. *Ibid.*, p. 160; 'Ireland: Securitisation in the Irish Financial Services Centre'. www.mondaq.com/ireland/x/5180/Corporate+Tax/Securitisation+In+The+International+Financial+Services+Centre+Dublin.
12. 'Tribunal Identifies £8.5 Million in Payments to Haughey'. www.rte.ie/news/2000/0524/7102-moriarty/.
13. 'Desmond Admits to Giving Haughey £125,000'. www.rte.ie/news/1999/1202/4513-moriarty/.
14. C. Keena. *The Ansbacher Conspiracy*. Dublin. Gill and Macmillan. 2003, p. 130.
15. 'Moriarty's Inquiry Takes Us Back to Telecom Deal'. www.irishtimes.com/opinion/moriarty-s-inquiry-takes-us-back-to-telecom-deal-1.257131.
16. D. Barrett, B. Godfrey and B. Golden. 'New Data Collection on Special Purpose Vehicles in Ireland: Initial Findings and Measuring Shadow Banking'. *Central Bank Quarterly Bulletin*. No. 4, October 2016. www.centralbank.ie/docs/default-source/publications/quarterly-bulletins/QB4-16/gns-5-1-15-new-data-collection-on-special-purpose-vehicles.pdf?sfvrsn=2.
17. *Ibid.*
18. Irish Funds. 'Industry Statistics', www.irishfunds.ie/stats/pdf/preview.
19. BlackRock. *Institutional Cash Series Prospectus*. 29 December 2017, p. 75.
20. PIMCO. *Global Investors Series Plc Prospectus*. 3 July 2017, p. 87.
21. PricewaterhouseCoopers. 'Structured Finance (Section 110)'. www.pwc.ie/services/tax/international-tax/structured-finance.html.
22. J. Stewart. 'Low Tax Financial Centres and the Financial Crisis: The Case of the Irish Financial Services Centre'. 2013, p. 7.
23. *Ibid.*
24. Pricewaterhouse Coopers. 'Structured Finance (Section 110)'.
25. *Ibid.*
26. Golden and Hughes. 'Shining a Light on Special Purpose Entities in Ireland', p. 5.
27. *Ibid.*, p. 9; Stewart. 'Low Tax Financial Centres and the Financial Crisis', p. 8.
28. 'No Desks. No Staff. No Tax'. www.irishtimes.com/business/financial-services/no-desks-no-staff-no-tax-ireland-s-shadow-banks-1.1388923.
29. *Ibid.*
30. *Ibid.*
31. *Ibid.*
32. *Ibid.*
33. Irish Funds. 'Facts and Figures'. www.irishfunds.ie/facts-figures/irish-domiciled-non-ucits.
34. This is dealt with more fully in Chapter 8 and Chapter 9.
35. 'New Irish Fund Vehicle to Facilitate US Investment: The ICAV'. www.walkersglobal.com/index.php/publications/99-advisory/209-new-irish-fund-vehicle-to-facilitate-us-investment-the-icav.
36. *Ibid.*

37. 'Global Monitoring Report on Non-Bank Financial Intermediation 2019'. www.fsb.org/wp-content/uploads/P190120.pdf.
38. Golden and Hughes. 'Shining a Light on Special Purpose Entities in Ireland', p. 9; 'A Third of Ireland's Shadow Banking Subject to Little or No Oversight'. www.irishtimes.com/business/financial-services/a-third-of-ireland-s-shadow-banking-subject-to-little-or-no-oversight-1.3077931.
39. 'Ireland Is World's Fourth-Largest Shadow Banking Hub'. www.irishtimes.com/business/financial-services/ireland-is-world-s-fourth-largest-shadow-banking-hub-1.3077914.
40. *Ibid.*
41. C. Doyle and J. Stewart. 'Financing Russian Firms: Ireland and Round Tripping'. *Critical Perspectives on International Business*. Forthcoming, p. 2.
42. *Ibid.*
43. *Ibid.*; C. Doyle. 'Russian Bank Collapse: Fictious Assets, Hidden Losses and the Role of the IFSC'. 2018. www.thejournal.ie/readme/russian-bank-collapse-fictitious-assets-hidden-losses-and-the-ifsc-4339432-Nov2018/.
44. F. O'Toole. *Ship of Fools: How Stupidity and Corruption Sank the Celtic Tiger*. London. Faber and Faber. 2009, p. 136.
45. *Ibid.*
46. IFSC. 'Insurances'. www.ifsc.ie/listing.aspx?id=74.
47. *Ibid.*
48. IFSC. 'The International Financial Services Sector in Ireland'. www.fsi.ie/Sectors/FSI/FSI.nsf/vPages/Media_and_Publications~Publications~fsi-accenture-ifsc-report/$file/FSI-Accenture+IFSC+Report.pdf.
49. O'Toole. *Ship of Fools*, p. 137.
50. *Ibid.*, p. 138.
51. *Ibid.*, p. 139.
52. *Ibid.*, pp. 140, 141.
53. Insurance Ireland and IDA. *Ireland for Insurance*. Dublin. Insurance Ireland. No date, p. 7.
54. PricewaterhouseCoopers. *Taking Flight: An Economic and Employment Analysis of the Aircraft Leasing Industry in Ireland*. Dublin. PwC. 2018.
55. S. Killian. 'Mantras and Myths: A True Picture of the Corporate Tax System in Ireland'. 2017, p. 17. www.oxfamireland.org/sites/default/files/upload/pdfs/mantras-myths-final.pdf.
56. *Ibid.*
57. *Ibid.*
58. Moore. *The Tax Treatment of Aircraft Leasing in Ireland*. Dublin. Moore. 2018, p. 1.
59. Department of Business, Enterprise and Innovation. *Focus on Aerospace and Aviation*. Dublin. Department of Business, Enterprise and Innovation. 2018, p. 5.

60. 'Aercap Net Income Jumps 19% Due to Asset Sale Gains'. *Irish Times*. 3 August 2017; 'Profits Soar by 833m at Aircraft Lessor GE Capital Aviation'. *Irish Independent*. 5 February 2019.

61. 'Aircraft Firms Pay Just 23m in Tax'. *Irish Examiner*. 22 October 2015.

62. 'Aircraft Leasing: Flying into the Future'. *Irish Independent*. 5 February 2019.

63. IFSC. 'Banking'. www.ifsc.ie/listing.aspx?id=70.

64. *Ibid.*

65. J. Stewart. 'Financial Flows and Treasury Management Companies'. 2006, p. 3. www.visar.csustan.edu/aaba/JimStewart2006.pdf.

66. *Ibid.*, p. 4.

67. *Ibid.*

68. *Ibid.*

69. *Ibid.*

70. *Ibid.*, p. 5.

71. Golden and Hughes. 'Shining a Light on Special Purpose Entities in Ireland', pp. 6, 7.

72. Doyle. 'Financing Russian Firms', p. 5.

73. Golden and Hughes. 'Shining a Light on Special Purpose Entities in Ireland', p. 6.

74. *Ibid.*, p. 20.

75. Shaxson. *Treasure Islands*, Chapter 9.

76. 'The Capture of Tax Haven Ireland: The Bankers Hedge Funds Got Virtually Everything They Wanted'. www.treasureislands.org/the-capture-of-tax-haven-ireland-the-bankers-hedge-funds-got-virtually-everything-they-wanted/.

77. D. Crowley. 'Tax Haven Comes of Age'. *Euromoney*. 1995, pp. 366–67. Cited in L. Murphy. 'Financial Engine of Glorified Back Office: Dublin's International Financial Services Centres Going Global'. *Area*. Vol. 30, No. 2, 1998, p. 160.

78. *Ibid.*

79. C. McCabe. *Sins of the Father: The Decisions That Shaped the Irish Economy*. Dublin. The History Press Ireland. 2014, p. 166.

80. *Ibid.*, p. 164.

81. 'Memoirs of the IFSC Finance Magazine'. www.finance-magazine.com/display_article.php?i=2303&pi=142.

82. 'Fresh Fodder for IFSC Machine Could Be Dodgy'. www.irishtimes.com/business/fresh-fodder-for-ifsc-machine-could-be-dodgy-1.1133089.

83. Department of the Taoiseach. 'Strategy for the Financial Services Industry in Ireland 2011–2016'. In Stewart, 'Low Tax Financial Centres and the Financial Crisis', p. 6.

84. *Ibid.*

85. 'IFSC Clearing House Group Minutes'. www.taoiseach.gov.ie/eng/Publications/Publications_2014/IFSC_Clearing_House_Group_Minutes_22_May_2014.pdf.

86. K. Allen with B. O'Boyle. *Austerity Ireland: The Failure of Irish Capitalism*. London. Pluto Press. 2013, p. 86.

87. *Ibid.*
88. 'Great Tax Race: Ireland's Policies Aid Business More Than Public'. www. ft.com/content/c638f73a-978f-11e2-97e0-00144feabdc0.
89. K. Allen with B. O'Boyle. *Austerity Ireland*, p. 86.
90. 'Inside the Clearing House Group'. www.irishtimes.com/news/politics/ inside-the-clearing-house-group-1.1487731.
91. 'Cost of R&D Tax Credit Soars to More Than €700 Million'. www.businesspost. ie/politics/cost-rd-tax-credit-claims-soars-e700m-394597.
92. 'The Capture of Tax Haven Ireland'.
93. www.lobbying.ie/organisation/767/blackrock-investment-management-dublin-limited?currentPage=2&pageSize=10&queryText=&subjectMatters=& subject.
94. 'Former Junior Minister to Head Funds Sector Lobby Group'. www.irish times.com/business/financial-services/former-junior-finance-minister-to-head-funds-sector-lobby-group-1.4365853.
95. *Ibid.*
96. 'Why Brian Hayes Went from Searing Critic to Chief Defender of the Banks'. www.irishtimes.com/business/financial-services/why-brian-hayes-went-from-searing-critic-to-chief-defender-of-banks-1.3953869.
97. O'Toole. *Ship of Fools*, p. 146.
98. *Ibid.*
99. *Ibid.*, p. 148.
100. Stewart. 'Low Tax Financial Centres and the Financial Crisis', p. 4.
101. O'Toole. *Ship of Fools*, p. 146.
102. 'Noonan Rejects Tobin Tax over Fear of Jobs Losses'. www.thejournal.ie/ noonan-rejects-tobin-tax-over-fear-of-jobs-losses-629138-Oct2012/.
103. 'Tax Havens Are Perfectly Legal – Yet Morally Murky'. www.businesspost.ie/ opinion/tax-havens-perfectly-legal-yet-morally-murky-403260.
104. *Ibid.*
105. *Ibid.*

7 FOREIGN DIRECT AVOIDERS

1. W. Isaacson. 'The Real Leadership Lesson of Steve Jobs'. *Harvard Business Review*. April 2012.
2. E. Dockterman. 'Read the TIME Magazine Story That Plays a Key Role in *Steve Jobs*'. *TIME*. 22 October 2015.
3. L. Brennan-Jobs. 'Growing Up Jobs'. *Vanity Fair*. September 2018.
4. 'Chinese Phone Factory Is Pretty Nice Says Jobs'. *Independent*, 3 June 2010.
5. D.C. Johnston. 'The Legacy of Carl Levin'. *American Prospect*. 30 December 2014.

6. S. Levin and J. McCain. 'Offshore Profit Shifting and the U.S. Tax Code – Part 2 (Apple Inc.) Memorandum to US Senate Sub Committee on Investigations', 21 May 2013, p. 33.
7. *Ibid.*, p. 4.
8. *Ibid.*, p. 4.
9. EU Commission. 'Decision of 30.8.2016 ON STATE AID SA.38373 (2014/C) (ex 2014/NN) (ex 2014/CP) Implemented by Ireland to Apple'. Brussels. EU Commission. 2016, pp. 13–14.
10. Levin and McCain. 'Offshore Profit Shifting', p. 20.
11. EU Commission. 'Commission Decision of 30.8.2016', p. 14.
12. *Ibid.*, p. 14.
13. *Ibid.*, p. 26.
14. *Ibid.*, p. 15.
15. EU Commission. 'EU Rules Apple State Aid €13 Billion Must Be Re-Paid to Ireland'. 30 August 2016. www.ec.europa.eu.
16. Since then, this judgement has been challenged in the General Court of the European Union. We take up this judgement in Chapter 9.
17. The Judgement of the Court can be found here: www.curia.europa.eu/jcms/upload/docs/application/pdf/2020-07/cp200090en.pdf.
18. *Ibid.*
19. The response to the Court Ruling by the European Commission can be found here: www.ec.europa.eu/commission/presscorner/detail/en/statement_20_1746.
20. S. Bowers. 'Leaked Document Expose Secret Tale of Apple's Tale of Apple's Offshore Hop'. *Reveal.* 6 November 2017.
21. S. Coffey. 'Review of Ireland's Corporation Tax Code: Presented to the Minister for Finance and Public Expenditure and Reform'. 2017, Chapter 9. www.finance.gov.ie/wp-content/uploads/2017/09/170912-Review-of-Irelands-Corporation-Tax-Code.pdf.
22. M.B. Christensen and E. Clancy. *Exposed: Apple's Golden Delicious Tax Deals.* Brussels. GUE/NGL. 2018, p. 5.
23. *Ibid.*, p. 40.
24. Coffey. 'Review of Ireland's Corporation'.
25. Christensen and Clancy. *Exposed*, p. 5.
26. R. Phillips et al. 'Offshore Shell Games: The Use of Offshore Tax Havens by Fortune 500 Companies'. 2017, p. 2. www.uspirg.org/sites/pirg/files/reports/USP%20ShellGames%20Oct17%201.2.pdf.
27. C. Kelpie. 'Leprechaun Economics: Ireland's 26% Growth Rate Laughed Off as Farcical'. www.independent.ie/business/irish/leprechaun-economics-irelands-26pc-growth-spurt-laughed-off-as-farcical-34879232.html.
28. '"Leprechaun Economics" Earn Ireland Ridicule, $443 Million Bill'. *Bloomberg.* 13 July 2016.
29. This is according to Richard Boyd Barrett TD (personal communication). (A Dail committee was also set up to look into the tax activities of multinationals, but rejected a proposal to publicly interview an Apple executive.)

30. EU Commission. 'Commission Decision of 30.8.2016', p. 2–3.
31. Phillips et al. 'Offshore Shell Games', p. 17.
32. C. Huang. 'The New Corporate Migration: Tax Diversion through Inversion'. *Brooklyn Law Review*. Vol. 80, No. 3, 2015. www.law.stanford.edu/wp-content/uploads/2015/09/Inversions-final.pdf.
33. D. Marples et al. 'Issues in International Corporate Taxation: The 2017 Revision (P.L. 115–97) Congressional Research Service'. www.fas.org/sgp/crs/misc/R45186.pdf 2017.
34. Dillon Eustace. 'Holding Companies in Ireland'. www.dilloneustace.com/download/1/Publications/Tax/Holding%20Companies%20in%20Ireland.pdf.
35. J. Stewart. 'Inversions as a Tax Strategy: Implications of Ireland'. 2015. www.tasc.ie/blog/2015/12/04/inversions-as-tax-strategy-implications/.
36. E. Solomon. 'Report to the Congress on: Earnings Stripping, Transfer Pricing and US Income Tax Treaties'. 2007. www.treasury.gov/resource-center/tax-policy/Documents/Report-Earnings-Stripping-Transfer-Pricing-2007.pdf.
37. 'Medtronic Press Release: Medtronic to Acquire Covidien for €49.2 Billion'. www.newsroom.medtronic.com/news-releases/news-release-details/medtronic-acquire-covidien-429-billion-cash-and-stock-0.
38. C.J. Polychroniou. 'Ventilator Shortage Exposes the Cruelty of Neoliberal Capitalism'. www.truthout.org/articles/chomsky-ventilator-shortage-exposes-the-cruelty-of-neoliberal-capitalism/.
39. P. O'Donoghue. 'It Makes No Sense Not to Take Advantage of the Tax: CEO of $30 Billion Company Moving to Cork'. www.fora.ie/johnson-controls-tyco-ireland-inversion-2975678-Sep2016/; M. Gannon. 'Eaton to Merge with Cooper Industries, Move Global Incorporation to Ireland'. www.hydraulicspneumatics.com/fluid-power-talk/article/21885471/eaton-to-merge-with-cooper-industries-move-global-incorporation-to-ireland; 'Perrigo Company to Acquire Elan Corporation, plc for $8.6 Billion Establishing Premier Global Healthcare Company'. www.businesswire.com/news/home/20130728005081/en/Perrigo-Company-Acquire-Elan-Corporation-plc-US8.6.
40. See History of U.S. Corporate Tax Inversions to Ireland (as at 21 November 2018) at www.en.wikipedia.org/wiki/Corporation_tax_in_the_Republic_of_Ireland#Corporate_tax_inversions for a whole series of information and further references; M. McCarthy. 'Hard to Swallow: Facilitating Tax Avoidance by Big Pharma in Ireland'. www.oxfamireland.org/sites/default/files/pharma-report.pdf 2018.
41. Phillips et al. 'Offshore Shell Games', p. 3.
42. *Ibid.*
43. S. McKee. 'AbbVie Completes Acquisition of Allergan'. 2020. www.pharmatimes.com/news/abbvie_completes_acquisition_of_allergan_1340086#:~:text=AbbVie%20has%20wrapped%20up%20its,by%20the%20Irish%20High%20Court.
44. McCarthy. 'Hard to Swallow'.
45. *Ibid.*, p. 2.

46. *Ibid.*, p. 1.
47. *Ibid.*, p. 4.
48. *Ibid.*, p. 2.
49. *Ibid.*
50. Phillips et al. 'Offshore Shell Games', pp. 1, 20.
51. *Ibid.*, p. 20.
52. *Ibid.*
53. *Ibid.*, p. 11.
54. *Ibid.*, p. 2.
55. *Ibid.*, p. 10.
56. Bureau of Economic Analysis. 'International Trade and Investment Country Facts'. www.apps.bea.gov/international/factsheet/factsheet.cfm.
57. *Ibid.*
58. '*Irish Times* Top 1,000'. www.irishtimes.com/top1000.
59. McCann Fitzgerald. 'Tax Attractions of Irish Holding Companies'. 16 February 2016. www.mccannfitzgerald.com/knowledge/international-tax/tax-attractions-of-irish-holding-companies-.
60. Oxfam. 'Analysis of Ireland's Corporation Tax Roadmap'. p. 7. www.oxfamireland.org/sites/default/files/ireland_s_corporate_tax_roadmap_final.pdf.
61. Pearse Trust. 'Irish Dividend Withholding Tax Exemptions'. www.pearse-trust.ie/blog/bid/77208/Irish-Dividend-Withholding-Tax-Exemptions.
62. 'Privacy Rights: It Is Natural That Facebook Would Choose Ireland'. *Irish Independent*. 22 February 2018.
63. 'Data Protection Commissioner Says No Action Will Be Taken against Apple and Facebook'. rte.ie. *RTÉ News and Current Affairs*. 26 July 2013.
64. B. Coyne and E. Denny. 'An Economic Evaluation of Future Electricity Use in Irish Data Centres TRiSS Working Paper Series No. TRiSS 02 – 2018'. Dublin. Trinity College. 2018.
65. Figures compiled from media reports on company earnings.
66. 'European Digital Taxation Proposal'. www.ec.europa.eu/commission/presscorner/detail/en/IP_18_2041.
67. *Ibid.*
68. P. Smyth. 'Ireland Joins Three Other Member States in Opposing EU Digital Tax Plan'. 2018. www.irishtimes.com/business/economy/ireland-join-three-other-member-states-to-oppose-eu-digital-tax-plan-1.3654619.
69. E. Burke-Kennedy. 'Digital Tax Could Reduce Ireland's Corporate Take'. www.irishtimes.com/business/economy/digital-tax-could-reduce-ireland-s-corporate-take-1.3954840.
70. P. Leahy and C Taylor. 'Pressure Mounts on Ireland to Accept EU Digital Tax'. www.irishtimes.com/business/economy/pressure-mounts-on-ireland-to-accept-eu-digital-tax-1.3681963.
71. 'Facebook Boss Happy to Pay More Tax in Europe'. www.bbc.com/news/business-51497961.

8 THE VULTURES HAVE LANDED

1. M. Norris and T. Fahey. 'From Asset Based Welfare to Welfare Housing? The Changing Function of Social Housing in Ireland'. *Housing Studies*. Vol. 26, No. 3, 2011, pp. 459–69.
2. C. McCabe. *Sins of the Father: The Decisions That Shaped the Irish Economy*. Dublin. The History Press Ireland. 2014, p. 31.
3. F. O'Toole. *Ship of Fools: How Stupidity and Corruption Sank the Celtic Tiger*. London. Faber and Faber. 2009. p. 119.
4. *Ibid.*
5. M. Reynold. 'The Land Scarcity Myth'. Dublin. MRD Architecture. 2018.
6. F. McDonald and K. Sheridan. *The Builders*. London. Penguin Books. 2009, p. 5.
7. *Ibid.*, p. 52.
8. *Ibid.*
9. *Ibid.*
10. *Ibid.*, p. 55.
11. O'Toole. *Ship of Fools*, p. 87.
12. S. Ross. *The Bankers: How the Banks Brought Ireland to Its Knees*. Dublin. Penguin Ireland. 2009, p. 123.
13. K. Allen with B. O'Boyle. *Austerity Ireland: The Failure of Irish Capitalism*. London. Pluto Press. 2013, p. 74.
14. O'Toole. *Ship of Fools*, p. 102.
15. 'Trichet Warned Me a "Bomb Would Go Off" Says Noonan'. www.independent.ie/business/irish/banking-inquiry/trichet-warned-me-a-bomb-would-go-off-says-noonan-31518658.html.
16. 'Statement by Minister for Finance, Brian Lenihan T.D. on the Motion on the EU/IMF Programme for Ireland'. www.archive.merrionstreet.ie/wp-content/uploads/2010/12/Statement-by-Minister-for-Finance-on-Motion-on-EU-IMF-Prog_15Dec10-2.pdf.
17. 'Irish Bailout Cheapest in the World, Says Lenihan'. www.irishtimes.com/business/irish-bailout-cheapest-in-world-says-lenihan-1.900393.
18. '42% of Europe's Banking Crisis Paid by Ireland'. www.irishexaminer.com/ireland/42-of-europes-banking-crisis-paid-by-ireland-219703.html.
19. F. Connolly. *NAMA Land: The Inside Story of Ireland's Property Sell Off and the Creation of a New Elite*. Dublin. Gill Books. 2017, p. 11.
20. *Ibid.*, p. 15.
21. 'NAMA Pays Developers €11 Million in Wages Every Year'. www.thejournal.ie/nama-pay-levels-developers-11-million-1491461-May2014/.
22. Connolly. *NAMA Land*, pp. 2, 44.
23. L. Fahra. *The Financialization of Housing*. New York. United Nations. 2017, p. 3.
24. N. Brooker. 'How the Financial Crash Made Our Cities Unaffordable'. *Financial Times*. 15 March 2018.
25. J. Ryan-Collins, T. Lloyd and L. MacFarlane. *Rethinking the Economics of Land and Housing*. London. Zed. 2017, p. 110.

26. Brooker, 'How the Financial Crash Made Our Cities Unaffordable'.
27. Bain Capital. *Global Private Equity Report 2019*. Boston. Bain Capital. 2019, p. 31.
28. 'Blackstone Billions on the Line and Out for Blood'. www.independent.ie/business/irish/blackstone-billions-on-the-line-and-out-for-blood-30507450. html.
29. Connolly. *NAMA Land*, p. 164.
30. *Ibid.*, p. 232.
31. *Ibid.*, p. 109.
32. 'The Vulture Fund Paying Very Little Tax on Its Billion-Euro Irish Incomes'. www.thejournal.ie/lone-star-ireland-2-2688497-Mar2016/.
33. 'Seen and Heard: Tax Avoiding Vulture Funds and Transfermate's Deal with ING'. www.irishtimes.com/business/economy/seen-heard-tax-avoiding-vulture-funds-and-transfermate-s-deal-with-ing-1.3579778.
34. 'With the REIT Stuff You Can Rake in the Money'. www.independent.ie/irish-news/gene-kerrigan-with-the-reit-stuff-you-can-rake-in-the-money-3716 8703.html.
35. 'Vultures Pay Just €8,000 in Tax on €10 Billion in Assets'. www.thejournal.ie/vulture-funds-2-3176030-Jan2017/.
36. *Ibid.*
37. Connolly. *NAMA Land*, p. 277.
38. 'SEI Global Finance Management Product Guide'. www.seicdrupalcdn. azureedge.net/cdn/farfuture/XPpPSt65QQ7pr6EXd2aiDcDftjrT_qOBBiyAth Aw78M/1518213101/sites/default/files/SEI_QIAIF_EU.pdf.
39. *Ibid.*
40. F. Reddin. 'Clampdown on Tax-Avoiding Property Funds Sees Tax Revenue Fall'. *Irish Times.* 14 June 2019.
41. 'Understanding Irish Real Estate Investment Trusts'. www.zurichlife.ie/DocArchive/servlet/DocArchServlet?docId=DOC_9948&docTag=&_ga=2.185368042.2117730838.1546872765-162169824.1546432940.
42. D. Donaghy. 'Real Estate Investment Trusts (REITs): Tax Policy Rationale'. www. taxpolicy.gov.ie/wp-content/uploads/2013/06/E3_DeirdreDonaghy.pdf.
43. Deloitte. *Ireland Introduces REIT Legislation: Finance Act 2013*. Dublin. Deloitte. 2013, p. 1.
44. M. Hennigan. 'Global Property Bubble: Dublin Tops 2014 Global Returns at 44.7%'. www.finfacts.ie/irishfinancenews/article_1028787.shtml.
45. S. McCabe. 'Blackstone Flips Prime Docklands Buildings Barely Two Years after Buying from NAMA'. *Irish Times.* 27 September 2015.
46. D. Buckley. 'Overseas Investment Firms Become Active in Flipping Irish Commercial Property'. *Sunday Business Post.* 26 January 2014.
47. J. Fagan. 'Starwood Flips Elm Park Block in Dublin 4 after Four Months for Tidy Profit'. *Irish Times.* 15 June 2016.
48. Cairn Homes. *Preliminary Results Presentation: Built to Last.* Dublin. Cairn Homes. 2018, p. 16.

49. 'Glenveagh Properties Unveils Latest Land Acquisitions in Dublin and Cork'. www.council.ie/glenveagh-properties-unveils-latest-land-acquisitions-in-dublin-cork/.

50. E. Burke-Kennedy. 'NAMA Chief Links Housing Shortfall to Land Hoarding'. *Irish Times*. 13 July 2017.

51. TaxStrategy Group. 'Real Estate Investment Trusts, Irish Real Estate Funds and Section 110 Companies as They Invest in the Irish Property Market'. Dublin. Department of Finance. 2019 p. 14.

52. 'With the REIT Stuff You Can Rake in the Money'. www.independent.ie/irish-news/gene-kerrigan-with-the-reit-stuff-you-can-rake-in-the-money-37168703.html.

53. 'Kuwaiti Stake in Green Reit Raises Eyebrows'. *Irish Times*. 18 June 2019.

54. Kennedy Wilson Holding Inc. 'Commercial Investment Summary'. June 2019. www.annualreports.com/HostedData/AnnualReports/PDF/NYSE_KW_2019.pdf.

55. M. Paul. 'Johnny Ronan: The "Sweat Equity" Comeback of a Flamboyant Businessman'. *Irish Times*. 8 December 2008.

56. 'Developer Who Sold Dublin Site for €70m Buys It Back for €22m-Plus'. *Irish Times*. 27 February 2019.

57. 'What Do Ireland's Biggest Builders and Landlords Earn'. www.irishtimes.com/life-and-style/homes-and-property/what-do-ireland-s-biggest-builders-and-landlords-earn-1.3665531.

58. Connolly. *NAMA Land*, p. 119.

59. *Ibid.*, p. 274.

60. 'What Do Ireland's Biggest Builders and Landlords Earn'.

61. 'Dublin City Council Built Just 74 New Social Houses Last Year'. *The Journal*. 8 March 2019.

62. E. O'Broin. *Home: Why Public Housing Is the Answer*. Dublin. Merrion Press. 2019, p. 138.

63. O. Hegarty. *Submission to Public Consultation on Draft Apartment Standards, Department of Housing, Planning Community and Local Government*. Dublin. UCD School of Architecture, Planning and Environmental Policy. 2018, p. 4.

64. E. Burke-Kennedy. 'Irish House Prices More than Nine Times the Average Salary'. *Irish Times*. 13 April 2019.

9 THE CASE FOR THE DEFENCE

1. G. Ní Aodha. '"That's a Joke", "Stealing": Ireland's Low Corporate Tax Rate Criticised at Davos'. 2018. www.thejournal.ie/ireland-corporate-tax-rate-davos-stealing-3817678-Jan2018/.

2. *Ibid.*

3. *Ibid.*; P. O'Donoghue. 'Eight of Ireland's Biggest Corporations Paid No Tax on Their Income. 2017. www.fora.ie/effective-tax-rate-ireland-3622827-Sep2017/.

4. G. McLoughlin. 'We're against Sweetheart Deals: Ireland's Tax Regime Criticised at Davos'. 2019. www.independent.ie/business/were-against-sweetheart-deals-irelands-tax-regime-criticised-at-davos-37745474.html.

5. N. Shaxson. 'How Ireland Became an Offshore Centre'. www.taxjustice.net/2015/11/11/how-ireland-became-an-offshore-financial-centre/; S. Killian. 'Mantras and Myths: A True Picture of the Corporate Tax System in Ireland'. 2017. www.oxfamireland.org/sites/default/files/upload/pdfs/mantras-myths-final.pdf.

6. G. Zucman et al. 'The Missing Profits of Nations'. *NBER Working Paper Series*. 2018. www.gabriel-zucman.eu/files/TWZ2018.pdf.

7. G. Reilly. 'Senators Insist Ireland Is a Tax Haven Despite Ambassador's Letter'. 2013. www.thejournal.ie/ireland-ambassador-letter-us-senate-corporate-tax-932838-May2013/.

8. F. Guarascio. 'MEPs Claim Ireland Is Among EU's "Tax Havens"'. 2019. www.independent.ie/business/irish/meps-claim-ireland-is-among-eus-tax-havens-37953907.html.

9. Fora Staff. 'Ireland Is Trying to Get off Brazil Black List for Tax Havens'. 2016. www.thejournal.ie/ireland-brazil-tax-haven-jbs-2-2990888-Sep2016/.

10. D. Dalby and S. Bowers. 'Lux Leaks and Panama Papers Spur EU to Better Protect Whistle-Blowers'. www.icij.org/investigations/panama-papers/lux-leaks-panama-papers-spur-eu-to-better-protect-whistleblowers/.

11. Zucman et al. 'The Missing Profits of Nations'.

12. M. Paul. 'Ireland Is the World's Biggest Corporate "Tax Haven", Say Academics'. 2013. www.irishtimes.com/business/economy/ireland-is-the-world-s-biggest-corporate-tax-haven-say-academics-1.3528401.

13. *Ibid.*

14. *Ibid.*

15. *Ibid.*

16. P. Vale. 'Peter Vale: 5 Reasons Why Ireland Is Not a Tax Haven'. 2013. www.independent.ie/business/irish/peter-vale-five-reasons-why-ireland-is-not-a-tax-haven-29287879.html.

17. G. Tobin and K. Walsh. 'What Makes a Country a Tax Haven?' *The Economic and Social Review*. Vol. 44, No. 3, Autumn, 2013, pp. 401–24.

18. *Ibid.*, p. 416.

19. *Ibid.*, p. 417.

20. *Ibid.*

21. *Ibid.*, p. 412.

22. IDA Ireland. '2018 Results'. 2018. www.idaireland.com/newsroom/ida-ireland-2018-results-highest-number-ever-emp.

23. Shaxson. 'How Ireland Became an Offshore Centre'.

24. J. Garcia-Bernardo et al. 'Uncovering Offshore Financial Centres: Conduits and Sinks in the Global Corporate Ownership Network'. *Nature*. Vol. 7, Article No. 6246, 2017. www.nature.com/articles/s41598-017-06322-9.

25. R. Murphy. *Dirty Secrets: How Tax Havens Destroy the Economy*. London. Verso. 2017, p. 96.
26. A. O'Reilly. 'Knowledge Development Box'. 2016. https://www2.deloitte.com/ie/en/pages/tax/articles/knowledge-development-box-ireland.html.
27. L. McCarty. 'Corporation Tax 2018 Payments and 2017 Returns'. 2019. www.revenue.ie/en/corporate/documents/research/ct-analysis-2019.pdf.
28. *Ibid.*
29. *Ibid.*
30. C. O'Brien. 'US Firms "Paid Effective Tax Rate of 2.2% in 2011"'. 2014. www.irishtimes.com/business/economy/us-firms-paid-effective-tax-rate-of-2-2-in-2011-1.1686733.
31. P. Bodkin. 'Turns Out Ireland Was Telling the Truth about Corporation Taxes. Unlike Nearly Everyone Else'. 2014. www.thejournal.ie/ireland-tax-haven-1796050-Nov2014/.
32. J. Stewart. 'MNE Tax Strategies and Ireland'. 2014. www.tcd.ie/business/assets/pdf/MNE-tax-strategies-and-ireland.pdf.
33. *Ibid.*
34. S. Coffey and K. Levey. 'Effective Rates of Corporation Tax in Ireland Technical Paper 2014'. 2014. www.budget.gov.ie/budgets/2015/documents/technical_paper_effective_rates_corporation_tax_ireland.pdf.
35. *Ibid.*, p. 3.
36. *Ibid.*, p. 12.
37. *Ibid.*
38. *Ibid.*, p. 37.
39. *Ibid.*, p. 38.
40. *Ibid.* p. v.
41. *Ibid.*
42. R. Boyd Barrett and P. Donoghue. 'Corporation Tax Debate Dail Eireann'. 2018. www.oireachtas.ie/en/debates/question/2018-05-16/37/.
43. T. Maguire. 'Ireland Is Not a Tax Haven'. 2018. https://www2.deloitte.com/ie/en/pages/tax/articles/ireland-is-not-a-tax-haven.html.
44. Revenue Commissioners. 'Summary of Corporation Tax Returns'. 2019, pp. 1–3. www.revenue.ie/en/corporate/documents/statistics/income-distributors/corporation-tax-calculation.pdf.
45. European Commission Ruling State Aid. 'Ireland Gave Tax Advantages to Apple Worth Up to €13 Billion'. 2016. www.ec.europa.eu/commission/presscorner/detail/en/IP_16_2923.
46. P. Leahy and H. McGee. 'Government Face Split after EU's Apple Ruling'. www.irishtimes.com/business/economy/government-faces-threat-of-split-after-eu-s-apple-ruling-1.2773654.
47. S. Coffey. 'Review of Ireland's Corporation Tax Code: Presented to the Minister for Finance and Public Expenditure and Reform'. 2017. www.finance.gov.ie/wp-content/uploads/2017/09/170912-Review-of-Irelands-Corporation-Tax-Code.pdf.

48. *Ibid.*, p. 126.
49. As we have stated on a number of occasions, Wikipedia has been an invaluable resource in understanding Tax Haven Ireland. See www.en.wikipedia.org/wiki/ Double_Irish_arrangement for more details in this instance.
50. M. Brehm Christensen and E. Clancy. 'Exposed: Apple's Golden Delicious Tax Deals'. 2018, p. 40. www.sinnfein.ie/files/2018/Apple_Tax_Deals_report_ final_21.06_.18_.pdf.
51. *Ibid.*
52. S. Bowers. 'Apple's Cash Mountain. How It Avoids Tax and the Irish Link'. 2017. www.irishtimes.com/business/apple-s-cash-mountain-how-it-avoids-tax-and-the-irish-link-1.3281734.
53. J. Brennan. 'Ireland Says EU Case on Apple €13 Billion "Fundamentally Flawed"'. 2019. www.irishtimes.com/business/economy/ireland-says-eu-case-on-apple-s-13bn-fundamentally-flawed-1.4020680.
54. *Ibid.*
55. A summary of the General Court of the European Union judgement can be found here: www.curia.europa.eu/jcms/upload/docs/application/pdf/2020-07/ cp200090en.pdf.
56. *Ibid.*
57. P. Ryan. 'Ireland Is Apple's Holy Grail of Tax Avoidance'. 2013. www.thejournal. ie/ireland-is-apples-holy-grail-of-tax-avoidance-918345-May2013/.
58. E. Loughlin and J. McEnroe. 'Noonan Moves to Close Tax Loophole for Vulture Funds'. 2016. www.irishexaminer.com/ireland/michael-noonan-moves-to-close-tax-loophole-for-vulture-funds-419714.html.
59. 'Noonan Is Accused of Rolling Out the Red Carpet for Vulture Funds'. www. independent.ie/business/personal-finance/noonan-is-accused-of-rolling-out-the-red-carpet-for-vulture-funds-31069286.html.
60. Mayson Hayes Curran. 'London Banking Seminar'. 2016. www.mhc.ie/latest/ events/london-banking-seminar-publications.
61. 'Government Moves to Amend Section 110 to Close Tax Loophole Used by Vulture Funds'. www.rte.ie/news/2016/0906/814471-revenue-nama-foi/.
62. J. Horgan Jones. 'Revealed: The Vulture Funds That Paid Just €250 in Tax'. www.businesspost.ie/more-business/revealed-the-vulture-funds-that-paid-just-250-in-tax-a6a2ed45.
63. C. Taylor. 'Department of Finance Closes Vulture Fund Loophole'. 2016. www.irishtimes.com/business/economy/department-of-finance-closes-vulture-fund-loophole-1.2781681.
64. J.P. Phelan et al. 'Houses of the Oireachtas Committee on Budgetary Oversight'. 2016, p. 25. www.data.oireachtas.ie/ie/oireachtas/committee/ dail/32/committee_on_budgetary_oversight/reports/2016/2016-10-31_ report-on-budget-2017_en.pdf.
65. C. Finn. 'Accountancy Firms Are Telling Vulture Funds How to Get Around Tax Loophole Closure'. 2016. www.thejournal.ie/vulture-funds-loophole-3009381-Oct2016/.

66. 'Irish Section 110 Special Purpose Vehicle'. www.en.wikipedia.org/wiki/ Irish_Section_110_Special_Purpose_Vehicle_(SPV)#cite_note-wf-82; www.matheson.com/news-and-insights/article/enhancements-to-irish- loan-originating-funds-regime-announced.

67. M. Paul. 'Tax Free Funds Once Favoured by Vulture Funds Fall €55 Billion'. 2018. www.irishtimes.com/business/economy/tax-free-funds-once-favoured- by-vultures-fall-55bn-1.3546101?mode=sample&auth-failed=1&pworig- in=https%3A%2F%2F.

68. OECD. 'Harmful Tax Practices: Peer Review Results'. 2019. www.oecd.org/tax/ beps/harmful-tax-practices-peer-review-results-on-preferential-regimes.pdf.

69. A. Cobham et al. 'The Axis of Avoidance'. 2020. www.taxjustice.net/wp-content/ uploads/2020/04/The-axis-of-tax-avoidance_Tax-Justice-Network_April- 2020-1.pdf/.

70. OECD. 'What Is BEPS?' 2020. www.oecd.org/tax/beps/about/.

71. *Ibid.*

72. R. M. Hammer and J. Owens. 'Promoting Tax Competition'. www.oecd.org/tax/ harmful/1915964.pdf.

73. *Ibid.*, p. 1.

74. *Ibid.*

75. *Ibid.*, p. 2.

76. S. Fung. 'The Questionable Legitimacy of the OECD/G20 BEPS Project'. 2017, p. 80. www.elevenjournals.com/tijdschrift/ELR/2017/2/ELR_2017_010_002.

77. Murphy. *Dirty Secrets*, p. 123.

78. N. Shaxson. 'Tackling Tax Havens'. 2019, p. 3. www.imf.org/external/pubs/ft/ fandd/2019/09/pdf/tackling-global-tax-havens-shaxson.pdf.

79. P. Donoghue. 'Check Against Delivery'. 2019. www.gov.ie/ga/oraid/dccc6c- speech-by-minister-donohoe-to-the-harvard-kennedy-school-and-irish-t/.

80. *Ibid.*

81. J. Lu. 'Activists and Experts Ridicule OECD's Tax Havens Backlist as a Farce'. 2017. www.humanosphere.org/world-politics/2017/06/activists-and-experts- ridicule-oecds-tax-havens-blacklist-as-a-farce/.

82. European Union. 'Directive on Administrative Cooperation'. www.ec.europa. eu/taxation_customs/sites/taxation/files/presentation_dac_evaluation_v3.pdf.

83. *Ibid.*

84. *Ibid.*

85. P. Hamilton. 'Ireland Delays Clampdown on Money Laundering'. 2017. www.irishtimes.com/business/economy/ireland-delays-clampdown-on- money-laundering-1.3280990.

86. S. McCárthaigh. 'State Risks Fines over Laundering Laws'. 2018. www. irishexaminer.com/breakingnews/business/state-risks-fines-over-laundering- laws-861491.html.

87. Oxfam. 'Analysis of Ireland's Corporation Tax Roadmap'. p. 3. www.oxfamireland. org/sites/default/files/ireland_s_corporate_tax_roadmap_final.pdf.

88. R. Neate. '12 EU States Reject Move to Expose Companies' Tax Avoidance'. 2019. www.theguardian.com/business/2019/nov/28/12-eu-states-reject-move-to-expose-companies-tax-avoidance.
89. Oxfam. 'Analysis of Ireland's Corporation Tax Roadmap', p. 6.
90. Department of Finance. 'Ireland's Corporation Tax Roadmap'. 2018, p. 6. www.assets.gov.ie/4158/101218132506-74b4db520e844588b3d116067cec9784.pdf.
91. *Ibid.*
92. J. Duffy and T. Bailey. 'The Anti-Tax Avoidance Directive: Winds of Change or an Easterly Breeze'. Matheson. 2016, p. 107. www.matheson.com/images/uploads/documents/The_Anti-Tax_Avoidance_Directive_in_Ireland_-_Winds_of_Change_or_an_Easterly_Breeze.pdf.
93. Department of Finance. 'Ireland's Corporation Tax Roadmap', p. 21.
94. C. Taylor. 'EU Services Notice on Ireland over Tax Avoidance Rule Delay'. 2019. www.irishtimes.com/business/economy/eu-serves-notice-on-ireland-over-tax-avoidance-rule-delay-1.3971144.
95. Department of Finance. 'Ireland's Corporation Tax Roadmap', p. 8.
96. Oxfam. 'Analysis of Ireland's Corporation Tax Roadmap', p. 7.
97. Department of Finance. 'Ireland's Corporation Tax Roadmap', pp. 14, 20.
98. Oxfam. 'Analysis of Ireland's Corporation Tax Roadmap', p. 10.

10 THE SOCIAL COSTS

1. 'Ireland Has Fastest-Growing Economy in the EU for Fifth Consecutive Year'. www.businessworld.ie/economy/Ireland-has-fastest-growing-economy-in-EU-for-the-fifth-consecutive-year-572117.html.
2. 'Bertie Ahern Advises Nigeria on Business'. www.bbc.com/news/uk-northern-ireland-13080947.
3. 'Tax Evasion Damaging Poor Country Economies'. www.oxfam.org/en/press-releases/tax-evasion-damaging-poor-country-economies.
4. 'Four Years on and Half a Billion Dollars Later: Tax Inspectors Without Borders'. www.oecd.org/newsroom/four-years-on-and-half-a-billion-dollars-later-tax-inspectors-without-borders.htm.
5. Oxfam Media Team. 'A Third of Tax Dodged Enough to Prevent 8 Million Deaths a Year'. www.oxfamireland.org/blog/tax-dodging.
6. *Ibid.*
7. 'IBFD Spillover Analysis Possible Effects of the Irish Tax System on Developing Economies'. 2015. www.budget.gov.ie/Budgets/2016/Documents/IBFD_Irish_Spillover_Analysis_Report_pub.pdf.
8. M. Lewis. 'Impossible Structure: Tax Outcomes Overlooked by 2015 Tax Spillover Analysis'. 2017, p. 8. www.christianaid.ie/sites/default/files/2018-02/impossible-structures-tax-report.pdf.
9. *Ibid.*, p. 11.

10. S. Killian. 'Mantras and Myths: A True Picture of the Corporate Tax System in Ireland'. 2017, p. 21. www.oxfamireland.org/sites/default/files/upload/pdfs/mantras-myths-final.pdf.

11. *Ibid.*, p. 22.

12. 'Ireland–Ghana Tax Deal Threatens to Fuel Profit Shifting and Avoidance: Report'. *Irish Independent.* 26 September 2019. www.independent.ie/business/irish/ireland-ghana-tax-deal-threatens-to-fuel-profit-shifting-and-avoidance-report-38535114.html.

13. *Ibid.*

14. *Ibid.*

15. 'Irish Officials Disregarded Dept of Foreign Affairs Concerns over Ghana Trade Deal'. www.irishtimes.com/business/economy/irish-officials-disregarded-dept-of-foreign-affairs-concerns-over-ghana-trade-deal-1.4031852.

16. M. Lewis. 'Impossible Structure'.

17. World Health Organization. 'Primary Health Care Systems: Comprehensive Case Study from Ghana'. WHO. 2017, p. 8.

18. 'Ireland–Ghana Tax Deal Threatens to Fuel Profit Shifting and Avoidance'.

19. 'Ireland's Tax System Undermining Developing Countries, Warns Aid Agency'. www.irishtimes.com/business/economy/ireland-s-tax-system-undermining-developing-countries-warns-aid-agency-1.3289238.

20. *Ibid.*

21. M. Smolyansky, G.A. Suarez and A.M. Tabova. 'U.S. Corporations' Repatriation of Offshore Profits: Evidence from 2018'. *Federal Reserve's Fed Notes.* 6 August 2019.

22. L. Emter, B. Kennedy and P. McQuade. 'US Profit Repatriations and Ireland's Balance of Payments Statistics'. *Central Bank Quarterly Bulletin,* Q2, April 2019.

23. D. Floyd. 'Explaining the Trump Tax Cut'. www.investopedia.com/taxes/trumps-tax-reform-plan-explained/.

24. J. Connolly. 'Socialism Made Easy, 1909'. www.marxists.org/archive/connolly/1909/sme-la/sme1.htm.

25. S. Killian. 'Mantras and Myths: A True Picture of the Corporate Tax System in Ireland'. www.oxfamireland.org/sites/default/files/upload/pdfs/mantras-myths-final.pdf. 2017, p. 8.

26. IDA Ireland. 'Highest Number Ever Employed in Multinational Sector'. 2018. www.idaireland.com/newsroom/ida-ireland-2018-results-highest-number-ever-emp.

27. The relevant information can be found in the following reports: www.revenue.ie/en/corporate/documents/research/ct-analysis-2019.pdf, p. 1, and CSO Stat Bank. www.statbank.cso.ie/px/pxeirestat/Database/eirestat/Nationalo.

28. KPMG. 'Employer Social Security Tax Rates'. www.home.kpmg/xx/en/home/services/tax/tax-tools-and-resources/tax-rates-online/social-security-employer-tax-rates-table.html.

29. 'Total Net Receipts by Tax'. head.www.revenue.ie/en/corporate/documents/statistics/receipts/net-receipts.pdf.

30. Irish Congress of Trade Unions. 'The Truth About Ireland's Taxation System'. www.ictu.ie/download/pdf/the_truth_about_irelands_tax_system.pdf.
31. 'Eurostat News Release: General Government Expenditure in the EU 2018'. www. ec.europa.eu/eurostat/documents/2995521/10474879/2-27022020-AP-EN. pdf/4135f313-1e3f-6928-b1fd-816649bd424b#:~:text=In%202018%2C%20 total%20government%20expenditure,stood%20at%2049.7%25%20of%20 GDP.&text=(4.4%25).
32. *Ibid.*, p. 6.
33. 'European Health Consumer Index'. 2017, p. 10. www.healthpowerhouse.com/ media/EHCI-2017/EHCI-2017-report.pdf.
34. 'Irish Mortgage Rates Still the Second Highest in the EU'. 2019. www.rte.ie/ news/business/2019/0614/1055338-interest-rates-figures/#:~:text=New%20 figures%20from%20the%20Central%20points%20on%20the%20previous%20 month.www.irishtimes.com/business/commercial-property/dublin-has-third-highest-residential-rents-in-europe-1.4037438.
35. European Commission. 'Eurydice Report: Key Data Early Childhood Education and Care in Europe – 2019 Edition'. Luxembourg. Publication Office EU. 2019, pp. 57–8.
36. 'Irish Primary School Classes among Largest and Worst Funded in Europe'. *Irish Independent*. 10 September 2019.
37. EU Commission. 'National Student Fee and Support Systems in European Higher Education 2018/19'. Luxembourg. Office of Publication EU. 2018, p. 10.
38. M. Reynolds. 'Two Houses for the Price of One'. 19 October 2018. www. passivehouseplus.ie/blogs/two-houses-for-the-price-of-one.
39. 'Dublin Now in Top 5 Most Expensive Places to Rent in Europe, Research Finds'. *The Journal*. 13 March 2019.
40. S. Calò and V. Herzberg. 'The Future of Global Financial Centres after Brexit: An EU Perspective'. 2019. www.centralbank.ie/docs/default-source/publications/ financial-stability-review/financial-stability-review-2019-i/financial-stability-review-2019-ii.pdf.
41. 'Depfa Saga Ends but at What Cost to Germany'. www.irishtimes.com/business/ financial-services/depfa-saga-ends-but-at-what-cost-to-germany-1.2042911.
42. *Ibid.*, p. 8.
43. European Commission. 'What Is the Common Consolidated Corporation Tax Base'. www.ec.europa.eu/taxation_customs/business/company-tax/common-consolidated-corporate-tax-base-ccctb_en.
44. *Ibid.*
45. J. Power. 'Brexit to Make CCCTB Harder to Block, UCD Academic Warns'. 2017. www.irishtimes.com/business/economy/brexit-to-make-ccctb-reforms-harder-to-block-ucd-academic-warns-1.3034086.
46. F. Barry. 'Cut to the Chase: US Corporate Tax Reform – The Implications for Ireland'. Dublin. IIEA. p. 8. www.iiea.com/publication/cut-to-the-chase-us-corporate-tax-reform-the-implications-for-ireland/.
47. *Ibid.*

48. 'How Tax-Free Irish Google Unit Paid \$50bn in Dividends'. *Irish Independent*. 2 January 2020.

49. N. Shaxson. 'Tackling Tax Havens'. 2019, p. 4. www.imf.org/external/pubs/ft/fandd/2019/09/tackling-global-tax-havens-shaxon.htm.

50. *Ibid.*

51. OECD. 'International Community Agrees on a Roadmap for Resolving the Tax Challenges Arising from the Digitalisation of the Economy'. www.oecd.org/tax/beps/international-community-agrees-on-a-road-map-for-resolving-the-tax-challenges-arising-from-digitalisation-of-the-economy.htm.

52. Grant Thornton. 'Say Goodbye to the Arm's Length Principle'. 2020. www.grantthornton.global/globalassets/1.-member-firms/global/insights/article-pdfs/2019/say-goodbye-to-the-arms-length-principle.pdf.

53. 'The Global Economic Outlook during the Covid 19 Pandemic'. www.worldbank.org/en/news/feature/2020/06/08/the-global-economic-outlook-during-the-covid-19-pandemic-a-changed-world.

54. *Ibid.*

55. 'The Great Lockdown: Worst Economic Downturn since the Great Depression'. www.blogs.imf.org/2020/04/14/the-great-lockdown-worst-economic-downturn-since-the-great-depression/.

56. *Ibid.*

57. 'Reopening from the Great Lockdown. Uneven and Uncertain Recovery'. www.blogs.imf.org/2020/06/24/reopening-from-the-great-lockdown-uneven-and-uncertain-recovery/.

58. Department of Finance. 'SPU 2020: Macroeconomic Outlook and Projections'. 2020, p. 30. www.gov.ie/en/publication/3639c3-spu-2020-presentation-to-ifac/.

59. *Ibid.*

60. P. van Doorn. 'Airlines and Boeing Want a Bailout. But Look How Much They've Spent on Stock Buybacks'. 2020. www.marketwatch.com/story/airlines-and-boeing-want-a-bailout-but-look-how-much-theyve-spent-on-stock-buybacks-2020-03-18.

61. M. Roberts. 'A World Rate of Profit: A New Approach'. 2020. www.thenextrecession.wordpress.com/2020/07/25/a-world-rate-of-profit-a-new-approach/.

62. R. Banerjee and B. Hoffman. 'The Rise of Zombie Firms Causes and Consequences'. *BIS Quarterly Review*. September 2018. www.bis.org/publ/qtrpdf/r_qt1809g.pdf.

63. *Ibid.*

64. *Ibid.*

65. OECD. 'State Owned Firms behind China's Corporate Debt'. 2017. www.oecd.org/officialdocuments/publicdisplaydocumentpdf/?cote=ECO/WKP(2019)5&docLanguage=En.

66. C. Taylor. 'How Much Can Ireland Borrow to Get Through This Covid 19 Emergency'. *Irish Times*. 2020. www.irishtimes.com/business/economy/how-much-can-ireland-borrow-to-get-through-this-covid-19-emergency-.

67. Department of Finance. 'Analysis of Private Sector Debt in Ireland'. Dublin. Government Publications. 2019.
68. B. O'Boyle. 'Paying for Covid: Who Says We Are in This Together?' *Irish Marxist Review*. Vol. 9, No. 27, 2020, pp. 50–60.
69. 'Irish Central Bank Macro Stability Review 2019'. 2019, p. 26. www.centralbank. ie/docs/default-source/publications/financial-stability-review/financial-stability-review-2019-i/financial-stability-review-2019-ii.pdf.
70. B. O'Boyle. 'Paying for Covid'.
71. *Ibid.*
72. See 'Planet before Profit' for a critique of Ireland's record on environmental initiatives alongside a series of suggestions to tackle climate change though progressive policies. The document can be found here: www.eco.pbp.ie/.

POSTSCRIPT

1. OECD/G20. Base Erosion and Profit Shifting Project. 'Statement on a Two-Pillar Solution to Address the Tax Challenges Arising from the Digitalisation of the Economy'. www.oecd.org/tax/beps/statement-on-a-two-pillar-solution-to-address-the-tax-challenges-arising-from-the-digitalisation-of-the-economy-july-2021.pdf.
2. W. Goodbody. 'Ireland not among 130 countries to back global corporation tax reform deal'. www.rte.ie/news/business/2021/0701/1232531-global-minimum-corporate-tax-of-at-least-15-agreed/.
3. C. Taylor & E. O'Riordan. 'Ireland one of 9 countries to hold out on signing OECD global tax deal'. www.irishtimes.com/business/economy/ireland-one-of-9-countries-to-hold-out-on-signing-oecd-global-tax-deal-1.4609129.
4. G. Percival. 'Ireland 'committed to global tax reform', despite not signing up to OECD proposals. www.irishexaminer.com/business/economy/arid-40327361. html.
5. S. Collins. 'With State Isolated on global corporation tax changes, Paschal Donohoe launches public 'consultation'. www.independent.ie/business/budget/with-state-isolated-on-global-corporationtax-changes-paschal-donohoe-launches-public-consultation-40674749.html.
6. *Ibid.*
7. KPMG. Proposed US Tax Reform. www.kpmg/ie/en/home/insights/2021/04/proposed-us-tax-reform.html.
8. OECD/G20. Base Erosion and Profit Shifting Project. 'Addressing the tax challenges arising from the digitalisation of the economy JULY 2021'. www.oecd.org/tax/beps/brochure-addressing-the-tax-challenges-arising-from-the-digitalisation-of-the-economy-july-2021.pdf, p. 4.
9. *Ibid.*
10. G. Percival. 'Ireland 'committed to global tax reform', despite not signing up to OECD proposals. www.irishexaminer.com/business/economy/arid-40327361. html.

11. OECD/G20. Base Erosion and Profit Shifting Project. 'Addressing the tax challenges arising from the digitalisation of the economy JULY 2021'. www.oecd.org/tax/beps/brochure-addressing-the-tax-challenges-arising-from-the-digitalisation-of-the-economy-july-2021.pdf, p. 5.
12. N. O'Leary. 'Ireland may support global tax deal, Donohoe Says'. www.irishtimes.com/business/economy/ireland-may-support-global-tax-deal-donohoe-says-1.4618497.
13. OECD/G20. Base Erosion and Profit Shifting Project. 'Addressing the tax challenges arising from the digitalisation of the economy JULY 2021'. www.oecd.org/tax/beps/brochure-addressing-the-tax-challenges-arising-from-the-digitalisation-of-the-economy-july-2021.pdf.

Index

Thanks to our Patreon Subscribers:

Lia Lilith de Oliveira
Andrew Perry

Who have shown generosity and
comradeship in support of our publishing.

Check out the other perks you get by subscribing
to our Patreon – visit patreon.com/plutopress.

Subscriptions start from £3 a month.

The Pluto Press Newsletter

Hello friend of Pluto!

Want to stay on top of the best radical books
we publish?

Then sign up to be the first to hear about our
new books, as well as special events,
podcasts and videos.

You'll also get 50% off your first order with us
when you sign up.

Come and join us!

Go to bit.ly/PlutoNewsletter